THE REAL VENEZUELA

The Real Venezuela

Making Socialism in the Twenty-first Century

Iain Bruce

PLUTO PRESS
www.plutobooks.com

First published 2008 by Pluto Press
345 Archway Road, London N6 5AA

www.plutobooks.com

Copyright © Iain Bruce 2008

The right of Iain Bruce to be identified as the author of this work has been asserted by him
in accordance with the Copyright, Designs and Patents Act 1988.

British Library Cataloguing in Publication Data
A catalogue record for this book is available from the British Library

ISBN 978 0 7453 2737 2 Hardback
ISBN 978 0 7453 2736 5 Paperback

Library of Congress Cataloging in Publication Data applied for

This book is printed on paper suitable for recycling and made from fully managed and
sustained forest sources. Logging, pulping and manufacturing processes are expected to
conform to the environmental standards of the country of origin. The paper may contain up
to 70% post consumer waste.

10 9 8 7 6 5 4 3 2 1

Designed and produced for Pluto Press by
Curran Publishing Services, Norwich

Printed and bound in the European Union by
CPI Antony Rowe, Chippenham and Eastbourne

This book is dedicated to Sofia Lashley, Marta Garcia, Maria Herrera and the many thousands of women, in the *barrios* and countryside of Venezuela, who have been the backbone of the Bolivarian experience. If socialism means anything in the twenty-first century, it will carry their seal.

CONTENTS

Acknowledgements   *ix*

Venezuela country facts   *xi*

Timeline   *xv*

Map of Venezuela   *xxii*

Acronyms and other terms   *xxiii*

Introduction   1

1. Oil for food, health, education …   17

2. The people's economy   40

3. War on the *latifundios*   64

4. Democracy at work   98

5. Who's in charge here? From local democracy to communal power   139

Conclusion: Making socialism in the twenty-first century   176

Notes   *194*

Index   *209*

ACKNOWLEDGEMENTS

It is impossible to thank by name all the people who made this book possible. In every place and in every sphere, dozens and dozens have gone out of their way to help. But some it is impossible not to name – their efforts went so far beyond anything I had the right to expect. At ALCASA, Marivit Lopez and Edgar Caldera took me under their wing, opened doors, and organised logistics; mayors Julio Chavez and Rosa Leon and their respective staff, in Carora and La Victoria, did the same – a special thank you for the hospitality given to me there. Jesus Ayala of the Urban Land Office gave up days to accompany me up and down the ranchos of Carapita. In Santo Domingo and Caracas, the unlimited generosity and friendship of Adele Williams, Claudia Jardim and Jorge Silva gave me both the space and the support to research and to write. Similarly, Carol Delgado and Greg Wilpert have been endlessly available to answer my many irritating questions. Finally, I want to thank my son, David, for patiently traipsing after me from one end of Venezuela to the other, sitting without complaint through hour after hour of interviews; and above all, my partner, Maria Esperanza Sanchez. She not only put up with my obsessions over the last two years, she both encouraged them and scrutinised them, demanding clarification and justification where these were long overdue. She is not responsible for the contents of this book. But without her contribution, it would be a lot worse.

Iain Bruce

VENEZUELA COUNTRY FACTS

Population

27.7 million (2007, UN estimate)

This makes Venezuela the fifth most populous country in Latin America, after Brazil, Mexico, Colombia and Argentina.

- Indigenous 2 per cent
- Black 8 per cent
- White approx 20 per cent
- Mixed approx 70 per cent.

At a bit over half a million, the indigenous population is only slightly larger than it was when the Spanish invaded at the end of the fifteenth century. It includes large, developed communities in the western, Andean highlands, as well as the almost totally quarantined and un-assimilated Yanomami in the southern Amazonian rainforest.

Venezuela had few large colonial plantations, so there are few black communities of almost exclusively African ancestry. The great majority of the Venezuelan people are of mixed ancestry, mostly African and indigenous, with a smaller European component. This is the overwhelming character of the 'Bolivarian' people that feature in this book.

Venezuela is almost the only country in Latin America to have experienced sizeable European immigration in the second half of the twentieth century. Poor white families, mainly from Spain, Portugal and Italy, came to make their fortune, drawn by Venezuela's oil wealth. They became the backbone of the country's burgeoning middle class. The latent racism in some of these sections of the population became a particularly ugly aspect of the anti-Chavez opposition.

Geography

Total land area: 882,050 square kilometres

Just over twice the size of California, and nearly a third larger than France, Venezuela includes everything from Caribbean coastline to high Andean peaks, from the cattle ranches of the vast central plains to dense Amazonian rainforest and the hauntingly beautiful savannah and table-top mountains of the Gran Sabana. It has land borders of over 2,000 kms each with Colombia and Brazil, and of almost 800 kms with Guyana, but the latter two are scarcely inhabited.

It has abundant mineral resources (oil, gas, coal, bauxite, iron ore, gold, diamonds), as well as water (80 per cent of domestic electricity comes from large hydroelectric plants on the Caroní river in south-east Venezuela) and high-quality agricultural land. However, less than a third of Venezuela's 2.85 per cent of 'arable' land is cultivated, and that arable area could arguably be greatly extended by reducing the large landholdings given over to cattle or left idle, and by making moderate investments in irrigation, etc.

Economy

- GDP: US$182 billion (2006, OPEC annual statistics).
- GDP growth: 8.3 per cent p.a. (2007 est.).
- GDP per capita: US$6,735 (2006, OPEC annual statistics).
- GDP by sector: agriculture: 3.5 per cent; industry (including oil): 40 per cent; services: 56.5 per cent (2007 est.).
- Labour force: 12.5 million (roughly half in formal employment and half in informal sector, although many more not officially included in the workforce figures effectively operate in the informal sector).

Non-oil exports

Aluminium and bauxite, steel, cement, agricultural commodities. (The government's demands that more be sold domestically was one issue feeding into the nationalisations of steel and cement plants in April 2008.)

Soaring international oil prices, and the highly political disputes over oil statistics, mean Venezuela's economic indicators have been hard to pin down in recent years.

Oil

Since the 1920s Venezuela's economy has depended massively on oil, which in 2007 represented:

- 90 per cent of export income
- 50 per cent of public revenues
- 30 per cent of GDP.

NB: These numbers do not account for the fact that much of the rest of the economy – e.g. banking – essentially 'services' oil or redistributes the revenue from oil.

For almost three decades, until 1970, Venezuela was the world's biggest oil exporter. In recent years, Venezuela's position in the world oil industry has been described as:

- fifth largest oil exporter in the world
- fourth largest supplier to the United States
- first largest proven oil reserves in the western hemisphere
- second largest reserves of natural gas in the western hemisphere.

The Venezuelan government claims it has the largest oil reserves in the world, including the estimated 130 to 270 billion barrels of super-heavy crude in the Orinoco Belt, currently classified as 'non-conventional' oil and not included in OPEC figures. Figures below are from OPEC's 2006 annual statistics and PDVSA:

- Crude oil production 3.1 million barrels per day (bpd)
- Proven oil reserves 87.04 billion barrels.

In 2005, before the government retook majority control of its various agreements with foreign oil companies, Venezuela's oil production split roughly as follows:

- 2 million bpd PDVSA's own production

- 500,000 bpd conventional crude produced by foreign companies in operating agreements with PDVSA
- 600,000 bpd synthetic crude from non-conventional super-heavy crude produced by strategic associations between PDVSA and a number of international oil companies.

VENEZUELA'S RECENT HISTORY: A BRIEF TIMELINE

1498 Christopher Columbus visits.

1521 First Spanish settlements in the north-east. After the first rush of interest in finding the gold of El Dorado, Spanish interest wanes and the area that is now Venezuela becomes something of a backwater among the Spanish colonies.

1810–29 The struggle for independence from Spain, led by Simón Bolívar, leads briefly to a union of independent South American territories reaching from Venezuela to Bolivia, *Gran Colombia*, but this soon falls apart. Simón Bolivar's 'unfinished task' is one Hugo Chavez aspires to take up again over a century and a half later.

1913 Venezuela's first oil well is sunk at Mene Grande near Lake Maracaibo. Large-scale production begins from the early 1920s and by 1929 Venezuela is the world's second-largest producer. In these years, the dictator Juan Vicente Gomez (1880–1935) hands over generous oil concessions to foreign companies, especially Standard Oil of New Jersey and Royal Dutch Shell.

1940s Venezuela becomes the world's largest exporter of oil.

1958 After the overthrow of the Perez Jimenez dictatorship, the leaders of the Democratic Action Party (AD), the Christian Democratic COPEI, and a smaller third party, sign the Punto Fijo pact which sets the framework for four decades of 'managed' democracy, with AD and COPEI alternating in office and sharing its spoils. Rómulo Betancourt of AD is elected president at the end of that year.

1974 As oil revenues boom, President Carlos Andres Perez of AD begins to nationalise the oil and steel industries.

1983 'Black Friday', 18 February: falling oil prices and mounting debt lead to currency crisis and devaluation. This marks the beginning of Venezuela's long and deep slide from the apparent 'affluence' known as 'Saudi Venezuela' to increasing poverty for most of the population, including sections of the middle class.

1989 The *Caracazo* revolt, 27–28 February, in response fuel price rises that are part of the IMF-inspired structural adjustment package introduced by Carlos Andres Perez just after the beginning of his second term as president. Ferocious repression by the military leads to many deaths: estimates range from 300 to 3,000 or more, with a figure of 396 killed reported by one of the most credible human rights organisations. Many on the left see the *Caracazo* as the birth of the Bolivarian revolution. This may be stretching a point, but it certainly signalled the beginning of an unravelling of the Punto Fijo system; it also served to radicalise a layer of young officers in the armed forces, Hugo Chavez among them, shocked at the use of the military against the civilian population.

1992 4 February, Colonel Hugo Chavez leads a coup attempt against Perez. This fails and Chavez is jailed for two years. However, in exchange for surrendering he is granted a one-minute TV address in which he promises that his cause has been defeated only 'for the time being'. It establishes him as a folk hero and a key reference point for growing dissatisfaction with the political establishment. A second attempted coup by another group of officers on 27 November is also defeated.

1997 Chavez' Movimiento Bolivariano Revolucionario 200 (MBR-200) decides to present Chavez in presidential elections and forms the Fifth Republic Movement (MVR) as a political movement for elections.

1998 6 December, Hugo Chavez elected president in first round with 56 per cent of vote.

1999 Chavez wins three major votes: to call a Constituent Assembly, to elect members of the assembly, and in December to approve the new Bolivarian Constitution. That December severe floods and mudslides on the Avila mountain outside Caracas kill thousands of people in the capital and on the coast just to the north. The exact number was never known. Estimates of 10,000, 15,000 or more abound.

2000 30 July, mega-elections under the new constitution give

Chavez a fresh six-year term as president as well as pro-Chavez majorities in the National Assembly (104 out 165) and among state governors (17 out of 23 states), but only about half of the country's mayors.

2001 In November, using temporary powers granted him by the National Assembly through an enabling act, Chavez introduces 49 decree-laws. Three of these in particular – the Land Law promising land reform, the Hydrocarbons Law stopping moves towards the privatisation of the state oil company and increasing royalties for foreign operators, and a Fisheries Law in favour of small fishers – seem for the first time to threaten the economic privileges of the old Venezuelan elite. It is this that opens the way to the coup attempt of 2002 and subsequent attempts to topple Chavez.

2002 25 February, Chavez appoints new board of directors to state oil company PDVSA in an attempt to retake control from the old elite and from the PDVSA executives close to its interests and those of foreign oil companies.

2002 9 April, the main business association, Fedecamaras, and the CTV trade union confederation, linked to AD and close to the PDVSA executive, announce a 'strike' to support the PDVSA executives.

2002 11 April, a large opposition march in support of the PDVSA executive heads for the Miraflores Palace where a counter-demonstration in favour of the Chavez government is taking place. A carefully choreographed sequence of events ensues. Shots, almost all of them from rooftop snipers, kill some 19 demonstrators, both opposition and pro-government. Opposition TV channels broadcast pictures purporting to show armed Chavez supporters as being responsible (these were later shown to be a fake montage, as the Chavez supporters with small arms were in fact trying to defend the pro-Chavez demonstrators from sniper fire). Members of the military high command rebel, and broadcast a statement dissociating themselves from the alleged 'governmental repression'. They demand that Chavez resign. (There is strong evidence that this video statement was recorded before any of the shooting happened.)

That night, military officers take over the Miraflores Palace and demand Chavez sign a resignation letter. He refuses. Chavez is taken into custody and flown to a military base on an island off the coast. The military commanders announce he has resigned. Most of the world's media broadcast this version of events. There is compelling evidence of co-ordination between all these moves and US military attachés and CIA station officers in Caracas.

2002   April 12, the armed forces commanders name Pedro Carmona, the head of Fedecamaras business association, as head of a transitional government. At an assembly of opposition, business and military leaders, he presents a decree suspending the constitution and dissolving the National Assembly. Several hundred of those present sign. Most of Chavez' ministers are in hiding but some get word out that he has not resigned.

2002   April 13, as word spreads, Chavez supporters in the poor neighbourhoods of Caracas mobilise and head for Miraflores. The palace is surrounded by tens of thousands demanding the return of Chavez. At the same time, military units and commanders loyal to Chavez begin to mobilise against the coup. As Chavez continues to refuse to sign his 'resignation' letter, there are suggestions that the military commanders may try to fly him into forced exile or even have him killed. Junior officers among those holding Chavez apparently learn by mobile phone from relatives in Caracas what is happening and block any such moves. Towards the end of the day, the interim government begins to collapse. The palace guard, which has remained loyal to Chavez, informs Carmona and his supporters that if they do not leave it will open the palace gates and let the people in. The 'interim government' and coup organisers flee in disarray. Late that night, a helicopter flies Chavez back into Miraflores and a rapturous welcome from the crowds outside.

2002–03   December to February, the opposition call a 'strike' or lockout, mainly in the oil industry, which begins to cripple the country, again demanding that Chavez resign. The nine-week stoppage is defeated by another huge popular mobilisation, of oil workers to keep the industry partially working, and of communities and soldiers to help keep transport moving and food supplies from grinding to a halt. After the 'strike' collapses, the government sacks 18,000 PDVSA managers, administrators and technicians who had taken part – the first and only purge of existing state personnel that the Bolivarian revolution has undertaken.

2003   In the months after the lockout, with oil revenues beginning to recover and now more clearly under public control, the government begins to launch its health and education Missions, with the aid of Cuban personnel and technology sent in exchange for Venezuelan oil supplied on preferential terms. The urban land committees, which have been mushrooming since 2002, provide the starting point for much of the community involvement in these Missions.

2003   Opposition begins to campaign for a referendum on Chavez' presidency, taking advantage of the provision for recall votes introduced by the Bolivarian constitution of 1999. In May there is an agreement with the government on how to proceed, followed by months of dispute over the collection of signatures to support the opposition's proposed recall referendum.

2004   August 15, President Chavez wins a clear victory in the recall referendum, defeating the third major attempt to unseat him and opening the way for a new phase of the Bolivarian revolution.

2004   October, Chavez supporters win all but two state governorships and a large majority of mayoral positions in local and regional elections.

2004   November, at a high-level workshop on 'The New Strategic Map', Chavez discusses with his new mayors and governors, and with ministers and other leading cadres, the ten objectives of this new phase of the Bolivarian revolution.

2005   January, President Chavez signs a new decree on land reform which aims to eliminate Venezuela's large estates, bring justice to the rural poor and boost the country's ability to grow its own food.

2005 January, at the World Social Forum in Brazil, Chavez for the first time declares that only a revolution can overcome the iniquities of capitalism and that the solution has to be socialism.

2005 May Day, Chavez talks of the need for workers to run their own workplaces through systems of co-management, a practice which has developed over the preceding months in the first two private companies to be expropriated, and at the state-owned aluminium plant, ALCASA.

2005 December, opposition parties boycott parliamentary elections, giving Chavez supporters a clean sweep of the new National Assembly.

2006 April, the National Assembly passes the Law on Communal Councils.

2006 December, Hugo Chavez wins a third term (second full term under the 1999 constitution) in presidential elections with 63 per cent of the vote. He says it is a clear vote for socialism.

2007 January, President Chavez outlines the 'five motors' of the revolution that should drive Venezuela's transition to socialism. They include an enabling law that he uses to renationalise the main telecoms company, CANTV, and the Caracas electricity company.

2007 May, the government takes majority control of the super-heavy crude oil projects in the Orinoco Belt, further consolidating national sovereignty over the country's oil industry.

2007 May, the government refuses to renew the franchise of RCTV, one of the channels involved in promoting the failed coup of 2002.

2007 August, Chavez presents his proposals for a reform of the Bolivarian constitution, intended to facilitate the promised transition to socialism. The opposition and the international media focus almost exclusively on the provision to remove presidential term limits, which would open the way for Chavez to stand again in 2012.

2007 December 2, Chavez suffers his first defeat at the ballot box, when voters reject the proposed constitutional reforms by a narrow margin in a referendum.

2008   April, Chavez renationalises the vast SIDOR steel plant after a 15-month struggle by the workers against the Argentinean-led consortium that held 60 per cent of the shares.

VENEZUELA

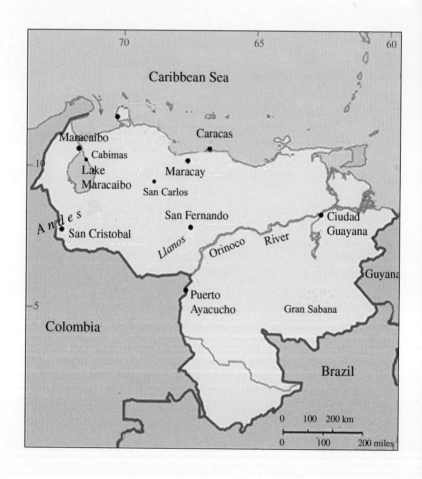

ACRONYMS AND OTHER TERMS

AD	Acción Democratica social-democratic party
CEBs	grassroots church communities (*Comunidades Eclesiales de Base*)
CLPP	local public planning council
COPEI	Christian Democratic Party
CTUs	urban land committees (Comites de Tierra Urbana)
CTV	Confederación de Trabajadores de Venezuela
CVA	Compania Venezolana Agraria
CVG	Corporación Venezolana de Guayana
ECLA	United Nations Economic Commission for Latin America
EPS	social production enterprise
ES	socialist enterprise
FBT	Bolivarian Workers' Force (FBT), later the Socialist Bolivarian Workers' Force (FSBT)
FIDES	Intergovernmental Fund for Decentralisation
FNCEZ	Ezequiel Zamora National Peasant Front
FONDAFA	government agency providing funding for forestry, fishing and agriculture
FSBT	Socialist Bolivarian Workers' Force
IMF	International Monetary Fund
INPARQUE	National Parks Institute
INTI	Land Institute
MBR-200	Movimiento Bolivariano Revolucionario 200
Mercosur	Common Market of the South
MST	Landless Workers' Movement
NUDE	Nucleus for Endogenous (self-sufficient) Development
OCV	Organisation for Home Credits
OPEC	Organization of the Petroleum Exporting Countries
PB	participatory budget
PDVAL	initiative to tackle food shortages, using PDVSA supplies

PDVSA	Petroleos de Venezuela S.A., Venezuela's state oil company
PPT	Fatherland for All Party
PRI	Institutional Revolutionary Party
PSOL	Party of Socialism and Liberty
PST	Socialist Workers Party
PSUV	Venezuelan United Socialist Party
PT	Workers' Party
SENIAT	federal tax authority
SINTRALCASA	Union of ALCASA workers
UBEs	electoral battle units
UBV	Venezuelan Bolivarian University
UNT	National Workers Union, Venezuelan trade union confederation

Adeco	supporting Acción Democratica social-democratic party
Asociaciones de Vecinos	neighbourhood associations
barrio	neighbourhood
Caracazo	uprising of February 1989 that signalled the beginning of the end of the Punto Fijo system
casa de integración	integration centre for community council's public service
cepalina	based on the theories and policies promoted by CEPAL, the UN's Economic Commission on Latin America,
Copeyanos	supporters of the traditional COPEI party
ejidos	public land belonging to the municipality
latifundios	large landholdings
mancomunidad	federation of communal councils
piqueteros	unemployed movements
ranchos	shanty-towns

INTRODUCTION

SNAPSHOT 1: PORTO ALEGRE, SOUTHERN BRAZIL, 30 JANUARY 2005

It was back in January 2005 that President Hugo Chavez first announced that the goal was socialism. I was there, along with 13,000 others, in the Gigantinho sports hall in the southern Brazilian city of Porto Alegre. Another 5,000 were watching on a giant screen outside. It was a moment that spoke volumes about Latin America's growing movement against neoliberal globalisation, and about Venezuela's special part in it.

It had been one of Porto Alegre's hottest summers on record. Dripping in perspiration, we'd already been waiting hours for the Venezuelan leader to turn up to this final session of the Fifth World Social Forum. But the political temperature was even hotter. People had high expectations of Chavez. And most of them expected something very different from Brazil's President Lula. Three days earlier, Lula had been booed in the same hall at the beginning of this annual gathering of the global justice movement. As the best known leader of the Brazilian Workers' Party, Lula had been one of the stars of the previous Forums in Porto Alegre. For 15 years or more, he and his party had been just about the brightest beacon around for the left in Latin America, even worldwide. But now, exactly two years into his first term as the country's first working-class president, many of Lula's former supporters were disappointed and angry. They felt betrayed by his refusal to break with the shibboleths of neoliberal economic policy – what in Latin America had become known as the Washington Consensus.

In fact, on just about every one of the big themes developed by the global justice movement and the World Social Forums since

Seattle, the Lula government had gone backwards. He'd kept interest rates and the budget surplus painfully high to service the national debt. He'd squeezed public spending and pushed through a reform of pension rights. Further market-friendly reforms were at different stages of preparation or completion. He'd lifted a ban on the planting of genetically modified soya by large-scale agribusiness, but made little progress in redistributing land to poor peasants and landless workers. He'd struck deals left, right and centre with the Brazilian political establishment to ensure support in Congress – although the full extent of the political corruption surrounding some of these deals only began to come to light a few months later. Perhaps most humiliating of all, his government had been repeatedly praised by the US Treasury and the State Department, the *Wall Street Journal* and the *Economist*, by Tony Blair, Condoleezza Rice and even Donald Rumsfeld, as a responsible and moderating influence in the region. And to prove it Lula had sent Brazilian troops to support an international military intervention in Haiti.

President Chavez, it seemed, was different – although it hadn't always been that way. A former colonel in the parachute regiment, he had led a failed coup attempt in 1992, spent two years in prison, and then won a decisive victory in presidential elections in December 1998 on a rather moderate, nationalist programme. After the oil boom of the 1970s, Venezuela had been suffering from a long but deep slide towards poverty. A turn to neoliberal austerity policies in 1989 had triggered an uprising – the *Caracazo* – that was bloodily put down. The country's two-party system of controlled, representative democracy, initiated with the Punto Fijo pact of 1958 and often presented as the most stable in Latin America, had all but collapsed in a heap of corruption and ineptitude.

Chavez promised a new start. He even called it a Bolivarian revolution. But it didn't look like a very radical one. The emphasis was on a thorough overhaul of the old, corrupt political system, as well as on education, national sovereignty and Latin American integration – all themes that went down well enough with Venezuela's disenchanted middle classes, who had voted for him *en masse*. It was only when Chavez really did call a constituent assembly to rewrite the constitution, began to curb the old elite's exclusive control of the oil industry and institutions like the Supreme Court, and introduced legislation on land reform that Venezuela's conservative establishment really smelt a rat, and began to draw most of the middle class back into its orbit.

Initially, this sharpening polarisation had had little impact outside the country. During his first three years in office, Hugo Chavez' government had stirred only a lukewarm response around the region. His military background was anathema to most of the left in Latin America, and in Europe and North America too. And anyway, Venezuela was a country where 'nothing much ever happened'. This attitude had begun to change, especially after April 2002. That was when the Venezuelan poor descended en masse from their shanty towns above Caracas to defend their president from a short-lived coup that almost everyone believed had been hatched in Washington.

In the following three years, it had become increasingly clear to the left and the social movements across Latin America – and eventually beyond the region too – that Chavez and the Bolivarian revolution unfolding in Venezuela really did hold out the promise of an alternative to neoliberal orthodoxy. They had not only begun to reassert national sovereignty over Venezuela's natural resources, especially oil. They had also begun to use the country's growing revenues from that oil to fund social programmes – known as Missions[1] – on a scale unseen anywhere in the region outside of Cuba: adult education and literacy for all, doctors' surgeries established for the first time in almost every poor neighbourhood. They challenged the primacy of market liberalisation with exchange controls and a chain of public mini-markets selling subsidised basic goods to more than half the population. Just three weeks before his appearance in Porto Alegre, President Chavez had announced a renewed drive for land reform as a 'war on the *latifundios*', or large landholdings. And he had been systematically and noisily challenging Washington's priorities for the region, including free trade pacts and military interventions like Plan Colombia and the occupation of Haiti.

Lula and Chavez, then, seemed to be two separate souls of the new Latin American left. The difference was between those who had and those who hadn't had the gall to stand up to the empire; to reject not only its wars and its free trade pacts, but also the whole framework of its IMF-backed, market-led, economic prescriptions.

Everyone was conscious of the difference. But the crowd in that sweltering Gigantinho sports hall was divided on its response.

On one side of the hall were the most radical opponents of the Brazilian government's new course – members of the new Party of Socialism and Liberty (PSOL), formed by supporters of the charismatic senator Heloisa Helena, and other members of parliament who had been expelled from the Workers' Party (PT) for refusing to vote for Lula's pension reforms. As the long wait for Chavez continued, between the performances of protest singers from Bolivia or Argentina, these critics began a barrage of chants against the Lula government's reforms. PT loyalists, concentrated on the opposite side of the hall, returned catcalls and chants of their own.

Somehow both sides seemed to hope that Chavez would be a part of *their* solution – either by marking his sharp difference with Lula, or by lending the Brazilian president some much-needed support from the left. In part, both sides turned out to be right.

The first half of President Chavez' two-hour speech was pretty much what everyone in the hall was expecting – praise for the young people who made up the bulk of this burgeoning international movement and who, he said, held the future of humanity in their hands; praise for Brazil's Landless Workers' Movement, who had taken him earlier in the day to visit one of their land occupations; and a commitment to work together against the common enemy: 'Let's make a worldwide conspiracy, a true, anti-imperialist, anti-neoliberal, anti-establishment conspiracy.' Then there was his familiar litany of role models: 'Somebody said I am a leader of a new type. ... Maybe, but inspired by some old types, like Jesus of Nazareth, one of the greatest anti-imperialist fighters in the history of the world ... like Simon Bolivar ... like Abreu de Lima ... and like that asthmatic Argentinean doctor who rode around the continent on a motorbike ... Che Guevara.'

Suddenly there was a less familiar flash – a hint of where he was heading: 'I am here as just one more revolutionary militant among you, because ... every day I feel more of a revolutionary, because every day I am more convinced that the only way we can break from capitalist domination, from the domination of the oligarchy in our countries, is through revolution, there is no other solution.'

Not that the word 'revolution' was new. It had long become

everyday currency in Bolivarian Venezuela. But this had a sharper edge. Chavez had not been in the habit of talking about an anti-capitalist revolution.

Still it was not until over half-way through the speech that the Venezuelan leader spelt out his new message: 'I am ever more convinced that ... it is necessary to transcend capitalism. But capitalism cannot be transcended within capitalism. Capitalism can only be transcended through socialism. That's the way for us to go beyond the capitalist model, true socialism. ... And I am also convinced that it is possible [to do this] in democracy. ... But not the kind of democracy that *Mister* Superman wants to impose on us from Washington.'

It wasn't much, but it echoed round the hall like a thunderclap. All of a sudden, Hugo Chavez and the Bolivarian Revolution were no longer to be seen as just the most militant expression of a nationalist, anti-imperialist, anti-neoliberal revolt spreading across Latin America. All of a sudden, here was a process that openly and deliberately claimed it was aiming for socialism. And that was something nobody in a similar position had dreamed of saying since long before the collapse of the Soviet bloc a decade and a half earlier.

From where I was sitting it sounded like it was the radical left on the far side of the Gigantinho that reacted first – with whoops and screams that immediately broke into a revised version of Lula's election theme: 'Ué, ué, ué, ué, Chavez, Chavez!' But looking around, the Lula loyalists on this side of the hall seemed to be just as delighted. It was as if they were hoping Hugo Chavez might pull their leader back to the left. And as he drew to a close, the Venezuelan leader himself seemed to reprimand the radicals. He'd already quoted Mao Tse Tung on the need to distinguish very clearly between friends and enemies. Now he held out a hand to Lula. 'And even if some of you start making strange noises, I want to say I like Lula, I value him, he's a good man, a good comrade. And I'm sure that together with Lula and the Brazilian people, with Nestor Kirchner and the people of Argentina, with Tabaré Vasquez and the people of Uruguay, we will move forward to the dream of a united Latin America.'

So the familiar, all-embracing, Bolivarian vision of continental unity was now combined with an emerging perspective of socialist revolution. This would become a constant theme over the following weeks and months. In speech after speech President Chavez would repeat and develop his invitation to debate Venezuela's future and the meaning of a new kind of socialism – not a repetition of any of the old models of socialism, not even of the Cuban experience, but a new kind of socialism for the twenty-first century.

This evolution reached another marker on May Day that year, when Chavez devoted much of his speech at a mass rally called by the new UNT trade union federation to the theme of co-management. It was time, the president said, for workers to get involved in running their own workplaces.

Of course, as soon as you look closely it's clear that this 'surprise' announcement of 'socialism' as the goal did not come out of the blue. A couple of months earlier, Chavez had told a 'high-level workshop' of ministers, parliamentarians and other Bolivarian leaders from across Venezuela, called to discuss 'The New Strategic Map', that the long-term, economic objective was to transcend capitalism. 'The capitalist economic model is not viable, it's impossible, and we leaders have to be clear about that.' But at that stage he stopped short of explicitly identifying the alternative as socialism, much less communism. 'No, that's not on the agenda at the moment. … We are not proposing to eliminate private property, the communist proposal, no. We're not going that far. Nobody knows what will happen in the future, the world is changing. But at the moment that would be madness. … This is not the time. At the moment … our aim should be to create the new economic system. And that's not something you can do in two years, or even in five.'

And just after that, in December 2004, I listened to him tell an international gathering of Intellectuals in Defence of Humanity that he'd just been reading Trotsky's *Permanent Revolution*, which he claimed he'd 'bought on a recent trip to Moscow', and that there were 'some important lessons to be learnt from the debates between Trotsky and Stalin'. 'I don't believe', he added, 'that there are any purely national solutions to a nation's problems.'

In fact, the ground on which Venezuela's Bolivarian revolution rested had been shifting in this direction for the last five months – ever since Chavez' decisive victory in the Recall Referendum on 15 August 2004.[2]

SNAPSHOT 2 – TACAGUA VIEJA, OUTSIDE CARACAS, 12 SEPTEMBER 2004

It was in the small rural community of Tacagua Vieja, half an hour from Caracas, that I got my first taste of this evolution within the Bolivarian revolution – what Chavez himself began to term variously 'the new stage', 'the leap forward' or 'the revolution within the revolution'. I'd arrived in Venezuela exactly nine days earlier to take up my role as foreign correspondent and I was keen to go along and see for myself the president's weekly TV show. I rang up the woman dealing with the foreign press in Chavez' Miraflores palace. She sounded a little surprised, but gladly sorted it out for me. It seemed going along to see *Aló Presidente* was not something foreign journalists did very often. As a professional chore, they'd watch it on TV when they had to. In fact for several members of the foreign press corps I'd already met, these marathon six-hour broadcasts – a strange mix of chat-show, phone-in, distance learning and tele-evangelism – were a favourite butt of their jokes. When one of them was leaving, he was given a T-shirt that read, 'I survived five years of *Aló Presidente!*' But I wanted to get a feel for the chemistry of this Bolivarian process, and there was nowhere better to see the interaction between leader and led than on location with *Aló Presidente*.

Tacagua Vieja turned out to be a rambling group of shacks just off the main road from Caracas down to the sea and the airport. The reason it had been chosen for that week's programme, only the second since the monumental referendum result, was that this was the site of a new 'endogenous development project' run by the Vuelvan Caras Mission for training and employment.[3] It was therefore an appropriate backdrop for the keynote message of the broadcast: that the only way to tackle poverty was 'to give power to the poor'.

There was, of course, a long wait – something I'd soon get used to. Under a white marquee roof, 50 or 60 representatives of the local community had already taken up their places. Others were still milling around. Most seemed to be from a group that had just finished a course on running their own agricultural co-operative, organised by the Vuelvan Caras Mission. The atmosphere was relaxed. 'Oh, this is the Minister of Labour,' someone I didn't know said to me, as they introduced an unassuming woman with a big smile. I later discovered that

Maria Cristina Iglesias was one of the key thinkers behind this new phase of the revolution. She excused herself and disappeared to talk to some of the international guests who were already sitting at the front: Shafik Handal, Nidia Diaz and a couple of other former guerrilla leaders from the Farabundo Marti National Liberation Front in El Salvador; some leaders of the Pachakutik indigenous party in Ecuador; some writers and intellectuals from Mexico. There was still a taste of euphoria from the referendum victory, as people started singing along to 'Maisanta', an example of Venezuela's typical 'Llanera' music, about a revolutionary hero from the beginning of the twentieth century, who happened to be Chavez' great-grandfather and who had been used as a motif of the campaign for a 'No' in the referendum.

Outside the marquee, and beyond the soldiers manning the security cordon, there was a similar atmosphere among the crowd of several hundred local residents gathered up on the dirt road and in the field behind, waiting for their president to arrive. Except here there was also a taste of those older styles of clientelism and personal patronage that have bedevilled Latin American political life for so long, and which the Bolivarian revolution did not seem to have entirely done away with. Individuals in obvious poverty held up cardboard messages asking the leader for some personal favour – an operation for their nephew, a job for some other family member or a solution to some dispute over a pension.

When he did arrive, and '*Aló Presidente* no. 203' got on air, President Chavez began to explain what he understood by this new phase of the revolution. 'Look at those wonderful organoponic gardens, and the people cultivating them! Three months ago, when I came by here, this was a dump. ... Now there are people everywhere.' The new phase, he said, meant deepening and consolidating the new structures of Venezuela, born from deep within these people. In the economic area, he said, the key was to be 'endogenous development'. 'That's "endo" from the Greek for "within", and "genesis" from the Greek for "creation", "created from within". ... That means we don't depend on the International Monetary Fund, we don't depend on what they say we should or shouldn't do. Here we depend on ourselves.'

And the political conclusion of such a project for self-sufficient development was, he said, clear: 'If we want to put an end to poverty, we have to give power to the poor.'

Still, the radical commitment in Chavez' approach was mixed with gestures of conciliation. The new phase would include a new emphasis on land reform. The concentration of land ownership was a curse from Venezuela's history. The big landholdings, or *latifundios*, had to be done away with. But there was no need for any expropriation, President Chavez insisted, much less confiscation. The Land Law introduced in 2001 provided for a punitive tax on idle property, which would encourage big owners to hand over their surplus land to peasant co-operatives. And even that might not be necessary, if only the landowners would sit down and talk. To make the point he called on Señora Maura to stand up. A woman who looked more like a peasant herself stood. With a mixture of embarrassment and pride on her face, she told how the land there belonged to her family and how they'd lent a part of it out to the Vuelvan Caras Mission to run their agricultural training and set up a co-operative. Everyone cheered and clapped.

Land reform was just a part of the bigger plan for 'endogenous development' and a people's economy, along with the training programmes, the co-ops, micro-credits and subsidised food shops. There was to be a new ministerial structure to promote these priorities. Chavez announced the creation of a Ministry for the People's Economy to integrate all this, working in tandem with a beefed-up Land Reform Institute and the Ministries of Food, Housing and Labour. The most radical proposal came at the end. Chavez suggested that, in order to get beyond the current 'bureaucratic state' and replace it with a 'social state, a people's state', the people in their co-operatives, or urban land committees or other kinds of grassroots organisations, should become part of the structure of these new ministries and help to run them. 'This is society, the people, taking power over the state. Power for the people. ... The people's time has come.'[4]

SO WHAT DID IT ALL MEAN?

Obviously something important was afoot. The political tone now was very different from what I had witnessed on a previous visit to Venezuela, back in April 2000. Then the government had been brandishing a much more moderate mix of Latin-American nationalism and Keynesian welfare measures. Then Hugo Chavez was just over a year into his presidency. The more far-reaching reforms entailed in the new Bolivarian Constitution had not yet taken effect, and he was battling to staunch a slide in popularity caused by falling living standards and a slow recovery from the catastrophic mudslides that killed as many as 15,000 people at the end of 1999.

Now, in 2004, the support for President Chavez could hardly be clearer. His 58 per cent victory in the Recall Referendum had meant a decisive defeat for the third big attempt to unseat him. It followed the failure of the April 2002 coup and the eventual collapse of an employers' lockout that tried to shut down the oil industry at the end of the same year. In the wake of these three defeats the Venezuelan opposition was now in disarray. It would spend the next year and a half tearing itself apart. Chavez might continue to make some conciliatory noises – repeatedly telling Venezuela's middle classes that there was 'room for everyone' inside the big Bolivarian tent. But here in Tacagua Vieja, one month on from that referendum, there was a clear declaration of intent: to push the revolution in a new and more radical direction.

A more fundamental question, however, was already taking shape in my mind. What did all this talk really add up to? There was no doubt that the rhetoric was impressive. It could be, by turns, enchanting, cajoling, inspiring and infuriating. It seemed to have an almost hypnotic effect, even on its opponents. The centre of everyone's attention almost always seemed to be what Chavez had *said*. Or what someone else, from the opposition or the US State Department, had *said* in response to what Chavez had said. Or what Chavez had *said* in response to that response. Endless news stories coming out of Venezuela began: 'The Venezuelan president Hugo Chavez has said, announced, declared, promised, threatened ...' I found myself writing quite a few of them myself. Certainly, for those of us who could still remember our years of training in the scholastic debates of the left, it was exciting to hear much of what was *said* – all those references to Rosa Luxemburg or Antonio Gramsci tripping off the tongue of a head of state. There had never been anything quite like it in our political lifetimes. But what did all this mean on the ground? Did the reality live up to the rhetoric? What was the real impact on the lives of ordinary Venezuelans?

Trying to find out became the main task of the rest of my stay in Venezuela – and of this book. But a year is very little.

I visited, of course, the Missions: the health mission, Barrio Adentro, which, with the help of more than 20,000 Cuban medical staff, has brought a doctor's surgery to almost every poor neighbourhood in Venezuela, usually for the first time; the education mission, Robinson I, which has taught about a million and half adults to read and write and effectively eliminated illiteracy from the country, as well as Missions Robinson II, Ribas and Sucre, which extend these new opportunities through primary and secondary education to the new Bolivarian University. These are at the heart of Venezuela's break with neoliberalism, and their popularity is at the heart of the mass support for Chavez and the Bolivarian revolution. After Tacagua Vieja, I visited a succession of other rural and urban co-operatives and 'endogenous development poles', where the basis of Venezuela's 'people's economy' was being laid out. And I spent some time with the peasants squatting on a vast cattle ranch belonging to English Lord 'Spam' Vestey – a ranch that had been singled out as the launch pad for a renewed drive towards land reform.

The people that I met in those communities, and the stories that they began to tell me, are the starting points for Chapters 1 to 3 of this book. Together their experiences are representative of the core content of Venezuela's revolution in its first half decade or more – the recovery of national sovereignty over many of the country's key resources, and the use of that wealth to reform and deepen the kinds of welfare provided to Venezuela's poor majority. These developments seemed to provide a practical demonstration that, contrary to Margaret Thatcher's nostrum, 'TINA', there *is* an alternative – and for that reason they are what first made the Bolivarian process an icon for the global justice movement. They are what had raised the spirits and the expectations of those 13,000 activists gathered in the Gigantinho in Porto Alegre.

But I also visited some of the less familiar developments, where a more radical, far-reaching alternative was gestating, where the first rough sketches for twenty-first-century socialism were being chalked out.

The co-management being introduced at the ALCASA aluminium plant in Ciudad Guayana was one of the most ambitious experiments in workplace democracy attempted anywhere in the world for at least a quarter of a century, arguably much longer. As those involved said themselves, it had many of the characteristics of workers' control on the way to workers' self-management. It was very different indeed from the kind of co-management promoted by social-democratic parties in the second half of the twentieth century in Europe, especially in West Germany.

In the tiny hilltop community of Galipan, I got to know one of the country's first Communal Planning Councils. Initiated by two young cooks and an ageing peasant leader, this had drawn up an ambitious scheme under which the local community would plan and manage its own future. When I first visited, they were fighting for support from a reluctant, pro-Chavez, local mayor. Soon they would become an example for what the president announced in January 2007 as the fifth and most important motor of the transition to Bolivarian socialism, the 'explosion of communal power'. These stories are the starting points for Chapters 4 and 5 of this book.

It is possible that in the course of that year I spent in Venezuela as a journalist I saw more and learnt more than many foreign correspondents have the chance, or sometimes the inclination, to do. But it was clear I had only begun to scratch the surface. It was also clear that beneath the surface, my initial question – what is the real impact on the lives of ordinary Venezuelans? – cascaded into a series of more profound questions. What, for their part, is the impact that these ordinary Venezuelans, with their desires and doubts, their questions and creativity, are having on 'the process'? How much of this comes from below, and how much from above? What, in the end, is the nature and possibility of socialism in the twenty-first century? And what strategies, if any, could plausibly lead there? As a working journalist facing the pressure of deadlines and programme editors, I was never going to get close to answering such questions.

The challenge was not just spatial – the need to dig deeper – but also temporal. Each of these stories that I had begun to unpick was only at a beginning. Each was crying out to be followed up later.

So this book has been a chance for me – and I hope for the readers too – to do just that, to scratch a little deeper beneath the surface, and then to watch the story unfold.

Readers may be relieved to find only occasional mention of

Chavez or the upper echelons of the Bolivarian movement in the central pages of this book. The aim is to look at the experience of ordinary Venezuelan women and men, and to listen to their voices, as a way of getting *inside* the process. Chavez and the other leaders appear only in so far as they figure as part of those people's experience and within their accounts – except in specific cases where more or less recognised leaders of the process are themselves among the protagonists of these grassroots experiences.[5]

In order to trace the unfolding of these experiences, I went back, in 2007 and 2008, to most of the people and places I'd been with earlier, and to a few new ones too. Of course, in almost every case, their stories had not come to an end – they were still unfolding. But they were unfolding in a context that was itself changing. Or rather, they were themselves, like Tolstoy's common people, just a few of the very many individual elements that were fashioning that changing context. In 2007, the re-election of Chavez to a second full term had given rise to a more forthright discourse about socialism. The beginnings of a new United Socialist Party, the PSUV (announced in December 2006) and the framework of the 'five motors' of the revolution and the transition to socialism (outlined in January 2007) were the official expressions of this more explicit commitment to socialism. In 2008, the surprise defeat of President Chavez' proposed constitutional reforms had produced a new mood of realism, expressed in the demand for the three 'R's – revise, rectify and re-energise. Had the project been fatally wounded? Would there really be a turn away from socialism of the twenty-first, or any other, century, towards an earlier, more limited horizon of nationalism? Chavez himself insisted that the objective had not changed, but the pace needed to be slower, more deliberate, more effective.

PRACTICE BEFORE THEORY

Seeking to ground this collective account in the concrete, lived experience of individual Venezuelans and the communities in which they live or work does not mean avoiding the more general, even abstract, realm of analysis and interpretation. On the contrary, many of the existing interpretations of the Bolivarian revolution err on the side of simplicity, not because they are too concrete but because they are too abstract. They often fail to take account of the multiplicity of lived experience that has found a place within it. And they often fail to measure the distance between intention and achievement, between rhetoric and reality. So for example, Tariq Ali's important interview, 'Changing the World by Taking Power', was a legitimate and timely rebuttal of some of the autonomist, would-be Zapatista, positions that could not cope with the phenomenon of a Chavez – a rebuttal taken further by D. Raby with her emphasis on the indispensable role of 'strong leadership'. But that is only half the story. It risks eclipsing the nonetheless real and also indispensable contribution of autonomist-type thinking and practice to the Venezuelan experience – and to its outlines of a socialism for the twenty-first century. This contribution has been very marked in some of the most impressive areas, like the urban land movement or the closely connected alternative media. And it has made a deep mark on some areas of government policy too, as in the way the attempts to develop a 'people's economy' have recycled lessons from the Brazilian Landless Workers' Movement (MST) and their '*economia solidaria*'.

Getting our understanding of these combinations right – or at least as right as we can – is no small matter. The significance goes well beyond Venezuela. And it goes beyond the immediate questions about what a government like that in Venezuela, or in Bolivia or in Ecuador, could or should do, because it begins to reveal much more generally where radical politics may be heading in the years to come. The experience in Venezuela is once again making it possible to ask some of the big political questions that have been off the agenda for half a generation.

In the decade since Seattle, we have seen a slow, cautious reappearance of radical thinking about political strategy. Old questions, about the who, where, when and how of fundamental change, are beginning to be asked again, but in new ways for a new period.[6] We are not, for the moment, in a situation similar to the one in the late 1960s and 1970s, which nurtured the generation, or generations, of '68. One of the main reasons we are not is obvious. Radical thought is not a purely intellectual construction. The explosion of thinking, discussing and writing then came out of more than 20 years of intensive and extensive struggle and upheaval in every continent of the world – during which the question of 'power' was posed with some frequency and urgency. The wave of post-Second-World-War decolonisation had fed through the Chinese Revolution, Dien Bien-Phu and the Cuban Revolution into a cycle of confrontations that raised enormous hopes, but which almost all ended in defeat: from the invasion of Santo Domingo and the 1965 slaughter in Indonesia, through the stifling of the multiple revolts of 1968 and the elimination of Latin America's guerrilla movements, to Popular Unity in Chile, the end of the Portuguese Revolution and the controlled transitions from dictatorship in Greece and Spain. In the few instances where there were successes, as in Vietnam, Angola or later Nicaragua, disappointment followed only too soon after. When the wall came down, the whole terrain seemed to have shifted.

The experiences since have been different. Some have been spectacular, like Seattle itself, or Genoa. Some have been extraordinary in scale, like the unprecedented worldwide anti-war marches on 15 February 2003. Some have come as a deep shock to the system, like the initial Zapatista uprising back in 1994, or the French 'Non' eleven years later. But none have carried with them a perspective of profound political, much less social, change.

This problem has been recognised within the new and diverse international movement against corporate globalisation. The early slogans of protest – 'the world is not for sale' – gave way to banners of promise – 'another world is possible' – and then a commitment to come up with concrete proposals. For more than five years in succession, the World Social Forums and their regional spin-offs – to take just the most obvious example – met in Porto Alegre, Mumbai, Florence, Paris, London, Quito, Bamako and Karachi, and promised to map out what another possible world might look like. There were fascinating, creative contributions. It began to look certain that many of the old assumptions – about the spaces, rhythms and subjects of radical change – would at least have to be reworked and relocated. But with few real experiences to go on, the contours of this new landscape remained abstract.

The single most important thing about Venezuela is that it has begun to fill that void. So far it is the only new example of a movement becoming a government that has not only avowed socialism as a long-term aim, but set itself the explicit task of building it here and now – 'build it now', in the words of Michael A. Lebowitz' book.[7] As such Venezuela has become *the* laboratory for a new cycle of revolutionary theory and practice. That is something that will remain, whether the Bolivarian experience ultimately succeeds or fails, or whether, as may be more likely, it ends up doing a bit of both.

It may be that 'socialism of the twenty-first century', as several on the left have argued, turns out to be a meaningless concept. But here and now it captures both the uncertainty of the moment, and its tentative, embattled, sense of promise. The aim of this book is to get the ordinary people of Venezuela to help us understand why that is.

1 OIL FOR FOOD, HEALTH, EDUCATION ...

In September 2004, Rodrigo Rato, the new head of the International Monetary Fund, advised oil-producing countries not to spend their rapidly rising revenue, but to save it. With the situation in Iraq going from bad to worse and China's economic expansion seemingly insatiable, world oil prices had been climbing sharply throughout the year. From around US$20 a barrel in January, the world benchmark price soared to over US$45 a barrel in October. The average price of Venezuelan crude – heavier and more difficult to refine than most – was a little lower. But by September it was still about 60 per cent higher than the US$20 a barrel on which the country's 2004 budget had been based.[1] The IMF's argument was that saving such windfalls rather than spending them would avoid stoking inflationary pressures and prevent the international economy from overheating. Oil-producing countries like Venezuela would then be better placed to invest in long-term projects to expand their capacity.

A DIFFERENT LOGIC IN CARAPITA

To José Gregorio Falcon and Greydaris Motta, in the Caracas slum of Carapita, this argument made little sense. It was just past 6 o'clock in the evening, early in October, when I met them. Along with 40 or so of their neighbours, they were beginning class in the local schoolroom in the San José sector of Carapita. They'd enrolled in Mission Ribas, one of a series of adult education programmes paid for directly out of Venezuela's oil income.[2]

At that time of day, with dusk falling fast, the view across the Caracas hillsides is spectacular. Tens of thousands of twinkling, low-wattage bulbs give it a Christmas tree appeal – concealing the reality of life for the million or more citizens who live in these precarious, gravity-defying shanty towns perched above the city centre. José Gregorio explained, 'I never got further than sixth grade, so I never had much opportunity in life. My father was very poor and didn't have any money for my schooling. But now it's free, so we're doing Years 1, 2 and 3 of Mission Ribas, which means we should be able to complete our *bachillerato* [high-school certificate] in two-and-a-half years. Then maybe I can go to university.'

Greydaris had her own story, similar but different. 'I didn't finish school because my parents didn't have much money and then I got pregnant.' Now Greydaris, with three boys, aged six, four and two, was hoping to become a lawyer. 'I'm doing this for my children's future,' she told me. 'If I study, maybe they'll follow my example.'

Both said the Missions had transformed the atmosphere in the neighbourhood. 'We've been encouraging more and more people to sign up. We try to persuade them. We lend them our books and materials. We help them with the exercises so they can catch up on anything they've missed. And the numbers are growing.'

Both agreed on something else too. 'It's thanks to President Chavez that we have these Missions.' 'This is being given to us by the president.' 'Our president is helping us students a lot with scholarships and so on.' About 10 per cent of those enrolled in Mission Ribas received a grant of about a $100 a month. The point was to make sure students with particularly difficult circumstances could concentrate on studying, without being distracted by the need to scrape together enough for the daily survival of themselves and their families. But there was a danger, as Greydaris pointed out. 'We are not studying because of these grants. We come to study because we want to be someone in life. But there are many who come just for the grant and nothing else. Then we say to them, don't come. Either you attend class regularly or you're out. If you want to come occasionally you can come as an observer, but without a grant. Because we're not having anyone strolling about the streets or sitting at home watching telly on a grant, while we're here working.'

José Gregorio pointed out proudly that he had never been paid a penny for his time over the last year as a member of the local health committee, helping the Cuban doctors of Barrio Adentro run the new local surgery. Barrio Adentro was perhaps the best known of all the social missions, through which more than 15,000 Cuban medical personnel had for the first time made primary health care easily and freely available in most of Venezuela's poor communities.

A little further up one of Carapita's steep, winding alleys, a dozen other local residents were crammed into Cecilia's front room. All but one were women. Like Greydaris and the others in the schoolroom, they sat facing a large TV. This one was playing the course video for Mission Robinson II. 'During the colonial period,' the female narrator stated, 'political and military power was exercised by the Captain General. ... Religion played a very important role ... and the main crop was cocoa.'[3] Magdalia explained to me: 'We've already learnt to read and write. Now we're learning where we came from.'

By the beginning of October 2004, the Venezuelan government calculated that its adult literacy programme, known as Mission Robinson I, had taught 1,314,788 Venezuelans to read and write in less than a year and a half.[4] A year later, on 28 October 2005, the government celebrated the certification of Venezuela by UNESCO as a 'territory free from illiteracy'. Kofi Annan, then Secretary-General of the United Nations, praised Venezuela's progress towards achieving the Millennium Development Goals. True, illiteracy levels had already been lower in Venezuela than in most of the region, at 7 per cent compared with an average of 11 per cent for the whole of Latin America and the Caribbean.[5] All the same, this still might be the world's most successful literacy programme ever. The Robinson II courses, like this one in Carapita, allowed the same students to go on and complete their primary education.

RETAKING VENEZUELA'S OIL

All this was possible precisely because the Bolivarian government had begun to re-assert control over Venezuela's oil industry, the fifth largest exporter in the world, and the fourth biggest supplier to the United States.[6] The industry had in fact been nationalised in 1976, with the creation of a new state oil company, PDVSA (Petroleos de Venezuela S.A.). But PDVSA increasingly came to be run as a giant bureaucratic empire in its own right – a state within the state – separate from any real government oversight, inhabited by the same managerial elite as before, and working in close symbiosis with the foreign oil majors which it had replaced, and with whom it now had a series of operating and exploration agreements – the terms of which were highly favourable to the international oil companies and often contravened the modest requirements of the existing legislation.

The first move by Chavez' supporters was to write into the 1999 Constitution a bar on any privatisation of PDVSA – something PDVSA managers and the previous government had certainly been moving towards. At the same time Chavez began an international campaign within OPEC, the oil producers' cartel, to raise world crude prices by ensuring production quotas were held to – something else that went in the opposite direction from previous PDVSA policy. He also began to curb the power of PDVSA managers by appointing a board made up of not PDVSA insiders but his own oil experts.

The last straw was the new Hydrocarbons Law introduced in 2001 which raised future royalty rates for foreign oil operators – to 30 per cent instead of the 16.66 per cent in the old law (or the 1 per cent many of them had actually been given exceptional licence to pay) – and stated that all state oil activities should be in the public interest and dedicated to 'the organic, integrated, and sustainable development of the country'. The response of the old PDVSA elite was support for the coup in April 2002 and a leading role in the opposition-led lockout at the end of that year. It was only after these two attacks had been defeated that Chavez moved to sack 18,000 PDVSA managers and technicians, and relaunch PDVSA as a Bolivarian state enterprise, 'belonging to everyone'. This, combined with the strengthening price of oil on the international market, is what freed up the resources to launch the Missions in 2003.

THE VISION OF AN ALTERNATIVE

The group gathered in Cecilia's front room were taking an obvious delight in their learning. Magdalia, still in her twenties, turned to Maribel, in her thirties or forties. 'Tell him how your life has changed!' 'Well, now that I can read and write, I can go out and I know where I'm going. I can see which bus to get on.' 'So you don't get lost, right?' And then she turned to Cecilia, who looked as if she might be past her sixties. 'I'm really happy because I knew very little. What we were taught when I was young was almost nothing. I never reckoned I would learn any more. And now I've really got on. But then I never imagined we'd get a president who was so much better than all the previous ones.'

Time and again it came back to this praise of President Chavez. 'If it wasn't for him, we'd never be here learning what we never knew before.' 'Before nobody could care less about the poor. They just shoved a piece of paper in front of you and said, sign here.' 'This is the first time in the history of Venezuela, in the history of the world, that a president has sat down in the Miraflores Palace and really thought about the poor, about the people up here on the hillsides. So that's why I ask the Lord and the Virgin to keep him in good health, so he can keep going.'

But this adulation went hand in hand with a vision of an alternative. 'Before the rich wasted the money, sending their children to study abroad and things like that. Presidents got into Miraflores and just divided the money among themselves and their mates. But now the president is spending it on us, the Venezuelans. And we also have the right. We are the inhabitants of Venezuela, we love our country and we want to serve it.' 'So I don't think the president's ideas, what he's doing, benefiting us the poor, can be bad for us or for the country.' 'He's giving the youngsters the chance to study in the universities, which they could never afford before. And later they will help the country. They are its future.'

And this alternative, which these three generations of women in a Caracas slum had begun to imagine, included a recognition of the limitations of the current oil bonanza. 'We cannot live only on oil. We need to learn more about other kinds of production, so that we can move the country forward. That's also what we are studying for.'

Two things begin to stand out from the way the people of Carapita – and tens of thousands like them in other neighbourhoods – talk about their experience of the Missions and the other social benefits that they perceive the Bolivarian revolution has brought them. They are two of the most enduring characteristics, or sometimes contradictions, of the Bolivarian process, and we shall return to them repeatedly in the course of this book.

One is this sense of an alternative. It is an alternative that obeys a logic very different to that of Rodrigo Rato and the IMF, with their recommendations of fiscal restraint. Here the priorities are inverted, with the poor neighbourhoods now in pole position. The terms of debate are also reversed. Spending on the poor is no longer seen as an expense, but as a form of investment.

The second is this peculiar identification with the figure of Hugo Chavez himself – universally recognised as both leader and incarnation of the Bolivarian process. There *is* a strong element of veneration here. At first sight this *does* seem to lend weight to what many opponents, and some friends, have described critically as the 'populism' or even 'personality cult' at work in Venezuela. But there is more to it than that. Something else can be detected, even in the words people here choose to describe their experience.

They talk of course about 'getting on', 'making progress' and 'improving themselves'. But one of the phrases you hear most often in these *barrios* is when people refer to themselves, and those around them who are taking part in the Missions and the other activities, as those who 'want to emerge' (*que queremos surgir*). And that is indeed what has happened. A whole section of Venezuelan society, the poor in general but in particular the urban poor of the Caracas hillsides, several millions of people who had been buried in silence, obscurity and neglect, have suddenly 'emerged' from the shadows and established themselves as actors, as protagonists both of their own individual stories and of the nation's collective drama.

What we need to understand are the great variety of ways they have organised themselves in the process; and the kind of alternative that points towards.

THE RING OF FIRE AROUND CARACAS

It was of course these poor, shanty-town communities of Caracas – in tandem with middle-ranking army personnel – that saved President Chavez from the coup of April 2002. In fact there is a case for saying that they have been *the* central actor of Venezuela's recent history, at least since the 1989 revolt known as the *Caracazo*.[7] Either way it is the combination of the charismatic figure of Chavez and these labyrinthine urban slums that has set the tone of the Bolivarian revolution. So it is worth trying to understand a little better where these urban communities, and the people who live in them, come from.

Carapita

Carapita is both typical and specific.[8]

Like many of the hills around the historic city of Caracas, Carapita – and the Antimano parish of which it is part – was once Indian land. It was granted by the Spanish crown as a reserve for a branch of Los Teques, an indigenous people of the Carib ethnic group, because the Spaniards wanted to keep the indigenous people safely outside their colonial capital. Later many of these indigenous inhabitants were moved further afield: first to Macarao, where there were other communities of Los Teques; then much further into Bolivar state in the deep south of Venezuela, which helps to explain why indigenous groups far into Venezuela's continental hinterland are descended from coastal Caribs. One community organiser in Carapita, Sofia Lashley, told me they had found indigenous artefacts at the top of the hill in the cemetery of the Heart of Jesus Church. By the beginning of the twentieth century there were almost no indigenous people left. A 1904 law called for these lands to be registered by the descendants of those indigenous communities, but in most cases no such register occurred. There was no one to do it. Much of the land became classified as *ejidos* – public land that belonged to the municipality and could not be sold.

But what followed in Antimano and some other of the most desirable areas was similar to what happened in much of the Venezuelan countryside through the first half of the twentieth century. Large landowners lodged a long and convoluted series of judicial claims, purchases and expansions – many of them almost certainly fraudulent – which were accepted by the courts. There was little or no oversight of the land registers. Most of Antimano parish became ostensibly private land.

When the first squatters began to build their homes in Carapita, in 1958, it was a *hacienda* or farm 'belonging' to the Baptista family. It grew potatoes, plantains and bananas. There were wild mangoes in abundance. In fact the first squatters were employees of the Baptistas.

They'd been brought in to guard fences built at the bottom and the top of the farm, to keep other intruders out. But when they stopped being paid, the employees decided to leave the farm shacks they'd been housed in down by the road, and move up the hillside to build their own homes. Sofia Lashley is 37 years old, so she wasn't around at the time. But from the tiny, two-room, breeze-block home she now inhabits with her partner and 16-year-old son, squeezed down a steep, narrow stone staircase from the Calle San José, she has learnt the history of her community in astonishing detail. 'The houses were very spread out then. There were only two on this road. In La Chinita there was just one, and that disappeared in the 1970s.'

The real building boom in Carapita came in 1973. It was part of a process affecting all the hillsides along the southern flanks of the central Caracas valley – driven by a mass exodus from the Venezuelan countryside and the first international oil crisis. The sharp rise in Venezuela's oil revenues deepened the economy's ever more exclusive dependence on hydrocarbons – and fuelled a frenzy of prestige construction projects in the centre of the capital. Agriculture was abandoned even further. The governments of Rafael Caldera and then Carlos Andres Perez were dreaming of a 'Venezuela Saudita' that could slide seamlessly into the first world. But the other facet of that Caracas dream was the ring of *ranchos* or shanty-towns that sprang up to surround it, both physically and eventually politically.

'What really triggered the growth of Carapita was that they'd begun quarrying rock here. They were dynamiting left, right and centre. In fact,' Sophia points out, 'that's one of the reasons so much of this *barrio* is on unstable ground now. The company was Cementos La Vega and they were taking as much rock and sand from here as they could, to make cement for the construction industry. From higher up in La Mamera they were taking coal too.'

Antimano parish was rich in minerals. That meant there was work there and land to live on. 'The peasants had been demanding credit to work the land in the countryside. But they were told there was no money. If they wanted work they'd be given it here in Caracas.' The process had begun earlier, in the 1960s under Caldera and even earlier under President Romulo Betancourt. 'When the peasants began to arrive behind the presidential palace, where they were finishing the 23 Enero neighbourhood, they put many of them into buses, brought them here to the lower part of Carapita and told them to go up the hillside.'

The process accelerated after 1973, especially under the first administration of Carlos Andres Perez. Antonio Briceno, now in his seventies, can remember first hand. 'Everyone moved to Caracas because there was no work anywhere else. We came from all over. We needed food. The police came to beat us up and tear down our shacks. So we came back at night to build the *ranchos*.'

Carapita, like almost all the Caracas *ranchos*, was self-built. This, of course, is not unique to Venezuela or to Latin America. One of the most extraordinary untold feats of the last half century is how the world's poor, with almost no resources and few formal skills, have built for themselves a great part of the planet's largest cities, from the *kampung* of Jakarta and the townships around Johannesburg, to the *favelas* of Rio de Janeiro.

In those early years, the homes in Carapita were almost all made of corrugated iron sheets, wood and reinforced cardboard. 'It was only towards the end of the 1980s, with the OCV (Organisation for Home Credits) that our community really began to emerge [that word *surgir* again].' That's when people began to see brick buildings on the hillsides, Sofia recalls. Some basic services were put in too. Sometimes they were financed by the OCV. Sometimes people just organised a *sancocho comunitario* (community meal) and raised the money themselves. But the work was done by the community. 'Everyone got together in one place and did it. The services were put in by the community. No government can claim to have paved the streets here. They were all dug out and cemented over by the people themselves. The same with the staircases and the drains. The fact that many of the services are now collapsing is because we didn't have sufficient knowledge and engineering skills to provide them for the whole community.'

For example, the main street (more of a steep, narrow alley) through the Manguito *barrio* of Carapita, was built, I am told, on the initiative of Senora Andrea Coba, '*el viejito*' ('the old man', who doesn't seem to have another name) and four people from the Fatima sector, including Antonio Briceno – because most of the others didn't want to contribute anything. Antonio confirms the story: 'We formed a junta and decided what to do. Each person put in 10, 15 or 20 bolivars, and we began to buy the cement, the stone, the earth. ...This has always been one of the most neglected parishes, by all governments, though not so much now.'

Sofia adds: 'That was a road that was going to benefit 1,000 families at the time. Now we have 3,000 families in the *barrio* using it. That's the kind of heroism that existed, that even then there were people thinking about the collective. They did it by their own effort.' For Avelino Montilla, one of the oldest activists in the neighbourhood, this explains another important characteristic: 'leadership in the community developed out of those who took the initiative. Because the government did nothing at all. Now Hugo Chavez Frias has given a big support. But there are still many things unfinished.'

It is important to grasp this tradition of self-help running through the recent history of Venezuela's poor communities. Domestic opponents of the Bolivarian revolution, and often the supposedly impartial international media as well, frequently depict President Chavez as using Venezuela's oil income to 'give' a series of benefits to the country's helpless and passive poor, and thereby to be 'buying' the political support that he so obviously enjoys. Whether wilfully or out of ignorance, this conveys an incomplete and seriously misleading picture.

For the Missions and other social programmes undertaken by the Chavez administration have slotted into a long history of community action and self-reliance. In Venezuela this may never have taken the form of well-structured, citywide or even national organisations of the urban poor, as it did in some other parts of Latin America. It was never the same as the grassroots church communities (*Comunidades Eclesiais de Base* or CEBs) in Brazilian cities like São Paulo and Porto Alegre, which in the late 1970s and 1980s, along with the newly militant industrial trade unions, helped to put an end to that country's military dictatorship and formed the backbone of the new mass Workers' Party (PT);[9] or those in parts of Central America like San Salvador, where they helped to sustain a clandestine guerrilla struggle and sporadic forms of dual power for the best part of a decade. In the years before the Bolivarian government was elected, Venezuela's *barrio* movement may never have acquired the political consistency of the urban poor movement that emerged from the rubble of Mexico City's 1985 earthquake, and which in turn helped

[26]

to bury the old politics of the PRI in the 1988 elections; and maybe it never consciously led an insurrection or toppled a series of governments, like the Argentinean *piqueteros* (unemployed movements) or the neighbourhood associations of Bolivia's El Alto did in 2001–02, 2003 and 2005.[10]

Certainly, the lack of strong co-ordinating structures in the Venezuelan urban movement has a price. Activists like Sofia Lashley in Carapita are painfully aware that, among other things, it makes it more likely that *some* local initiatives will fall prey to individual attempts at self-advancement, patronage or outright corruption.[11] But however localised and fragmented this Venezuelan urban movement has been, it has rather successfully combined a varying geometry of three key components: an impressive and more or less uninterrupted history of self-help initiatives, alongside a stream of demands and complaints levelled at local and national authorities, and a dynamic of rapid response to each and every opportunity opened up to it from above.

This combination is such a central pillar of the whole Bolivarian experience that we need to look more closely at the shifting forms of organisation that it has spawned in the *barrios*. In the process, we may also get a better insight into one of the secrets of President Chavez' political success – for he has shown he knows exactly how to engage with, and build upon, this pre-existing pattern of popular action.

FORMS OF SELF-ORGANISATION

Carapita is a good place to follow these shifts, precisely because it is *not* renowned for its history of militant organisation. Unlike the more emblematic *barrios* of La Vega or 23 Enero, it did not have a dense tradition of political struggle going back long before the arrival of Hugo Chavez. Its history of organisation is in that sense probably *more* representative.

In the early days, Sofia Lashley tells me, when there was plenty of work in the quarries and in the factories that multiplied at the bottom of the hill, people naturally organised themselves through trade unions. 'There was the Ronco pasta factory in Carapas, the industrial zone of Antimano parish.[12] That also processed rice and baby cereals. There was a flour mill, a soap factory and then a

General Motors car-parts factory. Now Carapas is just full of empty sheds.' Wages were low and to begin with the unions proved effective instruments of struggle. 'But they became politicised,' says Sofia, referring to the growing subordination of Venezuela's traditional trade union movement to the country's historic 'social-democratic' party, Acción Democratica (AD) – just as that party itself was becoming an increasingly integral part of the ruling establishment. 'The unions became a business, selling the sweat of our workers.'[13]

Something similar happened with the traditional neighbourhood associations (Asociaciones de Vecinos) that grew up alongside the community's efforts to build its own *barrio*. Avelino recalls that 'when there were community assemblies at the beginning, then you could talk of real community organisation. But later, when they legalised the neighbourhood associations, the community participation disappeared.' Like the trade unions, most of the neighbourhood associations became absorbed into the AD machinery. In fact, Carapita, and Antimano as a whole, became an important 'Adeco' base (a stronghold of support for Acción Democratica). 'The neighbourhood associations took care of some obvious things, a broken pipe here or there. But they became "personalised" and just served the interests of a few, not the collective. You saw their houses growing bigger while the community continued to suffer. The community as a whole no longer participated.'

At the same time, the more immediate organisational forms of everyday life in urban slums like Carapita had also changed greatly. Sofia likens the old family structure to that of an indigenous community. 'Before, our families were big, extended families with 13 or more children.' The flight from the countryside and the industrialisation in places like Carapita meant that 'the old peasant family began to disintegrate. You began to get nuclear families with a mother, a father, a child and at most one grandparent. I'm 37 for example, and I have just one child. You could say that capitalism destroyed the family community we had. This has been a struggle for our roots against industrialisation.'

The restructuring of Venezuelan capitalism through the 1990s, of course, added a further twist. As factories closed, jobs also disappeared. Sofia used to work as a receptionist in a city hotel, her partner as a builder. But neither has had a proper job for years. A typical

Caracas *rancho* now has maybe just 15 per cent of its adult population working in paid employment of some kind. More than 60 per cent survive doing bits and pieces in the informal economy.[14] As in so many other cities across Latin America, even the nuclear family has become something of a rarity, with single and abandoned mothers taking the strain. For many of the children, violence and crime became one of the few options available. Even now, almost a decade into the Bolivarian revolution, many parts of Antimano parish are no-go areas for non-resident males, as local drug gangs fight to mark out and defend 'their' territory.

In some of the more militant *barrios* of Caracas, like 23 Enero, the neighbourhood associations were effectively displaced from the late 1970s through into the 1990s by an array of more dynamic organisations. To begin with, some were religious, like the grassroots church communities (CEBs), inspired by the liberation-theology wing of the Roman Catholic Church.[15] Later, many were ostensibly cultural, organising educational, cultural and sports activities. One sector alone of 23 Enero, called Las Cañadas, had five separate family sports clubs. In addition there were folk culture groups, traditional drumming groups, community newspapers and the beginnings of what was to become Venezuela's rich experience with other alternative media – community radio, video and TV. Beyond these particular purposes, all had a strong social orientation, and increasingly they became the vehicles for grassroots political opposition. But according to Ivan Martinez, the head of the government's National Urban Land Office, and himself a long-time community organiser, they also had two other key characteristics that have left their mark on the popular movement that underpins the Bolivarian revolution.

Firstly, and partly in response to the way Acción Democratica and other mainstream parties had co-opted other popular organisations, they displayed a strong anti-party tendency. They tapped into the self-help tradition described earlier and sought to mobilise the communities to meet their own needs as far as possible. They wanted to avoid being used to serve interests or projects from outside the community. This distrust of political parties even extended to the few organised currents of the far left – groups like Bandera Roja (Red Flag), the GAR (Revolutionary Action Groups) and Ruptura (Rupture) – which did have serious links in the *barrios*.

[29]

Secondly, and partly as an extension of the first, these organisations were very localised. 'Localism was one of their defining characteristics,' says Ivan Martinez. 'There were attempts to co-ordinate between them, but most failed. The big common fronts of organisations came together at critical moments but then tended to disappear again. This localism reached the extreme of being resentful even of other grassroots organisations that began to overlap with their own sphere of action.'

Although these more active organisations did spring up in most of the *barrios* of Caracas, their presence in Carapita was never more than ephemeral. It was not until more than three years into Hugo Chavez' presidency that there emerged what were rapidly to become *the* fundamental organisations of Venezuela's urban poor – and the issue they organised around was *land*.[16]

URBAN LAND COMMITTEES

Land ownership had always been an issue in the *barrios*, because one of the reasons successive governments gave for not attending to the communities' needs was that they had no ownership rights. Right at the beginning of the urban explosion, when the *barrios* began to grow exponentially, the first government of Carlos Andres Perez had a policy of deliberately trying to camouflage their existence behind pretty, remodelled façades. Traditional urban planners worked on the assumption that sooner or later these popular neighbourhoods would have to disappear, because they were built on dangerous terrain and made the city look ugly.

But according to Ivan Martinez, after 50 years it has become clear that the *barrios* will not go away, that they have to be seen as part of the solution and not as part of the problem. In 2002, the Bolivarian government explicitly recognised this. In a rally at the Military Museum in 23 Enero, on 4 February 2002 – two months before the opposition tried to overthrow him in their failed coup – President Chavez announced Decree 1666, urging all public institutions to support the 'organised communities' in regularising land occupancy and ownership in the *barrios*. For Martinez, 'it was the first time any government had explicitly acknowledged that the *barrios* are not invisible, that they are there and that their residents have the same rights as everyone else, including the right to property.'

It was a strange battle cry for an administration that was already being accused by opponents of steering Venezuela towards 'Cuban-style communism'. The central slogan accompanying that decree – it still dominates the poster on the door to Ivan Martinez' office – would hardly have seemed out of place in the Central Office of Margaret Thatcher's Conservative Party: 'The Revolution creates millions of home-owners' (except of course for the word 'revolution'). Ivan Martinez explains: 'The strategy here is the democratisation of urban land. There's been a lot of propaganda suggesting the revolution would take away people's property. But on the contrary, we are recognising the right to own their land for 10 million people whose right to the place they live is in a precarious and uncertain state.'

The response from the communities was swift and far-reaching. All across Caracas, and in time in towns and cities across the country too, people began to organise urban land committees (CTUs or Comites de Tierra Urbana). The decree had identified these collective organisations as the one and only channel through which individuals could acquire title to their plots. This proved to be the secret of the land committees' success – that they took this core aspiration of the urban poor for individual security and improvement and turned it into the engine of collective community organisation.

Each CTU was meant to cover up to 200 homes, within an area whose natural boundaries would be defined by the community itself.[17] The members of the CTU should be elected in an assembly attended by at least 50 per cent of the inhabitants. They would then register themselves with the National Urban Land Office and begin a census of their community, gathering the information needed to begin regularising the land tenure of the various plots.

Sofia Lashley had never been involved in any kind of community organisation before that decree. She recalls that even in Antimano, with its relative lack of a militant tradition, 'there were three CTUs set up by the end of February, less than a month after the decree – one in Las Clavellinas at the entrance, one in Carapita itself, and one in the May First neighbourhood.' In El Manguito, she told me, it took them a bit longer. 'We hadn't fully understood the mechanisms. We were the seventh. We had the first assembly to form our CTU in

October 2002. We planned it as one big one for 3,200 families. So when we went to register they explained that was too many and they put us down as a "Promoting Committee" for the CTUs. So we began again and ended up with 13 CTUs in this neighbourhood.'

In some areas, the CTUs spread more quickly and with deeper roots. In the Cajigal sector of 23 Enero, Marta Garcia told me how they did it. 'Someone who knew how it worked came from the mayor's office, from the Libertador Municipality.[18] We put some announcements in the local and community media first. Then we just went out with megaphones and called people together. We got a massive turnout on the spot. People had been wanting to buy their land for years but couldn't. So we elected seven full members and seven auxiliary members there and then, in a very democratic process, by secret ballot. Our CTU represented 173 plots, with between 700 and 800 people living on them. The initial census we carried out recorded in great detail which homes were owned or rented, the state of each building, how many people lived in each, and so on. These were the first real organisations to come out of the revolutionary process. All the other local organisations that came later were based on these, and drew on the information that these had gathered.'

In Carapita, Sofia says it was a much harder slog. 'This was a strongly *Adeco* neighbourhood, so it took the devil of a struggle. At first people didn't believe in it at all. We had to organise land registry co-ops to draw up the registry of the whole parish. Some of these co-ops worked, others didn't. We had a right business when everyone wanted to be in the co-ops because they heard they were going to be paid. Then it turned out they weren't getting paid.'

For Ivan Martinez, the CTUs illustrate precisely that combination of initiative from above and spontaneous organisation from below. 'Yes, there was a decree from the state, from above. But then the CTUs were organised by the people themselves, spontaneously. Nobody went to the *barrios* to organise the CTUs. They did it themselves and then brought their registers here. We just set up a mechanism.'

In sheer numbers, this was the biggest initiative in self-organisation unleashed by the Bolivarian process in Venezuela (at least up until the new initiatives of 2007 around Communal Councils and the United Socialist Party). The National Urban Land Office reported a total of 6,494 urban land committees in 2006, covering almost a million dwellings and organising more than 1.4 million families or 7 million people. Between 2004 and 2006 these had succeeded in winning 281,578 title deeds benefiting more than 400,000 families or more than 2 million people. In the capital district of Caracas alone, where 60 per cent of the population live in *barrios* or popular neighbourhoods, there were 1,298 CTUs. About 75 per cent of these had completed their land surveys, and about half the families in these – that is, 90,000 families – had already legalised their land ownership.

PROBLEMS WITH PRIVATE PROPERTY

In Carapita, however, the CTUs faced a particular problem – one that reveals another of the contradictions in the Bolivarian process, and which is still playing itself out: the question of private property. Most of the *barrios* in Caracas, indeed most of the city itself, were built on public land. This made it relatively easy, once the CTUs had done their work, for the authorities to process the claims and grant titles to the individual occupants. In Carapita the situation was different. While overall in Caracas only 20–25 per cent of the land is ostensibly privately owned, in the parish of Antimano the reverse is true. About 89 per cent of the land belongs in theory to private landowners. And private property is of course protected by the Bolivarian Constitution of 1999. That makes the process of regularisation – even when the existing private claims are bogus – much more complicated.

The only ways in which such private ownership can be overturned under existing law are laid out in the Law on Expropriation and the Civil Code, which dates from 1989 and incorporates elements from the previous code of 1950. The main instrument is known as *prescripción* ('caducity'), which is a kind of penalty for a number of infractions, especially failing to take action against an occupation of the property for 20 years or more. In this event, title goes, in principle, to the occupant. In other words, people occupying such land as their own in the *barrios* for 20 years or more should have the right to acquire ownership. However the procedures for implementing this under the civil code are prohibitively slow and costly.[19] Firstly, each case (that is, each plot) has to be treated as an individual case. In every instance, notification has to be given by paid advertisement in two national-circulation newspapers, like *Universal* or *El Nacional*, once a week over four weeks, to allow the supposed owners to dispute the claim. At about 400,000 bolivars per advertisement, that means a cost of some 3.2 million bolivars (roughly US$1,500), which may be more than the market value of the plot. Assuming the 'owners' never show up, which is likely in most cases, each case then has to be ratified by the court. Obviously, most people are not prepared to go to this kind of expense or trouble. 'They know they've been living there for 20 years or more, so what's the point?' asks Ivan Martinez.

In 2006, there was an attempt to break this legal log jam. On the one hand, on the basis of the Urban Land Office's own legal investigations, a decree was issued reinstating the classification of 40 per cent of Antimano parish as *ejido* – that is returning it to its 1904 status as public land. More fundamentally, Ivan Martinez and others from the Urban Land Office had helped to draw up a new Special Law on the Integrated Regularisation of Land Tenure in Popular Urban Settlements. As a special law this would take precedence over the Civil Code. The draft law included several new measures for dealing with supposedly private land. Firstly, the period of occupancy needed for *prescripción* would be reduced from 20 years to 10. 'This isn't very radical,' points out Martinez. 'In Brazil and several other Latin American countries the period is five years.' Secondly, a new administrative mechanism would deal collectively with groups of plots or indeed whole neighbourhoods, not with individual plots. Thirdly, this administrative mechanism meant there would be no need to go to court unless the adjudication was challenged by the supposed private owners. After three years of public consultation, the Special Law was finally passed by the National Assembly on 17 July 2006. But, mysteriously, the entire mechanism for 'expropriation' of 'private' land was left out. Only the reduction to ten years was retained.

Why this happened is unclear. After the December 2005 legislative elections, which opposition parties decided to boycott on the grounds, never substantiated, that they would not be free and fair, Venezuela's National Assembly had become 100 per cent 'pro-Chavez'. So did the elected representatives simply make a mistake? Was pressure brought to bear by interested parties? Or were some more obscure forms of 'inducement' at play? Either way it raises questions about the ability of Venezuela's Bolivarian legislature to attend effectively to the needs and demands of the country's poor. All Ivan Martinez is prepared to say is that, 'this is a defect, which we are now trying to correct through the Enabling Law passed at the beginning of 2007.' That was the measure that gave President Chavez for 18 months the power to introduce new legislation in specified areas by decree. It was a measure that had been widely criticised in the opposition and international media as evidence that the government was heading in an 'authoritarian' direction. Government supporters, including interestingly many members of the National Assembly, had in turn insisted it was needed to set the country on its new course towards socialism of the twenty-first century. But they never quite got to explain why the *Chavista* National Assembly was incapable of doing this.[20]

These difficulties in dealing with private land took a toll on community organisation in Carapita. 'By 2004, we had 133 urban land committees in Antimano parish,' recalls Sofia Lashley. 'But two years later, we were in exactly the same situation. Nothing had happened. The only parish in Caracas where no land titles had been handed out was Antimano. I was responsible for the parish co-ordination of CTUs and I can tell you that no more than 20 of the 133 committees were still functioning.'

'Because there was no *respuesta* [response],' adds Avelino, pointing to another key characteristic of Venezuela's community organisations – their thoroughly pragmatic approach. 'No one is going to waste their time if there is no *respuesta*.'

FROM LAND COMMITTEES TO MISSIONS

But the channel set up by the urban land committees had already borne other fruits, including some in Carapita. The original decree in 2002 had only talked about regularising land tenure, but for the communities it had meant more than that. The initial censuses carried out by the CTUs had also looked at a range of other needs: water, building problems, families in acute poverty and with special health

and disability requirements. On this basis, the CTUs became a channel for almost all the Missions and other government social
programmes in the *barrios*. As Ivan Martinez puts it: 'with the CTUs
a channel was established, and people used it to raise a whole range
of issues.'

'Here in Antimano,' Sofia says, 'it was really the health committees that took over the baton from the land committees. Because
when the Missions began, the CTUs were no longer enough and new
forms of organisation began to emerge.' It was in June 2003 that
Cuban doctors began to arrive in the parish. 'That was a challenge for
all of us. There were no houses for the Cuban doctors to stay in. How
were we going to organise their accommodation? At first no one
wanted to be in the health committees, so we organised them with the
same representatives who had been elected to the land committees.
So then the CTUs began to die. Where before there had been between
14 and 28 people involved, now there were maybe just four left doing
the work.'

Again, the shift was eminently pragmatic. 'At that stage the
CTUs had still not achieved any *respuesta*, while the health committees were new and the benefits soon became obvious. Apart from
bringing the doctors and the medicines, there also came improvements in the surroundings. The health modules were built [a simple
two-storey building with the doctors' clinic and possibly a dentist's
surgery downstairs, and a couple of rooms for the Cubans' living
quarters upstairs]. So nobody listened to the land committees any
more.'

The basic literacy programme of Mission Robinson I began about
the same time, in July 2003. This also demanded community involvement. There was an appeal for volunteers, both as facilitators and to
provide rooms in their homes for classes. But in this case, the knock-
on effect for community organisation was less. As in several of the
other Missions, the basic organisational structure was provided by an
ad hoc combination of military personnel and bits of the civilian
administration (including, in some places, direct involvement of the
state oil company PDVSA) – usually working outside the traditional
ministerial structures, in this case of the Ministry of Education.[21]

A little later, it was Mission Ribas that became the driving force
of community organisation in much of Carapita. As part of their

accelerated secondary education, students like José Gregorio and Greydaris Motta had to draw up social projects for the community, and then get them implemented – things like improving school buildings or replacing water pipes. In Carapita this led to another organisational shift. 'The "Technical Water Boards" [linked to the Caracas public water company, Hidrocapital] had existed for 25 years or so. … With Mission Ribas these underwent another boom,' Sofia says, 'to allow us to get running water to all the houses that didn't have it.'

In better-organised areas, like 23 Enero, without the frustrations of being unable to obtain titles to private land, there was no difficulty keeping the land committees going as other forms of organisation flourished. Marta Garcia told me the CTUs in her area have continued to function, and that they help to promote the new forms of organisation around specific needs – the habitat and housing committees, the sports and recreation committees, since 2006 the new energy committees that have been putting in energy-saving light bulbs throughout the *barrios* – as well as supporting the whole gamut of new and old Missions.

UNFINISHED BUSINESS

Whether active or dormant, the urban land committees were both the starting point for a new cycle of community organising and the underpinning for almost all the varied and sometimes ephemeral forms of organisation that followed. They became, in a sense, the organisational heart of the Bolivarian revolution in its second, post-coup phase. As such, they provided a template for the Community Councils (Consejos Comunales), which were set to become the heart of its third phase, marked by the promise of a transition to twenty-first-century socialism.

Two key points emerge from all this: the peculiar relationship between Chavez and the people, and the pre-eminent role of the urban poor in the Bolivarian revolution.

As we have seen, it is clear that the Missions, about which a great deal has already been written, did not arrive to fill a vacuum in Venezuela's urban slums. On the contrary, they encountered, and interacted with, a dense history of self-organisation.

This 'encounter' – between a number of centralised policies issuing from above, essentially from the president, and a diverse field of initiatives bubbling up from below – has been one of the most enduring, and enigmatic, features of the Bolivarian experience. We need to try very hard to understand both sides of this combination, between Chavez and the Venezuelan poor. Equally importantly, we need to try to understand what happens when the two intersect.

The mainstream portraits of a maverick *caudillo* throwing around Venezuela's oil revenues in irresponsible populist gestures, or worse still, deliberately buying up popular support, utterly fail to do this. They fail to grasp the anti-neoliberal logic that guides these government policies – the idea that spending considerable amounts of oil revenue on social programmes may not be an expense at all, it may not even be just a repayment of the social debt; it may instead be an investment in social change. More importantly, they are completely blind to the real history, activity and contribution of the communities involved.

But it is not easy to come up with an adequate alternative. The conventional categories of the left are not well equipped to understand this combination either. With hardly anything in the way of organised social movements, parties or political programmes to engage with in the middle, many left-wing approaches to this core relationship between Chavez and the people are also haunted by the spectre of populism.

The second key point makes it doubly difficult to fit all this into an understanding of what Venezuela's twenty-first-century socialism might look like, and how it might emerge. This is the fact that this core combination – of initiatives from above and below – has not been centred on the traditional agents of socialist transformation, the wage-earning proletariat or the revolutionary peasantry – the political subjects that have framed most existing socialist thinking in both the twentieth and the nineteenth centuries. Instead the central subject of the Bolivarian process has been the under-employed urban poor.

It may seem strange. After all the idea that we live on a planet of slums is hardly new – and a number of social revolts in recent decades have been spearheaded by urban masses organised, if they are organised at all, not at the point of production, but in the places they live. Yet this is a section of society that existing socialist theories and strategies still do not quite know what to do with. And Venezuela is arguably the first place where they have done more than rebel, where they have taken the lead in what purports to be a process of socialist transformation. It is not that the traditional subjects are irrelevant in Venezuela. On the contrary, in the coming chapters we shall make some important detours through farms and factories. But this is a challenge to which we shall return.

2 THE PEOPLE'S ECONOMY

The long billboard above the gate showed President Chavez on one side saluting on the other the figure of Fabricio Ojeda. He was a member of parliament who quit Venezuela's National Assembly in 1962 to join the guerrillas and was later killed. Between these two emblematic, heroic portraits, the sign read: 'The Revolution is the fusion of the Missions.' This was October 2004 and the entrance to the Fabricio Ojeda Endogenous Development Nucleus – itself set to become an emblem of that new phase of the Bolivarian revolution.

Inside the gate, a broad, neatly swept square was bordered on three sides by clean, new or rebuilt buildings. In the middle, a covered meeting area had steep stand-seating for maybe a couple of hundred people. Alvaro Blanco and two others were laying a final line of kerb stones around the edge. He seemed to be the one who knew what he was doing. 'I have about 15 years experience in the building trade. But most of us were unemployed. We had no jobs, nothing. So we got organised in co-operatives and now we've been working here for four months. We've been fitting out the whole complex, this central area, the sports ground, the Mercal super-market outside the gate, the building on that side for the clinic, and those two for the textile workshop and the shoe-making factory. They will be run as co-operatives too. This is a project for the whole community. But PDVSA (Venezuela's state oil company) is in charge of the whole logistical part. They pay for the materials and everything, because we are just beginning and we don't have the resources for a construction project on this scale. We had 360 people working here day and night when we began. Now there are only a few of us left because we are just doing the finishing details before the *nucleo* is inaugurated. Later we'll be back to work on the second phase, building the school up on the hill there, and a library.'

Fabricio Ojeda was the first nucleus for endogenous (or self-sufficient) development (NUDE) launched by the Bolivarian revolution. Alvaro and his colleagues were laying those final paving stones at just about the time that President Chavez was summoning all his ministers, all the country's governors and mayors, all the heads of state enterprises and public institutions, senior military commanders and members of parliament, to that two-day high-level workshop mentioned in the Introduction, to discuss 'The New Strategic Map' for the Bolivarian revolution. That 'map' identified ten 'strategic objectives'. Objective Number 7 was to 'speed up the construction of a new model of production, as a way of moving towards the creation of a new economic system'.[1] Fabricio Ojeda was a prime example, perhaps *the* prime example, of this 'new model of production'. But how was it meant to work? And in exactly what sense were Alvaro and the others 'moving towards a new economic system'?

As we saw, at this stage, although Chavez did mention the need to go beyond capitalism, he was not talking explicitly about socialism, much less about the elimination of private property. 'No', he told his assembled leaders, what was needed at the moment was 'a social economy, a humanist and egalitarian economy', and that would have a good deal to do with these nuclei of endogenous development, with the Vuelvan Caras job training mission, and with the new Ministry for the People's Economy. So was this it? Was this how the Bolivarian revolution planned to 'transcend capitalism' – with networks of co-operatives integrated into nuclei of endogenous development, all held together with revenues from the state oil company? Was Fabricio Ojeda to become the starting point for socialism in the twenty-first century?

PDVSA CALLS ON THE COMMUNITY

The Fabricio Ojeda Nucleus was built on the site of a disused fuel depot belonging to the state oil company, PDVSA, in the western Caracas neighbourhood of Catia, in Sucre parish, a dense network of urban slums that is home to some 1.2 million people. The location was chosen by President Chavez himself at the end of 2003. They told me he used to fly directly overhead in his helicopter on the way to the airport. He'd repeatedly asked his aides what this apparently empty, 13-hectare space was doing lying idle in the middle of a sea of poverty.

A few months later the project began. The idea was to combine the unused resources of Venezuela's powerful oil industry with the active engagement of local communities to generate a new model of self-sufficient, people-centred development. The Fabricio Ojeda Nucleus was to be a pioneer of the principle that we heard President Chavez spell out in the Introduction, just after his August 2004 referendum victory, that 'the only way of combating poverty is to give power to the poor.' Combined with endogenous development, it was to be the founding principle of his proposed 'people's economy'.

Neither the idea, nor the practice, of endogenous development was entirely new in Latin America. The word 'endogenous', as President Chavez had explained to his TV audience at that *Aló Presidente* broadcast from Tacagua Vieja, means 'created from within'.[2] It had been used to describe a theory of development that had its roots in the work of the United Nations' Economic Commission for Latin America (ECLA) from the 1950s through until the 1970s. That was the period immediately before the neoliberal orthodoxy took hold, when import-substitution and national industrialisation programmes were meant to strengthen and diversify the productive capacity of Latin American nations and reduce their dependence on imported goods.

Much of this philosophy had been resurrected right at the beginning of the Chavez presidency, notably in the 2001–07 development plan.[3] What was new now was the increased emphasis on involving local people in the design and implementation of these development plans, and the political situation which made such involvement possible and necessary.

For, if the defeat of the April 2002 opposition coup had marked the start of a fresh cycle of community organising among Venezuela's poor (as we saw in Chapter 1 with the urban land committees as its backbone), it was the defeat of the opposition-led oil shutdown at the beginning of 2003 that opened the way to implementing a new set of economic priorities – with this emphasis on a 'people's economy' and 'endogenous development nuclei' as its most ambitious expression. With the dismissal of thousands of managers and technicians who had supported the lockout, PDVSA came, almost for the very first time, under government control. On the one hand, oil revenues were steadily rising. On the other, the government now had the freedom to spend this revenue as it wished – with a significant share going to the social missions in the *barrios* and to development projects like Fabricio Ojeda. The state oil company, it argued, was no longer a private fiefdom managed in the interests of the Venezuelan elite and its transnational partners. In the words of the propaganda posters that adorned billboards, bus stops and subway stations across the capital: 'Now PDVSA belongs to everyone.'

THE SHAPE OF THINGS TO COME

Felicia Hidalgo, better known as Licha, from the adjoining neighbourhood of Frederico Quiroz, was one of the first members of the local community to get involved in the Fabricio Ojeda nucleus. 'PDVSA called the first assembly. They went out into the neighbourhoods, put up posters and people heard through *radio bemba* [the grapevine]. At that time the community wasn't well organised. The fuel depot here had been closed for about twelve years. The assembly took place on 28 February 2004. There was a big turnout. We appointed a number of working groups and began to identify what we wanted to include in the first phase of the Nucleus. Three months later, the work began. First the new approach road and entrance, then all the buildings you can see.' The first phase was completed in just over four months. 'It was quick because we had the support of the armed forces. We had a battalion of more than 120 naval engineers to support those of us who were forming co-operatives.'

This was a combination that had become familiar in the preceding years. President Chavez first used the armed forces to advance projects in poor communities right at the beginning of his presidency in 1999, with Plan Bolivar 2000. This was reinforced by the military's participation in relief efforts after the Vargas mudslides that killed thousands at the end of that year. But at that stage the level of community involvement and participation was limited. It was more a case of 'sit back and watch the army build our Bolivarian school'.

In 2003, the military involvement came together with a much more active community participation, *plus* the financial, material and organisational resources of PDVSA, to launch the Missions. It was a combination deliberately designed to bypass the inertia and bureaucracy of the old, largely untouched, administrative apparatus of the ministries and local government.

The Fabricio Ojeda Endogenous Development Nucleus reproduced this pattern. Sitting in the central meeting area at the end of 2004, Hugo Moyer, who was then National Co-ordinator of Endogenous Development Nuclei for PDVSA and the Energy Ministry, told me: 'we really want to break with this paternalist scheme where it's always the state that's supposed to meet the communities' needs. The communities need to come up with the answers to their own problems.'

Fabricio Ojeda also set out to combine the different social Missions – health, education, leisure – with economic activities – job-skills training, construction and production co-operatives and a subsidised retail outlet – into an integrated development centre whose impact would, in theory, radiate outwards, having a multiplier effect in adjacent communities.

On the social side, the first phase included a spanking new Popular Clinic – one of the first of the Barrio Adentro II Missions, intended to back up the front-line health care provided by the mostly Cuban doctors in the neighbourhood surgeries of Barrio Adentro I. When I first visited in October 2004, the dentist's chairs, still wrapped in shiny cellophane, were just being bolted into place. Here there were to be 16 doctors, all of them Venezuelan. They'd cover general medicine as well as specialist paediatric, gynaecological and trauma services. There would be a laboratory and an X-ray section, immunisation and epidemiological units, as well as an accident and emergency department and the dentists' surgery. All this was to be entirely free to anyone who turned up. All they needed to bring with them was their identity card. There was also a People's Pharmacy that would be dispensing drugs at an 85 per cent discount. (When I returned in mid-2007 they told me the clinic was seeing on average 1,800 patients a week and that they'd treated about a quarter of a million people since opening on 25 January 2005.) In the second phase of the Fabricio Ojeda Nucleus, this health centre was expected to expand its laboratory and its range of specialist services, and to build a new rehabilitation centre, the first of its kind in the Caracas slums.

Most of the educational facilities of the Nucleus were scheduled for the second and third phases – a *liceo* or secondary school, a Bolivarian primary school and a *Simoncito* pre-school. A library, an info-centre with internet and computer facilities, a community radio station and a cultural centre were also planned, as well as a sports hall, a baseball pitch and a gymnasium. Licha told me that skills training had already been supplied to more than 600 people who wanted to take part in the construction co-ops. More than the same number again were still being trained to take part in the various other co-operatives. The second phase would also see the completion of Venezuela's first 'Popular Building School', a purpose-built, appropriate-technology complex of its own that would bring students from across the country to help develop and refine the often self-taught construction skills that already exist in abundance in the country's *ranchos* and poor neighbourhoods, as we saw in Chapter 1. At the same time that PDVSA was putting these resources into the Nucleus itself, the state oil company had also refurbished a number of primary schools in the neighbouring communities and was supporting a programme of community soup kitchens.

On the consumption side the super-Mercal, just outside the main gate, was almost finished. This was to be part of the Mercal network of some 4,000 government food stores which gave almost half the population access to basic necessities at reduced prices. There was also a small cafeteria and a recycling point. In later phases there was to be a much larger community canteen attached to a community bakery, alongside a community laundrette, all charging solidarity prices, and public baths for those in the area who still didn't have adequate access to running water at home.

But the heart of the complex – and of the whole idea of endogenous development – was production. Apart from the building work itself, this had three main components.

The first two were the shoe-making and garment workshops. Their purpose was to provide new skills and jobs for some of Venezuela's swollen army of unemployed, and at the same time contribute to a network of local suppliers that in time could eliminate or reduce the country's need to import so many of its basic consumer goods.

More than 300 people were just completing their training in the government's new Vuelvan Caras Mission to work in these two small factories. Most were women, with little formal education and only a patchy record of work in the informal sector behind them. They'd spent the last six months learning the skills of the industrial cobbler and seamstress. When the government start-up credits came through, they should begin making school shoes and uniforms for the new school year, as well as boots and uniforms for oil workers or the armed forces, and meeting similar orders from a range of other co-operatives in the area – including outfits for local transport workers and street cleaners.

But Vuelvan Caras was not meant to be just about job creation. For Moises Duran, a young left-wing activist who had been put in charge of the Vuelvan Caras Mission a few weeks earlier, just as it was incorporated into the new Ministry for the People's Economy, the aim was not to alleviate poverty but to eradicate it. For him, that meant putting the poor themselves in the driving seat. 'Vuelvan Caras is not just about giving unemployed people the chance to acquire new job skills and become skilled workers. It *is* that of course. But it's also about giving people the chance to develop new values and become productive citizens. This is not just any kind of endogenous development. The neoliberals also have their own version of that. What we want to do is change the economic model.'

He explained the logic of this new economic model to me in more detail. 'For years Venezuela has been totally dependent on its oil income, which powerful groups have used for their own benefit through their control of the state machinery. This mass of oil money has sat alongside a highly inefficient productive sector, grown used to easy credit, a big service sector and a very depressed primary sector, with agriculture all but disappearing. Venezuela became a port economy, with most goods being imported from abroad. We believe that this model is no longer viable, in part because we have such a chronic deficit of jobs.'

For him, the alternative had to be based on extending the Bolivarian revolution's principle of participatory democracy into the economy. 'We need to allow the Venezuelan people to participate in the economy through a variety of forms of production, including co-ops, producers' associations and more. We don't want to create state enterprises but to encourage the formation of co-operative enterprises by these sections of society that have been excluded in the past. That's what we are training them for. It's an alternative that is much more attractive to those who have little or no experience of formal employment.'

Another constant theme of this new people's economy has been the emphasis placed on achieving food security. That means reversing the process whereby Venezuela, with large expanses of some of the most fertile land in the western hemisphere, has come to depend on imports for around 70 per cent of the food it eats. Agrarian land reform is obviously a key issue here, as we shall see in Chapter 3. But in the heart of the Caracas city slums too, the issue of food security is keenly felt. The third strand of production built into the Fabricio Ojeda project sought to address precisely this need. For alongside the training in construction skills, shoemaking and garments, another group of local people was being trained in agricultural skills. The idea was that most of them would then move back to the countryside.

On my return to Fabricio Ojeda, Licha's friend Olga told me how it had worked. 'There were 418 of us in all that did the agricultural training. That was the first stage of Vuelvan Caras. We were divided into 13 groups. At the end of the training, most of these groups were given land and loans to set up agricultural co-operatives a few hours outside Caracas, in Cúpida and Barlovento in Miranda state. They got provisions, tools, beds, tents, and then set about building their own homes and farm buildings. I couldn't go because of my health. So I stayed in the Nucleus here to help the community set up a *Clube de Abuelos* or older people's group.'

Sixteen of those who didn't move out to the countryside, most of them in their fifties and sixties, had set up two small market-gardening co-operatives inside Fabricio Ojeda. They'd rehabilitated a couple of plots of unused land on the hillside leading down from the main complex. 'Now they're growing cabbages, lettuce, radishes, spring onions, watercress and pumpkin. Most of this stuff goes straight to the staff canteen at the PDVSA headquarters in La Campiña – where they put a little label on it saying "Produced by the grandparents at Fabricio Ojeda Endogenous Development Nucleus". Over there is a nursery for ornamental plants. There's a hydroponic seed bank down there. And over here there's going to be the Grannies' Herbal Plot, growing purely medicinal plants for sale in the local community.'

For Hugo Moyer, the man in charge back in 2004, this was the shape of the future. 'We see these nuclei', he told me, 'as spaces where we can map out the kind of Venezuela we want – spaces where all the different Missions come together. I've no doubt that the endogenous development nuclei will become a new model of development for the world. They will not only attack the cancer of unemployment, which corrodes any democracy. They will also allow us to innovate with new ways of producing things. And they will even allow us to innovate with new ways of producing culture, the ways people live and think.'

So who was meant to be in control of this new people's economy, this new way of producing and of living? Hugo Moyer thought the control would evolve through three distinct phases. In the first, the initiative would lie essentially with the state, in the form of the oil company PDVSA. As quickly as possible, however, he thought this should move into a second phase of shared responsibility, a kind of 'co-management' between PDVSA and the community. At some point in the future, Fabricio Ojeda, like the other nuclei, should cut the umbilical cord and become wholly autonomous, the exclusive responsibility of the local communities. He couldn't say for certain how long it might take to reach this third phase, but he was certain that the pattern of small and medium-sized co-operatives already set up in Fabricio Ojeda was the route that would lead there.

Fabricio Ojeda was, and remains, a showcase. It's where foreign journalists, visiting heads of state and other prominent guests get taken. It has featured several times on Hugo Chavez' weekly TV programme, *Aló Presidente*. Not that this diminishes its importance. But is it typical?

Hugo Moyer had told me that PDVSA had identified 16 sites for possible endogenous development nuclei, that twelve had been selected, and that six were given priority status. So I decided to visit a couple of others and make the comparison.

USING THE ORGANISATIONAL MUSCLE OF THE OIL INDUSTRY

In November 2004 Cabimas, on the eastern shore of Lake Maracaibo, was, as always, a hive of activity. Tugs sounded deafening hooters as they churned across the harbour. A seemingly endless stream of boats deposited their cargoes of oil workers on the jetty, then promptly steamed out into the lake taking another load with them. There was the constant noise of hammering and welding from the boat sheds behind. And out on the lake in front, dotted across the horizon, the towers of dozens and dozens of drilling platforms silhouetted against the sky.

This had been the heart of Venezuela's oil industry for the best part of 90 years. It was on the shores a little further south, at Mene Grande, that the country's first commercial oil well had been sunk in 1914 – part of a concession that was rapidly bought up by the Royal Dutch Shell group. Standard Oil of New Jersey, forerunner of Exxon and other US oil majors, soon moved in alongside. When Venezuela became the world's biggest oil exporter in the 1940s – on the back of Lazaro Cardenas's nationalisation of the Mexican industry and the Second World War's intensified demand for safe supplies – it was from here that most of the oil came. Right up until 1970, when Venezuela was overtaken by Saudi Arabia and Iran, this had been the world's single most important source of fossil fuel.

I'd come to the Central Maintenance Department of PDVSA's Western Division, because this was the site of what I had been told might be the most exciting example of all of PDVSA's endogenous development nuclei.

The department manager, Manuel Troconis, doubled up as director of the Las Salinas endogenous development project. Sitting on the wharf outside the main boat-building and repair shop, he explained the idea. It sounded impressive. 'The oil industry cannot employ everyone in the area,' he explained. 'In fact we have a community here of around 300,000 people. Only 6,000 or so work in the industry. For the others, poverty levels are surprisingly high, compared with the wealth you can see around you here. These facilities behind us are not used in the afternoons or evenings. So we reckon we can take advantage of that and put them to use, either by or for the local communities, to help them become more productive and improve their standard of living.'

Manuel spoke in almost fluent English. Like a number of the senior managers and technicians here, he'd spent time studying in Aberdeen, looking at how the Scottish oil industry had developed 'endogenous' community outreach programmes. 'The boats we use for the oil industry: we repair them here and some of them we build here too. So why not build boats for the local fishing industry too? It's very expensive for the fishermen around here to get a boat. Most of them have to rent one from an entrepreneur who owns a whole fleet. Then they make almost nothing on their catch.' If they formed co-operatives and acquired their own boats, things could only get better.

But that was just a first step, he explained. The local Vuelvan Caras programme had started six months previously and there were many local people looking to learn new skills. After their initial classes, many came here to the PDVSA repair sheds to get their practice in welding, carpentry or engine maintenance. 'So why not get our welding trainees from the community to learn to build the boats for the local fishermen, rather than PDVSA itself? Then outside PDVSA they can set up a business, a co-operative, to build boats for the fishermen and for other users too. There's a proposal for industrial tourism, involving boat trips out on the lake, for example. And we've had requests for river barges to serve communities down in the Amazon region.'

As Manuel spoke, a smart new launch swung into view, hanging from one of the gantries. It was painted in sparkling red, blue, gold and white, the colours of the Venezuelan flag. As it reached the end of the boat shed, two men in hard hats guided it down into the water. 'That boat has just been built,' Manuel said. 'Now we put the motor in, send it to the area where the fishermen are, and just give it to them. The fishermen actually helped to design the boat to their own requirements,' he added. 'That's why there's the ice-box in the middle.'

It sounded even more impressive. I said I'd like to go and talk to the fishermen. There was a moment of consternation because no one seemed sure if the fishermen were around. Then it was decided we should visit another group who were just beginning to set up a co-op.

On the way, we stopped at the local job-skills centre. One group of 13 women – there was one man amongst them – were just coming to the end of their training in carpentry. Surrounded by furniture they had made themselves, they were in the middle of a session on their 'rights and duties' as members of a co-operative. 'No', they said, 'none of us has ever done any carpentry before.' Further down the corridor, Ender Contreras had just replaced his first ventilator motor on an air-conditioning unit. None of this mixed group had ever done any of this kind of work either. But now, Ender told me, 'we are going to be useful to the nation.'

When we arrived at the lakeside to meet the fishermen, we were met by Giovanny Villareal, who introduced himself as president and representative of PESCACOL, the Cabimas fishermen's co-operative. The others were local fishermen who were not yet organised in any co-operative. They certainly agreed with Giovanny about their difficulties. As Raúl Navas mended the mesh on a lobster pot, he told me he was aiming to catch some crab to make a soup. 'We live from a bit of everything here, crabs, shrimps, harpoon fishing. But business is bad. Before there was a lot of fish. Now there is very little. The lake is contaminated with algae.' Raúl and his neighbours also seemed to agree with Giovanny's account of who was to blame. 'We've been fleeced by the bandits who control the fish trade. If we try to sell directly to the public, we get attacked by the traders and even the local authorities who say we don't have permission to sell direct. We are ripped off and abused even by those who claim to represent us at the National Fishing Institute.'

They seemed to agree with his argument that forming a co-op might help them to get their own boats and motors and sell their fish to the community for 20–40 per cent below the market piece. 'That would help everyone.' But they were a lot less convinced that PDVSA was helping them to move in this direction. 'We need support,' Raúl told me. 'But we're fed up of having meetings with PDVSA and nothing coming of it. Meeting after meeting after meeting, and they solve nothing. Let's see if PDVSA is really prepared to help.'

I also visited the Caigua endogenous development project, in the eastern state of Anzoategui, an offshoot of the vast José refinery complex, where PDVSA in 'strategic associations' with several big international oil companies, was refining petrol from the superheavy crude that lies in vast quantities below the banks of the Orinoco River.[4] This was a more modest proposal, to work with one of the local indigenous communities, the Caigua, to grow and process aloe vera for export, and then expand this to neighbouring communities. The man in charge, Egly Ramirez, told me the underlying principle was 'to use the organisational muscle of PDVSA' to promote a new development model based on the 'co-responsibility' of the communities involved. The aim was to have, in 20 years time, the José refinery at the centre of a network of prosperous, non-oil, small businesses, developed with the local communities.

[51]

But here too, as we walked among the aloe vera plants, accompanied by staff from the PR office and a variety of other PDVSA departments, I was left with a number of questions. How far were the people from the local Caigua community truly engaged? Had they had really taken on the project as their own, or did they just see it as somebody else's good – or not so good – idea? Did this have anything at all to do with a 'new production model' and a 'people's economy', or was it just the conventional kind of exercise in social responsibility carried out by big companies and mainstream NGOs all over the world?

It did not particularly surprise me to learn, three years later, that the Endogenous Development Nucleus at Cabimas no longer existed. It hadn't worked out, I was told, although no one seemed able to say exactly why. The Caigua project was, I gathered, still 'just about to start' producing aloe vera.

THE FRUITS OF ENDOGENOUS DEVELOPMENT

It shouldn't have been any surprise to find that progress towards the 'new economic system' had thrown up some contradictory results. Indeed, when I arrived back in Venezuela for the first time in 2007, the mixed messages of the Bolivarian revolution were on very public display. As the airport shuttle bus sweeps up the *autopista* into Caracas, it passes the giant, dilapidated apartment blocks of 23 Enero. They always have immense hoardings blazoned across the top. That summer, two of these dominated the city skyline. One shouted loudly the new slogan of the moment: 'On the Road to Socialism of the twenty-first century.' Right next to it the other, in letters only slightly less huge, said: 'Toyota, Moving Forward Together.'

Fabricio Ojeda, however, did seem to be making impressive progress. There was little doubt that it *was* being used *by*, as well as *for*, the local community. This was clear, even before I entered the main gate. In fact every time I went, morning, afternoon and weekend, there were a hundred or more people queuing on the approach road, at the entrance of the Super-Mercal supermarket. 'It opens at 8am but there are always some of us queuing from 6am.'

Not surprising perhaps, when people explain that here they can buy chicken, oil and milk for just over a third of what they'd have to pay in other shops, and that sugar costs less than a fifth its normal price.

On the first Sunday afternoon I went back, a group of communal councils had just finished a training course for their elected spokespeople. They were now gathering in that central meeting area where I'd first met Alvaro Blanco, to discuss what should be done about the private media and their persistent campaign against the revolution. The new PDVSA Co-ordinator of Fabricio Ojeda, Omar Orsini, told me: 'the Nucleus offers its space for the activity of these community organisations.'

When I returned during the week, the central square was bustling with more everyday concerns. People coming and going from the clinic on one side, several others waiting for their medicines at the window of the People's Dispensary next door. Near the gate, a line of school students queuing for their subsidised bus passes. Behind the clinic, building work continued on the new Rehab Centre. And up the hill, the sound of more hammering and welding as the skeleton of the new Popular Building School took shape across an area the size of half a football pitch.

But the key measure of Fabricio Ojeda's success or failure had to be what had always been at the heart of its endogenous development proposal – production: in other words, the two co-operatives making shoes and garments on the two other sides of that central square.

Inside one of those large sheds, the garment factory was now called the 'Venezuela Advances Co-operative'. Compared with the empty shell I'd seen in 2004, this was a working enterprise. Yet the atmosphere seemed relaxed, even playful. 'There are 148 members of this co-operative,' one of them told me. 'And 147 of us are women. We have one man, who cuts the cloth,' she said. 'He's very happy, he feels like he's in a bed of roses!'

In Area A, a group of women was sewing shirts for the military. 'We produce 100 shirts a day. Each uniform we sell for 38,000 bolivars.'

The trousers were being done by another group in Area B on the other side. There were polo shirts being done for some other ministry further down, but the uniforms seemed to be the main order at the moment. The factory had 122 sewing machines – '116 of them are working properly at the moment' – and the women worked part time, in two four-hour shifts.

Each member of the co-operative received an advance of 465,000 bolivars a month – that's a little less than Venezuela's full-time minimum wage of 615,000 bolivars – with each member getting a 5-million-bolivar share of the profits at the end of the year. I tried to do some mental arithmetic and came up with a rough estimate that maybe three-quarters of the co-op's income was going in payments to the women who worked there. Was that reasonable? Was it sustainable? Above all, how was this changing their lives, and could it be a part of changing the way a society like Venezuela's was organised?

Four of the women agreed to sit down and explain it to me, step by step. 'You have to remember that almost all of us here are mothers, grandmothers and wives,' they told me. 'Ninety-five per cent of us had never touched a sewing machine like these in our lives.' In fact, as their own stories showed, most of them had never even had a proper job before.

At 67, Leonza Amaro was one of the older ones. She'd gone into domestic service at the age of twelve, and spent the rest of her life cleaning, cooking and looking after children – other people's as well as three of her own, one adopted child and four grandchildren. Before the revolution and Fabricio Ojeda, she'd never been in formal employment and had never been to school. She'd finally learnt to read and write in Mission Robinson, studying there in the evenings at the same time as she came to the Nucleus to learn to work as a seamstress. No, she wouldn't be going on to do Robinson II or Ribas. 'At 67 that's enough, with the little I've learnt!'

Two of the others had also worked as domestic servants. Rosa Guaikirima grew up in the countryside of Anzoategui. Her parents live there still, growing a bit of coffee and keeping a couple of cows, but with no electricity. She wasn't sure if her indigenous surname, inherited from her grandmother, came from the same Caigua people I'd visited there. She'd come to the city in her teens to work in a family, and was now 36 years old with two kids and a husband who was still looking for work. Thirty-eight year-old Yanira Belmont had also come to Caracas as an adolescent to work as a maid. That family had actually taught her to read and write and she had been hoping to go on to study computing, but she had to give up studying in order to support her younger sister. After getting married at 19, she'd begun to work from home, as an out-worker stitching shoes for a local factory. They paid her piecework, 150 bolivars a pair, and she could do 400 a month. 'I only ever went out to fetch the shoes and return them. Until this revolution came along, I was entirely a *house*wife.'

The only one of the four who had ever worked in the garment trade, indeed who had ever earned a regular wage at all, was Estela Verdiospino. She'd worked in a couple of private textile factories in the 1970s, but after a few years she had to leave to look after her mother who was ill. She hadn't had another job since. Now aged 54, she was one of just five members of the co-op who had experience of working as a seamstress – so people regularly turned to her for help and advice. 'The fact is,' she told me, 'none of us would ever get a job like this in a private factory now, either because we don't have the experience, or because we are too old, or both.' She told me she had gone along to a private company a few weeks earlier, 'just out of curiosity'. They gave her a test, which she passed. Then they asked her how old she was. 'I said nearly 54. They said, "that's a shame. You work well but we can't give you a job because you are too close to retirement." They don't want to pay the pension.'

Here at Fabricio Ojeda, the women told me, there was no discrimination like that. So how had they become enrolled in that Vuelvan Caras training programme three years before? Leonza had first heard of it on TV: 'You know how you hear about the president's projects on *Aló Presidente!*' The others had all heard through friends. 'You just turned up and put your name down. Then they called you from the training institute, INCE.' It seemed to be a case of first come, first served. The only requirement was that you come along the following day with black shoes, a white shirt and blue trousers. 'I didn't have any. It was a Sunday and I had to be there on the Monday, so I had to race around trying to get hold of the clothes,' recalled Estela. 'I'm so grateful to the president, because at our age you don't often get a chance like this.'

'It seemed like a lot of hot air to me,' Yanira remembered. For her, governments had always ridden roughshod over people like her, and she didn't believe this would be any different. Her friend assured her that this time the president was making sure these projects were for real. So she agreed to go along to the very first meeting PDVSA had called with the community, just to see. 'I thought it was really interesting, what they discussed there. So we decided to stay. There were four or five more meetings like that before the whole shape of this project for Fabricio Ojeda was decided on.'

This sense of responding to what people themselves identify as their needs has continued to be critical to the survival of Fabricio Ojeda. Early in 2006 a dispute broke out and most of the women in the garment co-op walked off the job. They accused members of the co-op's elected board of misuse of funds and failing to pay the members their monthly advance. It was only through calling a mass meeting, with the Vice-Minister of the People's Economy in attendance, that the matter was cleared up. Yes there had been sloppy book-keeping, receipts had been mislaid and the members had not been fully informed of what was going on. But there seemed to be ample evidence that the money *had* been spent on what it was meant to be spent on, nobody had stolen anything, and the suspension of advances to the members was down to a failure to meet production targets in time to replace with real income a government credit that had run out. In the end the meeting reached an agreement on how to overcome this problem too, and the crisis was resolved. 'This is precisely the kind of debate you should be having,' Vice-Minister Juan Carlos Loyo told the mass meeting, 'because it's very easy to talk about working collectively, but a lot more difficult to do it.'

For Estela, the atmosphere is very different from the places she worked in before. 'Most of those private companies have a list on the door of the things you can't do. Here nobody stops you from going to the bathroom and you get regular breaks.' Leonza pointed out how the co-op had given her a loan to make up her missing pension contributions, even though there is still no law on social security arrangements for co-ops. 'Now I'm drawing my pension and paying back the co-op at the same time. Nobody else would have lent me that money free of interest. So it truly is a blessing.'

It is not just that the women feel they are being treated like human beings. The point is, they feel they are in charge. As Leonza puts it: 'I am the businesswoman, I am the boss of this company. What I earn is what we, among ourselves, have agreed to share out.' The sovereign body of all the members of the co-operative, the

General Assembly is held every three to six months. It elects a co-ordinating committee of eight, whose major decisions come back, in turn, to the assembly. 'Nobody is the chief here. We are the owners of our own decisions.'

This sense of control has not come easily for all of them. I asked them if their new roles had caused any friction at home. 'Oh no,' Rosa said, 'my husband irons and cooks and looks after the children. It depends how you get them used to it from the beginning.' Yanira was looking thoughtful. I had noticed the dark shadow across her cheekbone, but I wasn't quite sure if it was a bruise.

'I've been with my husband for 19 years,' she offered. 'But when he saw me getting really involved in the revolution, giving it 100 per cent, it hit him pretty hard.' Like other men, she recalled, he had been happy when she'd stayed at home the whole time and didn't have any 'moral sustenance' of her own. He'd wanted her to be there for him, and for no one else. 'Because all this is new for us, even for those of us who had studied a bit before. So you grow as a person, you learn to understand your fellow human beings, and the men don't want that. Within this revolution you are struggling for your fellows, even for other communities than your own. There are projects and meetings and they are not interested in you being a socialist. They're just interested in you staying within those four walls.'

Her husband wasn't exactly against the revolution, Yanira said, but he didn't like all this stuff about it being 'participatory', because he didn't like *her* participating. And he didn't like to see the benefits she got at the end of the year, because he wanted to be the one wearing the trousers. Still, he'd have to get used to it. 'If he wants to be with me, he'll have to adapt to my rules.' Fortunately, she said, she did have the support of her children. The eldest boy, the twelve-year-old, helped her look after the six-year-old. 'Whatever you want, Mama. You go where you need to go. If I can go with you I will, but if not I'll stay at home.'

That was the important thing for her – that and the belief that she and the other women were 'making this project work for all of us'.

But what did 'making it work' really mean? The new feeling of 'being in control' was obviously of key importance to these women, both in the factory and in the home. But how would this feeling of control translate into productivity and quality? Could this kind of co-operative enterprise be viable in the long run? Could it ever survive without the organisational and financial support of PDVSA? Or then again, why should it have to? Maybe these were the wrong questions.

SELF-SUFFICIENCY WITHOUT PDVSA

Certainly, as I walked around the shop floor, it looked and felt quite different from the garment assembly plants I had often visited in the free-trade zones of the Dominican Republic. Here there was none of that sense of intense, eyes-down urgency, of sinews stretched to meet the next target before the bell rang. Here there were no employers or supervisors pacing up and down between the lines of sewing machines, peering over the women's shoulders. The finished items were not neatly stacked and labelled according to customer, but bundled in slightly chaotic fashion in piles of black plastic bags. If anything this was a little more like some of the Cuban factories I'd visited more than a decade and a half earlier. There were not quite as many people standing around chatting and laughing. Most of the women *were* sitting at their machines. But I was reminded of the old soviet joke: 'You pretend to pay us and we pretend to work.' That was unfair. Surely it was a *good* thing that here no one was busting a gut, that people could get on with their work in an amiable and relaxed manner, without being tyrannised by deadlines or the demands of perfect packaging?

Yet the questions remain. Does this mean that a 'social' production enterprise like the Venezuela Advances Textile Co-op at Fabricio Ojeda cannot compete in the market place with a conventional capitalist garment factory? Could its tops or trousers ever begin to replace items imported from big textile plants in Central America, Colombia or China? Do they need to? It may be true, as some critics have argued, that NUDEs like Fabricio Ojeda, and especially their core production activities, will never be able to cut their umbilical cord with PDVSA, because this would cause the whole project to collapse. But why should this cord be cut? If Venezuela's oil, and its state oil company, is indeed now '*De Todos*' ('everybody's'), then surely everybody has a right to benefit. Is it not perfectly reasonable to decide to use that resource to subsidise, if need be indefinitely, projects of social production like these?[5]

CO-OPERATIVES, NEW FORMS OF PRODUCTION AND THE POSSIBILITY OF SOCIALISM

Over many decades, and in different parts of the world, there have been two separate but parallel debates about co-operatives as a strategy for the labour and progressive movements.[6] Both seem relevant to Venezuela and the Bolivarian revolution's 'New Strategic Map', with its plans to 'transcend capitalism' and move towards a 'people's economy' through combinations of co-ops, endogenous development nuclei (NUDEs) and social production enterprises (EPSs).

The first of these debates we have already mentioned. It's about whether or not co-operative forms of production can be efficient and productive enough to be able to compete and survive without large state subsidies or other external support.[7]

The other debate comes from the opposite direction. It revolves around how far co-ops neutralise their members' ability and will to struggle for more fundamental social change, by turning groups of workers into separate units of capitalist production, competing with each other; how far they are pushed into applying and thinking in terms of market criteria and production for profit, rather than in terms of production that meets the needs of the environment and the community as a whole, including both those who consume and those who produce.

These debates about the place of co-operatives, and co-operation, in any imaginable socialist future, and in any plausible plan for reaching it, have taken on even more importance amid the recent resurgence of discussion on socialist theory and strategy. Not surprisingly, this has been fed by the ignominious collapse of the soviet command economy in Russia and eastern Europe. But it has also been fed by the appearance of a wide variety of local, environmentalist, feminist and other initiatives for alternative, people's economies that has been such an important feature of the worldwide anti-globalisation movement. In Latin America, these have often been expressed as proposals for an *economía solidaria* (literally an 'economy of solidarity', as opposed to one of competition), drawing much of their inspiration from the co-operative projects developed by Brazil's Landless Workers' Movement (MST) on their many land settlements, as well as by some of the region's indigenous movements. But, yet again, Venezuela is the first place in decades where it has become possible to test out how such initiatives might fit into a transition to socialism.

A number of Marxist economists, in France for example, have looked back at the some of the classic texts and come up with rather surprising accounts of Marx's own attitude to co-operatives.[8] It is true, they suggest, that in *The Communist Manifesto* and other early texts, Marx emphasised the need for state control of the economy, and either ignored co-operative forms of appropriation, or attacked them as a dangerous diversion for the workers' movement. This hostility or disdain has been repeated by many orthodox Marxists ever since. However, Marx's own position, they claim, is more complicated. After 1850, as his critique of political economy became more sophisticated, and as the co-operative movement itself developed, they suggest his attitude to co-operatives also became more nuanced. On the one hand he came to see them as possible precursors. In the words of a resolution to the First Congress of the International Working Men's Association, in 1866: 'Their great merit is to show in practice that the despotic and impoverishing subordination of labour to capital can be supplanted by the republican system of the association of free and equal producers.' On the other hand, they say his more developed view of the socialisation of the means of production included co-operative forms of appropriation, alongside and in complex combination with forms of public or state ownership. A socialist economy, in other words, would not be necessarily or entirely the same thing as a state-controlled one.

But how far, in either of these two cases, could or should co-operatives remain subject to the logic of the market, governed by the law of value?

Both these aspects have come up in debates of a more contemporary kind. One interesting example in relation to the Venezuelan experience, took place in the Brazilian Workers' Party (PT) in 1999 and 2000. It was between two of the most prominent thinkers of that party's moderate left and radical left wings.[9] Lula da Silva himself took part in some sessions of this discussion, which took place just a couple of years before he came to the presidency and opted to implement neither perspective. For Paul Singer, co-operatives were a central element in what could be called his 'strong reformist' argument. He saw them as the most important of several 'socialist implants within capitalism'. He criticised earlier generations of

Marxists for centring their attention on a purely political revolution, on a 'seizure of power' that would then begin to build socialism through the promotion of central planning, which he argued was inevitably authoritarian. Co-operatives, on the other hand, built from the bottom up, already clash with the logic of capitalism. Reinforcing them and other forms of *economia solidaria* was therefore for Singer a central aspect of socialist strategy today, a part of the growing over of these implants into a socialist economy – the result less of a momentary political revolution than of the maturing of a more gradual social revolution. The resulting socialist economy would, for Singer, continue to operate a significant market sector, but subject to a set of other, non-market priorities. It's worth registering, in passing, the similarity between these arguments and some of the most interesting theorisations of the Bolivarian experience.

Singer's critic from the revolutionary left, João Machado, accepted almost all the first part of this argument – from the idea of co-operatives as a 'socialist implant' to the need to incorporate their extension into any serious socialist strategy today. But he differed over the market. The great weakness, he argued, of co-operatives and other forms of *economia solidaria*, is that within capitalism they are acutely vulnerable to deformation. As soon as you subject them to the criteria of capitalist efficiency, to the logic of the market, they are lost. They cannot 'compete'. They either accommodate or die. For Machado, if co-ops were indeed to 'pre-figure' a socialist future, they would have to go hand-in-hand with implacable opposition to the rule of the market. And for that to be possible, he argued, it is necessary to build a broad political and cultural movement in favour of socialism, one that can serve as a point of reference for all those involved in these initiatives and help to counteract the pressure of the market. As the best available exemplar of such a movement, he pointed to the MST Landless Movement.

One conclusion of such debates – shared by both 'reformist' and 'revolutionary' sides of this particular discussion in Brazil – is that within most capitalist societies, including for example Brazil, co-operatives can provide a strong argument in favour of socialism because they point the way towards other ways of organising production. They begin to educate people in both the possibilities of collective enterprise and the idea of producing for need (use values) rather than profit (exchange values). In other words, they plant the seed of a possible future.

But how might that apply in the different context of Venezuela, where a revolutionary process is already under way, where at least some of the key levers of political power have already been wrested from the old, capitalist class? How far, here, could co-operatives be the instrument of transition from one way of organising production to another? Or would there still need to be a rupture, sooner or later, where the domination of the market, of capital, of the law of value, is broken and replaced? And is there any way, in the concrete circumstances of Venezuela, that such a rupture could take place without a large-scale takeover of the economy by the state?

THE QUESTION OF CONTROL

There is one other criticism of Fabricio Ojeda – and the route it suggests towards a people's economy – which may eventually help us to solve this dilemma. It comes from someone who has himself been deeply involved in the strategic debates of the Bolivarian process as a theoretician of its participatory democracy and of twenty-first-century socialism, as Chief of Staff to President Chavez in that critical period of 2005, and, from January 2008, as the Venezuelan Minister of Planning. For Haiman el Troudi, the whole model of endogenous development adopted in 2004 belongs to 'the second phase of the Bolivarian revolution'. This involved a significant and positive break with the fundamentally developmentalist, paternalist and *cepalina*[10] vision of the first phase, embodied in the 2001–07 development plan. There was a real move towards getting people to participate in managing their own processes. He told a seminar at the International Miranda Centre in August 2007 that the endogenous development nuclei 'tried to achieve a balance between organised communities participating in production and the state with all its policies'. But the break was incomplete. 'They never finally succeeded in tapping the potential resources in a given zone.' There wasn't enough community organisation. The 'marked absence of participation' meant that the NUDEs 'became a mechanism for the state to transfer its policies and programmes, Mercal, the Missions and so on'.

[62]

In other words, it's a question of control. There wasn't enough of it from below. According to this argument, the whole approach adopted in 2004 in fact gave far too *little* 'power to the poor'. Too much of both the shape and content of these nuclei was determined from above and beyond the communities concerned, by PDVSA or some other state body. This criticism may seem harsh in the case of Fabricio Ojeda, where there clearly has been a significant level of grassroots involvement – although the failure of Las Salinas and a number of other NUDEs may seem to corroborate it. The target of El Troudi's criticism, however, is not this or that co-operative, but the model of economic management and planning that lies behind the Fabricio Ojeda and the other NUDEs.

What he was pointing towards, in the middle of 2007, was an incipient 'third phase of the Bolivarian revolution, the phase of the transition towards socialism', in which a more deliberate system of participatory planning would respond much more effectively to the specific needs of local communities, formulated and expressed by them through their communal councils and other bodies of popular power.

As always, however, real life has a habit of outstripping the theories that seek to explain or guide it. There were already other stories of endogenous development – more modest and less well-known than the showcase of Fabricio Ojeda – but probably more genuinely self-sufficient and responsive to local needs. I'd stumbled across one of these back in 2004 in the tiny hilltop village of Galipan. It was a fascinating tale of how a 77-year-old former peasant leader and a 23-year-old restaurant administrator had led their community in a four-year battle against the bureaucracy, before finally realising their dream of a building a pole for eco-tourism. But it is also the story of what may have been Venezuela's very first 'communal council'. And that is a story that must wait for Chapter 5.

3   WAR ON THE *LATIFUNDIOS*

I first saw Maria Herrera on a small screen in one of the edit suites at Vive TV. It must have been February 2005. Just a year old, Vive was Venezuela's second state-funded television channel, set up as an extension of the country's vibrant tradition in community TV. Its *raison d'être* was to give a national voice to ordinary people from grassroots communities and movements. A friend with close links to Brazil's Landless Workers' Movement had just been given the job of producing a new, weekly programme on land reform.[1] I told her I wanted to do some work on El Charcote, the cattle ranch owned by British meat magnate Lord 'Spam' Vestey, in the central plains of Cojedes state – it had exploded onto the national and international scene that January when the Venezuelan government made it the launch pad for a new drive against big landholdings. 'You must come and see the stuff our people down there have been filming,' she said. 'They found some very strong characters.'

She was right. Maria Herrera was a woman who clearly knew what she wanted. 'I haven't got my "Right-to-Remain Certificate" yet. But I know I will.' She was sitting in front of what looked like a substantial, but simple, wooden house. There was a cage with a parakeet just behind her. 'We were the first to occupy land here. We are certain it doesn't really belong to the English. When we get that certificate, the government will help us work in co-ops and then we can develop a strong, sustainable agriculture. That's what will provide a future for our children. The oil isn't going to last forever.'

From the screen, Maria talked eloquently of Venezuela's long dependence on its oil, the need for the country to stop importing so much of its food, her dream of co-operatives building new homes here, producing their own organic fertiliser, banding together in an endogenous development nucleus.[2] Better still, they might set up one of the new *Fundos Zamoranos*, the model collective farms and integrated rural communities that the government was just beginning to promote. 'All this will change a lot.' Obviously I would have to go and meet Maria Herrera in person.

Of course the story of El Charcote – and of the Venezuelan government's renewed emphasis on land reform – was not unfamiliar. The very first report I did from Venezuela, at the beginning of September 2004, had been about the new moves in this direction following President Chavez' victory in the Recall Referendum. I still hadn't unpacked my suitcases. The internet in our newly rented, empty flat was not yet connected. The Intake Desk in London called me and asked if I could do a live commentary on Chavez' latest threats (or promises, I mused) – his suggestions that now the government was 'going for the idle land' and his demands that local governors and the National Land Institute begin to apply the 2001 Land Law with rigour. Much of the international media was already in a spin over land reform in Zimbabwe. They wanted to know if there were parallels.

I hadn't read a lot about the background, but after a few frantic phone calls I felt I had enough to speak for two minutes without making a fool of myself. There were two main facts I'd found, and both surprised me. Firstly, yes, the land reform had already benefited a significant number of families in the Venezuelan countryside. 130,000 seemed to be the widely used figure, and most of these had been settled on the land in 2003. Secondly, it seemed that more or less all of the land handed out so far had been state land. To date it appeared that not a single large, private land-holding had been confiscated. So the obvious question seemed to be, was this about to change? Was there now going to be a real confrontation with the country's landed elite?

The naming two weeks later of an allegedly 'hard-line' army captain, Eliezer Otaiza, as the new head of the country's Land Institute (INTI), seemed to suggest there might be.

LAND REFORM AND TWENTY-FIRST-CENTURY SOCIALISM IN LATIN AMERICA

Land reform had been the single most contested issue in Latin America's political and social life throughout the twentieth century

– from Zapata and the Mexican revolution in the early decades, through Bolivia and Guatemala in the 1950s, Cuba in the 1960s and Nicaragua in the 1980s, to the new cycle of anti-neoliberal struggles of the 1990s, with Brazil's landless movement and the indigenous uprisings in Chiapas and Ecuador at the forefront. In 1928, a young Peruvian communist called José Carlos Mariátegui had put 'the land problem' at the centre of his *Seven Essays on the Interpretation of Peruvian Reality*, a work that later became recognised as the foundation of an emerging school of specifically Latin American socialist thought. His interpretation saw the land problem as both the underlying form of the 'Indian problem' and as the key to 'the problem of eliminating feudalism in Peru'. But both of these he saw as fundamental contributions to 'the creation of Peruvian socialism'.[3]

An assortment of Latin American socialists, communists and other revolutionaries had continued to place land reform at the heart of their plans. First and foremost, of course, they presented it as an instrument of basic social justice. In the face of abject poverty and a staggeringly unequal distribution of ownership, the cry of 'land and bread' addressed the immediate needs of many millions, just as it had in Tsarist Russia or Republican China. But from these varying points of view on the left, land reform had also been given a variety of strategic roles. For some it was just a first step, a means to break the grip of the semi-feudal landed oligarchy that had been stifling the region's development, and to liberate the productive force of capital. Others insisted it would immediately go beyond that, acting as a lever to establish an alliance that would bring the support of the rural masses behind a comparatively small urban working class. Others again saw it as the political counterpart to a more or less prolonged armed struggle that would start in the countryside and eventually surround the cities and draw in the rest of the population.[4]

From the opposite direction, centre-right and moderate reformist governments across the region, encouraged by the Kennedy administration in Washington with its Alliance for Progress, introduced land reform programmes in the early 1960s in an attempt to mitigate rural poverty and head off any repetitions of the Cuban revolution. The previous Agrarian Reform Law introduced in Venezuela in 1960 by the social-democrat Rómulo Betancourt was in exactly this mould. But as soon as any of these reforms began to gather real momentum (which was not the case in Venezuela), they often provoked a violent backlash from the right, in turn backed by the return of a more hawkish mood in Washington. Hence President João Goulart's increasingly radical land reform in Brazil was the main detonator for the 1964 military coup that began a cycle of dictatorial regimes around much of the region. By the 1990s another drive for land reform had began to take shape among some of the new generation of centre-right, civilian governments in Latin America. This time it was driven by the World Bank priorities of opening up the countryside to a maximum dose of the free market. But almost all these twentieth-century approaches were premised on the understanding that an absolute majority of the population, or at least a very large minority, lived on and off the land.

What relevance could this have to Venezuela in the twenty-first century? Venezuela had long ceased to be an agricultural country. Perhaps only 6 per cent of its GDP came from this sector, while 12 per cent or less of its population lived in rural areas. Rural poverty might be a real enough problem, but it could hardly be one of the most pressing priorities in this most urban of Latin American countries. Yet land reform was shaping up to become a leading edge of this new phase of the Bolivarian revolution. Why? The reason has partly to do with the promise of more jobs, including ones for at least a few of the urban poor, whom it was hoped, as we saw in the previous chapter, would choose to move back onto the land. In parallel with this was the aim of greater food production, regarded as key to securing both social welfare and national sovereignty. Breaking the dominance of the *latifundios* or vast rural estates might also help to reshape social relations and redraw class boundaries, though this was never stated as an explicit objective. But above all, land reform itself was seen as the cradle of something new. Bringing together many of these earlier and specific concerns, it was seen as a starting point for an alternative model of production and development. It was here that the project to build a co-operative, endogenous, socially responsive, non-statist 'people's economy' must begin. As such, Venezuela's rural land reform would become a first test ground for its promised move towards a new kind of socialism. In this, as we shall see, it owed less to the big socialist movements that had marked the twentieth century, than to the landless and indigenous movements that had begun to emerge in other parts of Latin America as that century drew to its close.

MARIA'S STORY

It was the Vive TV crew themselves who eventually took me to meet Maria Herrera – in March 2005 – just a few weeks after I'd seen her on their TV monitors. To get there we had to drive through a military checkpoint at the farm entrance, past the El Charcote farm office buildings on the right and then halfway down the 17-kilometre-long main farm road – what they call the *carretera negra* because of its shiny black tarmac surface. The ranch stretched several kilometres into the distance on either side. At 12,950 hectares – or nearly 130 square kilometres – El Charcote was far from the biggest ranch held by Lord 'Spam' Vestey and his family in Venezuela. Further south, in Apure state, they had nine breeding farms, some of them occupying more than 50,000 hectares, or 500 square kilometres, apiece. My friends from Vive TV told me they'd visited one of these, Los Cocos, and it took them nearly two hours on a tarmac road to drive from the ranch entrance to the main ranch buildings. There was an entire indigenous community living in a state of semi-feudal abandon in the middle of the ranch. In all, Agroflora, the Vestey Group's Venezuelan subsidiary, laid claim to over 300,000 hectares, or 3,000 square kilometres across the country. But El Charcote was special. This was prime pasture land where the cattle were sent on for fattening.

You could see small groups of them in each of the fields off to the left. But in almost every one of these fields you could also see one or maybe two makeshift shacks housing the most recently arrived peasant families. Many had the yellow, blue and red Venezuelan flag fluttering from a pole. Several displayed posters of Che Guevara. They made strange companions, Vestey's cattle and these emblems of nationalist or revolutionary struggle – a slightly surreal image of dual power, perhaps. Further along, up a rise on the left, we passed the farm manager's pleasant home, with a swimming pool in the garden. I met the incumbent later, an affable cattleman from the north of England who lived there with his children and spoke fluent

Spanish with a heavy Yorkshire accent. Tony Richards told me he used to have 14,000 head of cattle on the ranch attended by 28 full-time workers and producing 1.5 million kilos of meat. But with this latest wave of occupations in the part known as New Charcote, *Charcote Nuevo*, he was down to 5,743 cattle. 'We've got a very complex rotational grazing system here which at the moment isn't working very well because obviously all my fields are full of people.' And he didn't believe this land could or should contribute to diversifying Venezuela's agriculture: 'In my opinion, this land is only good for what it's doing at the moment and that is raising cattle. There's another 49 farms below us and everyone raises cattle. People have tried with rice, they've tried with maize, they've tried with other crops and they've always come back to cattle, because that's what this land is good for.'

To get to Maria's house, in the Las Pacas sector of Old Charcote, we continued a little further then turned off the farm road to the right, following farm tracks across fields for several kilometres more.

Maria was out in the yard, tending her animals. 'I've got turkeys, hens and ducks, as well as the parakeets and of course these cows.' She gave me a short tour. 'The fence is new, the rest I've had for years. In fact I put the fence up with the grant money I got from doing the Vuelvan Caras training programme.' Beyond the enclosed yard she pointed to a series of plots. 'Over there we grow coriander and peppers, and that's for the cows to graze.' There was a wooded area too. 'That's good for water and shade, and a reserve of wood when we need it.' Beyond the wood she said there was another area where they hoped to plant up to a dozen hectares of maize. In all, Maria Herrera and her husband Germán Perez were occupying 21½ hectares of El Charcote. 'Originally we did all this on our own. It was only much later that we got any help from the government.'

We sat down to talk more in front of Maria's house, which also seemed to double as the village shop. There were occasional interruptions from people drifting in to buy tobacco or sugar. It was exactly the same location as I'd seen in the Vive TV interview, only now I saw that on the front wall next to the parakeet cage Maria had hung her own portrait of Che Guevara.

Maria's story sounded like that of Everyman or Everywoman of the Venezuelan countryside – the tale of an entire class. She had been born on the land. But while she was still a child her parents had to move to the city. That was the period, following the failure of Venezuela's previous land reform in the early 1960s, and fuelled by rising oil revenue in the 1970s, when the agricultural sector shrank to its current skeletal state. Maria spent the rest of her youth and most of her adult life in the city. That was where she raised her five children. Perhaps fittingly, the city was Maracay, capital of Aragua state. I say fittingly, because I recalled Ivan Martinez of the Urban Land Office citing Maracay as a symbol of Venezuela's peculiarly insane form of urbanisation – vast expanses of concrete slapped across some of the finest, highest-grade arable land on the planet.

'We first arrived here at El Charcote at the beginning of 2000. Or maybe it was the end of 1999.' Maria said they'd tried to return to the land before, in the south of Aragua state, but the water sources had turned out to be brackish.'Then with the new president and the opportunities he brought us, I said again, I'm off to the countryside. We heard through the grapevine that people were recovering land here. So I came with some friends. We were six women on our own to begin with, looking for who was in charge.'

This old part of El Charcote, she recalled, was completely unused by the English. 'All this was thick bush and scrubland with some wooded areas. There were no roads or even tracks. We had to open a path ourselves.' But it seemed there had been people in the area before: 'Right here there were four big mango trees and they don't grow like that by themselves. And there was a sort of cemetery nearby too. But there were no local people left. The English had taken over the whole area and expelled anyone living here.' There was a widespread belief that this was the nation's land, she said, and people had tried to 'invade' it for years. But previous governments had just thrown them out again.[5]

'When we first came we camped in groups of 15 or 16, waiting to see who would settle where. Many of the people couldn't even read or write. But there were a few leaders who knew what to do. So eventually each family occupied its own plot and measured it out.' Maria and Germán had first settled on another bit of land nearby, before moving to their current home two and a half years previously. 'We began to plant a bit, beans, cassava, things like that. And we kept calling on the Land Institute, INTI, to come and measure the plots and give us some papers. Because without papers you can't go to the bank and get credit.' It seemed that early on the English cattle company had agreed to turn a blind eye to this occupation by Maria and the others in El Charcote Viejo.

It had only been since 2003 that government offices had begun to take some notice of them. 'That was when INTI finally turned up and took some initial measurements.' After that they came back and did some surveys and socio-economic studies, and gave the peasants in Old Charcote '*avales*'. These were letters that didn't lend any official status to their occupation of the land, but did recognise that their cases were being looked at and might in time merit the *cartas de permanencia* or Right-to-Remain Certificates that would finally give them a legal status. More recently, the Vuelvan Caras Mission had begun to teach the settlers improved agricultural techniques – how to plant and use insecticides without slashing and burning or damaging the environment. Of the more than 200 families occupying land here, there were now 62 graduates from these training programmes ready to form a co-operative in Maria's sector, and more than 30 in the other sector. Most recently, the state governor had also taken up their case.

'What about the newly arrived peasant families that I'd seen along the main farm road?' I asked Maria. 'Ah, no,' she said. 'It's a lot more conflictive over there in El Charcote Nuevo, because that's where the English have their cattle. I get on with the people over there fine, they like me and they come to meetings over here. But they don't have good relations with the governor.'

Back in one of the fields alongside the *carretera negra*, Pablo José Flores soon told me why. He and some other peasants were stacking sesame into bundles to dry. They'd occupied this part of the ranch 15 months before and this was their first harvest. 'We had to clear the land, hoe and plant at night, in secret. Because if we used a tractor during the day they'd come and arrest us.' He accused the state governor of sending the police to knock down their shacks and prevent them from bringing in materials to build any more. He accused the English company of harassing them too. 'This bit of land was empty. But after we'd planted our crops they let their cattle loose to destroy them.'

'We have more than 800 families registered here in this sector, along the main farm road. All we want', he insisted, 'is for them to implement the Land Law. Not this show that the governor is putting on now!'

THE AGRARIAN REVOLUTION IN STAGES

To understand the significance of these developments at El Charcote in the early months of 2005, it is necessary to rewind to an earlier stage of the Bolivarian revolution. For land reform was the very first issue that got the wind up the Venezuelan establishment – suggesting there might be more to the Bolivarian project than had first met their eye. True, Hugo Chavez had spoken often enough of land reform even before he came to power. The new constitution passed by referendum in December 1999 also contained several articles that refer to the need for land reform. Article 307 starts with the words: 'The system of large land-holdings is contrary to the interests of society.' (It may have been these early expressions of intent that, at least indirectly, motivated the land occupations undertaken by people like Maria and her family.) But all of this was quite vague about what exactly was to be done. There was talk of a tax on land left idle, but the delicate question of expropriation was not mentioned directly.

It was not until November 2001, almost three years after he was elected, that President Chavez used the special 'enabling' powers given to him temporarily by Congress to pass 49 decree-laws, amongst them the Land and Agrarian Development Law. We shall return to the details of this legislation later. Suffice to say here that it was this law that did more than any other single thing to inflame the Venezuelan elite and provoke them into staging their short-lived coup the following April. The main reason was that for the very first time they saw something that looked as if it might threaten the sanctity of private property, *their* private property. The Land Law made it clear that both the large expanses of state land *and* the large private estates were liable to find themselves redistributed to small peasant farmers. The curious truth, however, was that three years further on, the latter had still *not* happened. Private property remained untouched – at least by the government.

This explains the brief flurry in September 2004, when that

threat seemed to reappear, and when I had been asked to file that first report. But the opposition had just been crushed in the referendum – it hardly had the stomach for more skirmishes in the short term. For three months things went quiet. The government had mayoral and gubernatorial elections to attend to, as well as a new 'Strategic Plan' for the 'New Phase of the Revolution' to draw up. So it was not until December 2004 that the newly re-elected Governor of Cojedes state, Jhonny Yánez Rangel, a former military comrade of Chavez, took up the gauntlet and announced his own, regional, Zamoran decree.[6] A month later, on 8 January 2005, El Charcote became the first private farm to be 'intervened' by the Venezuelan government. With much fanfare, local state and federal authorities, accompanied by a contingent of National Guard and several helicopters, moved onto the Vestey Group's ranch about half an hour's drive from the Cojedes state capital of San Carlos. They were almost outnumbered by the swarms of domestic and international media.

Much of the coverage all this produced – both at home and in the international media – gave the impression that the Venezuelan opposition's worst fears were finally being realised, that the government had begun down the slippery slope of confiscating private property. Even the usually measured *Financial Times* sounded a note of alarm: 'The government's first target was seized at the weekend, with the official "takeover" of El Charcote, a 32,000-acre cattle ranch belonging to Lord Vestey, an English meat tycoon.'

President Chavez himself added grist to the mill two days later. On that Monday, 10 January, he gathered 10,000 peasants in the Poliedro sports hall on the southern edge of Caracas for the announcement of Presidential Decree No. 3408 – a declaration of war on Venezuela's *latifundios* or large land holdings. It was presented as a national counterpart to and continuation of the local Zamoran decrees issued by Jhonny Yánez and two other state governors the previous month. It was intended to give presidential backbone to a nationwide effort to kick back into life the land reform law of 2001. This was of course just three weeks before that speech in Brazil where Chavez first came out in favour of socialism and the date had been chosen carefully. 'It was 145 years ago today,' he told the crowd, 'on 10 January 1860, in San Carlos, Cojedes, that they spilled the libertarian, revolutionary and peasant blood of Ezequiel

Zamora.' It was Zamora, he explained, who had grown up with the betrayal of Simón Bolivar's revolutionary dream by a new oligarchy of landowners. It was Zamora who had organised and led the peasants to resist that new liberal oligarchy, and whom they had had shot down, 'so that everything could continue as before'. 'A century and a half later, we are taking up the banner of Zamora once again.'

Chavez paid tribute to the significant numbers already settled on state-owned land since the 2001 Land Law. 'But this is not nearly enough to ensure food security and sovereignty for our people.' There were structural obstacles, he said, and the biggest of these was the huge inequality of land ownership. He referred to the last land census, carried out in 1997, which indicated that almost 80 per cent of the land was in the hands of just 5 per cent of the landowners, while three-quarters of the country's farmers owned or occupied just 6 per cent of the land. 'It's an aberration,' he roared, and the crowd went wild. No genuine democracy, no genuine revolution, he continued, could tolerate such injustice. A new leap forward was needed. That was why they had just drawn up the 'ten big objectives' of 'The New Strategic Map' of the revolution, including the 'war on the *latifundios*'. 'We've already begun: the leap forward, 2005 and 2006. We're going to take a gigantic leap forward. Hold on tight, because this leap is going to be a big one, and we're only just beginning.'

The president's promise was radical. Among the thousands of peasant activists gathered in the Poliedro his enthusiasm was infectious. The rally ended as it had opened, with a rendering of Zamora's stirring nineteenth-century anthem: '*El cielo encapotado, anuncia tempestad. ... Oligarcas temblad, viva la libertad.*' ('The heavy skies foretell a storm. ... Tremble oligarchs, let freedom live!') To conservative ears at home and abroad, the declaration of 'war' sounded only too real.

The truth on the ground, however, was a little more complicated. Governor Jhonny Yánez reiterated tirelessly, to the few journalists who were ready to listen, that the 'intervention' at El Charcote was not intended to interfere with private property, much less abolish it. Yes, he said, 'we need access to land if we are to carry through our plans to overcome exclusion and poverty.' But, he added, 'private property is a right we respect in Venezuela, as President Chavez has said many times, and as the Constitution guarantees.' The only thing he wanted to abolish was the 'eternal anarchy' that prevailed in much of the countryside. The application of his *Zamorano* decree should in fact *help* both landowners and small producers to clarify who had a right to what, and thereby increase investment in 'endogenous development' and promote 'food security'. There was no question of anyone being 'expropriated'. Agroflora, along with the owners of a couple of other big estates in Cojedes, had another 60 days to produce the documents needed to prove their legal titles to the land. If they could not, then the land would be considered to belong to the nation. But even then, there was room to negotiate over whether Agroflora might continue to raise cattle for meat on at least part of the land.

I travelled to Cojedes just as those 60 days expired. There was a bit of confusion about dates and about who was deciding what. It is worth dwelling on this for a moment, because it illustrates three kinds of difficulty that have dogged many of the initiatives taken by the Bolivarian government. One is the difficulty in joining up in a coherent way the actions of different parts of the public administration. Sometimes this is a purely practical problem. Sometimes it reflects personal or institutional rivalries. Sometimes there are real differences of orientation. Another difficulty is the complex and often intractable nature of the laws and other legal instruments that have to be applied. Thirdly, there is the gap that can easily open up between even the best-intentioned public servants and the real needs and experience of the people they are there to serve. Whether these difficulties are inherent in any attempt to work *within* existing institutions, and how far they can be minimised or overcome, are questions of interest well beyond the Bolivarian experience in Venezuela.

First it was announced that on that Tuesday, 8 March, the new presidential committee for land reform would visit El Charcote to announce the results of the two months' investigations. In the event, most of the commission, including Captain Otaiza, the new head of the Land Institute, INTI, didn't turn up. There was mention of bad weather and transport problems. We were told the event would be rescheduled for the following Tuesday.

That Saturday, 12 March, INTI issued its own communiqué, announcing its decision on the status of El Charcote and three other ranches under inspection.[7] The verdict, in line with the legislation itself, was complex. This complexity, combined with a desire in much of the media to over-egg the story, led to further, inaccurate, confused and confusing coverage, most of it centring on the government's alleged (but non-existent) 'decision to expropriate 110,000 hectares'.

In fact, for each of the four farms INTI combined rulings on two different aspects. The first was whether the land was being used productively, or whether it was idle, in which case it could be legally classified as a *latifundio*.[8] If the latter were the case, then the authorities could *begin* the complicated series of procedures that might eventually lead to expropriation, in accordance with the Land Law.[9] The second aspect was whether or not those who claimed to be the owners had been able to demonstrate their legal title. If they couldn't, then it was not legally private property and didn't need to be expropriated. INTI ruled against the supposed owners of all four farms on both these aspects, but in varying degrees. In the case of El Charcote, INTI first ruled that 'much of the 12,950 hectares is idle, with no productive activity, and is therefore considered to be *latifundio*' (rather strangely INTI did not specify exactly *how* much). At the same time, INTI judged that Agroflora had not produced adequate papers to sustain their claim to the property, and it therefore considered that El Charcote as a whole belonged to the nation. The part of the ranch where more than 230 peasant families were already growing a variety of crops would be classified as productive. Those families would be given the right to remain and helped to form a *Fundo Zamorano* collective farm.

The event promised for the next Tuesday never happened. But the following week, on 22 March, I was back at El Charcote for the formal ceremony where the entire Presidential Land Commission flew in by helicopter to hand out the first of the Right-to-Remain Certificates. It took place right outside Maria Herrera's house in Las Pacas.

THE SITUATION ROOM

Before the ceremony took place, I wanted to understand exactly who had been investigating what at El Charcote, and what they had come up with – so I visited the Situation Room of the Regional Land Commission with Leopoldo Lugo, the Land Commissioner for

Cojedes state. He was a gentle-mannered, immensely knowledgeable man. And as he guided me from one area to another, he was evidently proud of the work they had been doing. The room was large and windowless. Small groups of people were working at clusters of tables and cabinets, in almost separate pools of light, surrounded by charts and maps and diagrams. It seemed to have taken on the deliberate air of a makeshift command bunker. We walked over to the far corner. 'This is where the team doing the technical study on El Charcote works. We have six teams in all, each dealing with several estates.' He explained how they processed all the information from the field. They weren't just tracing back the title deeds. They were also checking the topographical measurements and compiling a comprehensive register of soil quality, condition and usage. 'We check exactly what the "presumed owners" are producing where, and we do the same for the small land claimants or "precarious occupiers" – we don't like using the terms "invaders" because of course as well as small "invaders" you can also have very big ones.' He pointed at a pile of files. 'Those are all the interviews done by Team 1. We've already completed 600 and we're aiming to do another 200.'

Then he produced a diagram with a timeline representing the history of the property deeds for El Charcote. 'As you can see, in 1920, the Lancashire Investment Company bought 22 properties from the Rotondaro family. Since then, there have been several stages, but it's all the same people. They just change their name.' His finger followed the sequence of names, all representing the Vestey family: the Venezuelan Meat Company, the New Holding and Finance Company, Rosalinda – 'that was in the 1980s when there was a very nationalist mood and the government decreed that radios had to play Venezuelan music, so they chose the name of a favourite Venezuelan folk song, Rosalinda' – right down to Agroflora. There are two big problems, he said. Firstly, what the Rotandaros 'sold' to Lancashire Investment in 1920 was something they had no legal right to sell. Like so much land in Venezuela, this was land that had been appropriated for himself by the dictator Juan Vicente Gomez. On the tyrant's death, all this land was returned to the state. 'Things were very arbitrary in those days. So this guy Rotondaro supposedly "bought" the land back from the state, but with not even the most basic legal procedures. Then he "sells" it on to the Lancashire Company.' In other words, legally, according to Leopoldo Lugo, it never stopped being state land. The second problem, was that the English company had started selling to others much of this land which wasn't legally its to sell – over 40,000 hectares in all. 'They left themselves with just the current 13,000 hectares, which was the area with fewer legal problems.' Technically speaking, if it were decided once and for all that El Charcote belonged to the nation, then all the land that Vestey's had sold would also belong to the nation. The English company might be liable for vast amounts of compensation.

I was beginning to understand what people meant by the 'anarchy' of land ownership in Venezuela and recalled a comment made to me by peasant organiser, Jhonny Milan: 'the powerful landed interests never wanted this Land Law because it would mean re-examining a large number of murky property deeds, huge areas of land where they just put up barbed wire, said it was theirs, and threw out the peasant families living there.'

Then there was the environmental aspect. Leopoldo Lugo pointed to a series of coloured charts on the wall. 'These were supplied by Agroflora. The different colours represent different qualities of soil. They claim they are using the land as legally specified: using for cattle what is legally specified for cattle, and so on. But what we have found so far is that they are all wrong. Both the British company and the small farmers have been using protected land for production. In some conservation areas the company has introduced grass, or the grass sown for the cattle has spread. So now there are, for example, no fauna like *chiguira*, capivara or deer left there, because they can't eat the hard cattle grass. Similarly, small farmers have destroyed saman seedlings, where monkeys and rodents thrive, or they've cleared areas of everything but the biggest saman trees, and nothing grows beneath them.' It is difficult, says Leopoldo, to strike a balance between the needs of production, nature and society, but it has to be done. 'Nobody has the absolute truth. It's got to be a combination of all these truths.'

So was Agroflora's farm manager Tony Richards right to say the land on El Charcote was only good for cattle? 'Well, that too is half truth, half lie,' Leopoldo answered. 'It depends how you look at it and what you want. Of course it is good for cattle, because grass grows very well in this good soil. But farmers growing sugar cane or rice will tell you it's perfect for that too if you pick the right place. Don't forget that 15 or 20 years ago Cojedes used to export rice. And just consider what sugar cane or rice can do for a society compared with cattle!' He pointed to the very few jobs generated by cattle ranching – maybe two or three cowboys for a thousand or more animals – compared with the 20 to 30 people needed to harvest a hectare or two of sugar cane or rice.'Here in Cojedes state we have 50–70,000 people who need a job, out of a total population of 300,000. We're right in the centre of Venezuela, with good access to the main population centres. But we're not producing enough. And there are other crops that produce more protein and greater social and economic benefits. We cannot just depend on meat. Meat is not the healthiest source of protein, and it is not very cheap for the poor.'

Endogenous development should begin with what you have. 'We have grass, so let's use it in some places. But we also have better land, so let's use that for what Venezuela really needs – better nutrients for our population.'

This seemed like a coherent, well-grounded argument, and one that led to conclusions a good deal more moderate than most of the rhetoric for and against land reform might have suggested. 'You cannot think this has anything to do with communism,' said Leopoldo, 'because we are responding to the market.' Meat, he claimed, had become very monopolistic.'We need more competition, we need more farmers, we need more cattlemen, not only a few big ones. We need those big cattlemen whose unit costs are probably low. But we also need a lot of small cattlemen and small farmers who make the general economy grow.' In the specific case of El Charcote, this pointed to some kind of negotiation with the Vestey family. 'We need their herd, we need their production, but under new legal conditions. If the land belongs to them, fine. But if it belongs to the nation then we'll let them produce on part of the farm under "land of the nation" conditions.' He was aware that the authorities might have to pay a high political price for this. 'Some of the peasants are not going to like it. The radicals are not going to like it.'

In fact not even Maria Herrera liked it, and she was supposed to be in the governor's camp. When I put it to her that the government might invite Agroflora to continue raising cattle on the other part of El Charcote, she said quietly but firmly: 'I don't think they contribute much to our country. If it doesn't belong to them, I think it would be better if they left.' Pablo José Flores and the peasants occupying New Charcote certainly didn't like it, because that was precisely where the English were likely to be invited to stay. They would probably be declared illegal squatters and forced to leave.

These tensions, or at least differences of approach, were simmering below the surface at the ceremony outside Maria's house. The event was certainly intended to show that the new phase of land reform had truly begun. And in a sense it did. In this remote corner of an immense and prestigious, up-until-now 'private', cattle ranch, Governor Yánez, Minister Albarran, INTI head Otaiza, and half a dozen other state governors, ministers and senior public officials, stood facing several hundred peasant squatters, and together, with feeling, they sang the Venezuelan national anthem: *'Gloria al Bravo Pueblo, que el yugo lanzó'* ('Glory to the brave people, that threw off its yoke'). Then they handed out the crucial Right-to-Remain Certificates to most of the peasants who like Maria had been occupying Old Charcote for years. Nothing quite like this had happened before. Jhonny Yánez called it 'historic'. This time, he promised, Venezuela's peasants would not be abandoned as they had been by the Fourth Republic after the land reform of the 1960s. This time they wouldn't get just a piece of paper and an abandoned shack. This time there would be proper homes, health care and electricity; there would be agricultural services, credit and production, an endogenous system of production. Very shortly, here in El Charcote Viejo, the country would see a new Nucleus of Endogenous Development take shape. Captain Otaiza told them that the name of this NUDE, or *Fundo Zamorano*, would be 'Independence'.

But the peasants from the other side, from El Charcote Nuevo, were already feeling abandoned. Why weren't they being given the right to remain too? Their anger was mostly contained, but at the end of the ceremony it spilled over into chants against the governor. And even among the squatters in Maria's area, there were moments of discord. One old man receiving his certificate used his moment in the limelight to praise President Chavez and at the same time

very publicly call on Captain Otaiza and Minister Albarran to investigate whether some local official wasn't ripping them off – he told
the TV cameras that he and 100 others still hadn't been paid for the
maize they'd delivered to the public silos five months before. The
minister looked embarrassed and directed him towards the State
Agrarian Prosecutor who was also present. But overall, the mood
was upbeat.

INTERREGNUM

For most people who had read about El Charcote in those early
months of 2005, it was and remained a symbol of the Bolivarian
government's radicalisation, of its resolve to take on, once and for
all, the power and interests of the big land holders. But for anyone
able to follow more closely developments on the Vesteys' cattle
ranch during the rest of that year and into 2006, El Charcote
became an emblem of frustration. In effect, there *were* no developments. The English company did not seem inclined to compromise.
The convoluted legal process appeared to be heading nowhere.
Local appeals procedures then international arbitration remained in
the air, paralysing any change on the ground. Agroflora continued
its cattle operations at much the same level as before. The two
groups of peasants continued to occupy their different parts of the
ranch, with hardly more or less state attention than before. The
moves towards forming an endogenous development nucleus or a
Fundo Zamorano were virtually non-existent. El Charcote seemed
to illustrate the distance between rhetoric and reality, between
intention and achievement.

Part of the difficulty facing any more robust approach to land
reform was the Bolivarian government's own Land and Agrarian
Development Law. Once a piece of land had been identified as idle and
therefore a *latifundio*, the law laid out what seemed like a very reasonable mechanism for its expropriation – but one that in practice proved
to be virtually inoperable. First, if the apparent owners couldn't
bring it into productive use themselves, they would be invited to
negotiate handing over some or all of the land to peasant co-operatives.
If that failed, the law proposed a scale of taxation that they should

pay on their idle land. In most cases, it was only if they failed to pay those taxes that the government could move to expropriate. As far as I was able to discover, by the middle of 2007 the federal tax authority, SENIAT, was still working out how it might implement this tax and it seems that no landowner has ever actually paid it. One of the aims of Chavez Decree 3408 in January 2005 was to seek a way around these difficulties by emphasising the examination of the validity of the big owners' property titles. If it could be shown that the land didn't really belong to them, then clearly the *latifundistas* would not need to be expropriated. And this indeed has been the mechanism – known as *rescate* or recovery – that the Bolivarian government has used to tackle the big landed estates. But even this, as El Charcote was proving, could get bogged down in a labyrinthine sequence of legal challenges.

It was not until well into 2006 that there was any kind of breakthrough. It got only a passing mention in the press, but at the insistence of the new Agriculture Minister, Elias Jaua, Vesteys made up their mind. Not prepared to accept the government's offer that they continue raising cattle on just part of the ranch, they finally agreed to a deal that would see the English company abandon El Charcote entirely. There are contradictory versions of the exact terms of this deal. This was probably because the two sides disagreed about what exactly the deal was over – Vesteys never accepting the government's version that El Charcote wasn't legally theirs. Nonetheless, it seems the government agreed to pay Agroflora some US$4.2 million. This, it was said, was for the farm's installations and improvements, since the authorities did not recognise that Agroflora had any legal title to the land itself.[10] In return, the English company would abandon the whole of El Charcote and would also turn over to the Land Institute (INTI) another of its ranches, San Pablo Paeño, occupying a massive 47,000 hectares of much poorer quality land in the more remote southern state of Apure. It was reported that for its part the government would undertake to remove the peasants who were 'illegally' occupying parts of Agroflora's nine remaining ranches in Venezuela. Whatever the detail, the Vestey Group seemed quite pleased with the deal. Within a few weeks, the English had left, and taken their cattle with them. It was more than a year after that when I returned.

RETURN TO EL CHARCOTE

As the *por-puesto* (mini-bus) pulled into the small town of Las Vegas, the graffiti was still there on the wall: *'Fuera los ingleses'* ('Out with the English')! A cheap sound system on a pavement opposite was blasting out the mournful tones of a *llanero* – the singer was lamenting how much he missed his sweetheart, his home on the plains and his cattle. But a couple of kilometres beyond town, at the entrance to the El Charcote ranch, where Agroflora had had their offices, everything was changed. The compound had been taken over by the Compania Venezolana Agraria (CVA), set up to provide production and marketing support to peasants under the land reform programme. In the yard there were rows of shiny new tractors and harvesters, bright yellow bulldozers and diggers, brought in from Brazil and Argentina under agreements with the government.

The back road to Las Pacas was greatly improved – still packed earth for most of the way, but easily passable now, without the potholes and boulders that had made progress so painful two years before. Maria Herrera's house did not seem to have changed much. Her husband Germán was out at the front tinkering with a motor. 'I just do the mechanics stuff on the side.' Maria wouldn't be back till later. She'd been to visit her daughter in Maracay. As we sat down to talk, a neighbour passed and asked Germán for some cheese. He walked across to a wooden press and took out a tray of simple, rustic cheese covered in a cloth. This seemed to be one of their main lines of business now. It's true, Germán told me, that the NUDE and the *Fundo Zamorano* never happened. That would have come with all the benefits and services integrated – houses, school, agricultural machines and support. But they couldn't do it then because the issue of who owned the land still hadn't been sorted out with the English. Later Maria told me that the planned *Fundo* or collective farm had been switched to Paraima, one of the other big ranches in Cojedes state that the government had 'intervened' at the same time as El Charcote. So yes, it had been hard. And for much of the time they'd had little support. Few of the co-operatives had worked out either. Those that survived were mostly just family co-ops. Like many of the 200 or more families who'd been given provisional titles in Old El Charcote, Germán and Maria had ended up working on an individual basis. 'It's mostly down to people's level of awareness. Co-operatives are a very new idea for most people. They're not used to the idea of working together. For 40 years everyone just looked out for themselves.'

Nonetheless, in the last year and a bit, things had got a lot better. The government had begun to sort out the access roads. 'There's still a lot of work to do,' says Maria, 'but at least we hope that this year we won't lose the harvest like we did before.' Germán described how their own business had developed. 'I'm very happy because we got a credit for one year for 15 beef cattle.' Maria explained that they'd paid off that credit before it was due and had been offered a second credit for another 15 beef animals. They'd also bought 16 dairy cows with their own savings, and from these they were selling milk, cheese and whey to the local community. 'Things have really changed here,' Maria told me. 'We've made a corral and sown pasture for the cattle to graze.' There seemed more than a little irony in the fact that land-reform beneficiaries like Maria and Germán – pioneers of the war on the big ranches and of the battle for food security – were turning back to cattle to make their living. But she said the point was that it wasn't just cattle. 'We're also growing eight hectares of maize and some yam.' Germán pointed out that others on El Charcote were growing sorghum, *yautia* and rice, as well as a variety of fruit and herbs. I remembered Leopoldo Lugo back in the Situation Room with his insistence on a balanced approach – 'a combination of all these truths'. Maybe he had been right.

Even though the peasants settled in the old part were mostly working separately as individual smallholders, two things had begun to draw them back together. One was the arrival of the machines. 'It's a state company, of course,' Germán said, 'and the machines belong to the state, but they rent them out to us at about 30 per cent below the market rate. They'll plough your field for 28,000 bolivars, for example, rather than the 40,000 it'd cost anywhere else. In fact they helped me with my maize planting just a week ago. They came and ploughed, sowed and spread the fertiliser.'

The engineers were making regular visits to see who needed what. But it wasn't really worth bringing the machinery all the way over to Las Pacas, say, just for one smallholder. It was much better if they could combine four or five in one visit. 'So we had a meeting and began to organise by sector. So each area now has someone who takes responsibility, a spokesperson for the community, who keeps a list of who needs a tractor, who needs a plough, and so on, and arranges it in groups with the company. Doing it as a co-operative would be much better, of course.' The request also had to be approved by the communal council. 'Everything like that needs to be signed off by the council.'

This was the second thing that was now bringing them to together. The development of communal councils since the beginning of 2006, and their explosion across the country since January 2007, had not missed out this corner of Cojedes. 'We formed the first one here in Las Pacas, almost two years ago. Later four others were set up in other parts of El Charcote Viejo. We do small projects.' Maria described how they call together the community, almost 60 people in their area, when something needs doing, and discuss the proposals. Their first project had been a pick-up truck. 'We got 29 million bolivars and bought a "350" four-wheel-drive, because of the state of the road. It's to take our produce to market, but it also serves to ferry the kids to school and take anyone who's ill to the doctor.' The community were managing the truck through a co-op they set up, and the driver was appointed from the community. Next they applied for 30 million bolivars to build a school in Las Pacas, so that the children wouldn't have to walk eight kilometres to the nearest primary school. 'Now our school is almost finished, we'll apply to the town hall or the state government for a teacher.'

The next project, Maria explained, was to bring electricity to Las Pacas. 'We don't know how much that will be yet, but it's a big project so we're going to link up with the other communal councils for that, and we'll get technical advice from the local government engineers.' Other projects were in the pipeline, or just being considered: more connecting roads and tracks within the farm, drainage channels and wells, irrigation too. They were also receiving technical support from the Cuban agronomists and vets of Campo Adentro – a Mission started in 2006 that brought 700 Cuban specialists to advise Venezuela's new land-reform settlements.

By a roundabout route, and more slowly than had been promised, Maria seemed to think that Old Charcote might be on its way to becoming something like a *Fundo Zamorano* collective farm after all. But they still had a long way to go. Ironically, she thought New Charcote – the area along the main farm road whose squatters had felt abandoned two years before – had done better out of the changes than Old Charcote had.

'They already have a school, they've built bridges and they've got good co-operatives that have received plenty of credit. So we tend to think, damn it, now we're the ones who have been forgotten!'

ALONG THE BLACK ROAD

I walked by chance into one of the wattle huts just on the other side of the *carretera negra*, the main farm road. I was looking for someone else – a name I'd been given – but 76-year-old Regina de Ribas insisted I sat down and waited for her son to come home. It might not be much, she told me, but here they were living like kings compared with how things had been when they first arrived. Regina's story was very much like Maria's and so many others: born in the countryside, moved to the city to scrape a living for most her life, always dreamt of returning.'Four years ago in Mission Robinson, where I was learning to read and write, my teacher, Mercedes, asked me if I'd rather get a house in the city or a bit of land in the countryside. I answered her without hesitation, "What do you think? I can't eat four walls!" Mercedes said No way – I wasn't up to working the land. But look at me now!'

When he arrived, Regina's son Claudio Ribas recounted how things had turned around for them. He was a member of the Contraoloria Agraria, a citizens' oversight body checking on corruption and irregularities in credit and land, set up by the previous agriculture minister, 'so I have a lot of information, both written down and in my head. ... There was a lot of uncertainty among the more than 300 families on this side. They'd given papers to the 150 or so families on the Las Pacas side, but not to us. The governor and some other authorities were against us, they were threatening to kick us out. The situation wasn't too good in Las Pacas either, with no government help and no roads. They lost thousands of kilos of maize because they didn't have access to a threshing machine. A lot of people left.' He said it went on like that and there were press reports that the authorities were just counting the days until they threw out the peasants from New Charcote. 'Then at the last moment word must have come from above to sort this situation out for all the people on El Charcote. I think it came directly from the presidency.'

They still hadn't got their provisional titles, or Right-to-Remain

Certificates, which could enable them to get credit from private or state banks. But from the end of 2006 and the beginning of 2007, most of the peasants squatting in New Charcote had been given the 'letters of recognition' that showed their cases were being dealt with and allowed them to apply for limited credit from FONDAFA, a specialised government agency. 'We've set up quite a few co-operatives of five to seven families each. I'm the secretary of one of these. But the members can also sell their produce individually if they want to.' The arrival of the heavy machinery of the CVA had been a great help too. 'Now we're growing maize and rice. Rice you can sell anywhere, but if you get credit you usually have to sell it to the state silos. However, rice needs irrigation, wells, infrastructure.' For Claudio, this was now the top priority, getting the right infrastructure in place. 'I can't irresponsibly ask FONDAFA for credit to grow rice if I don't have the wells. It'll be lost in the ground. If there are no access roads and you don't have access to the machinery you need, you won't be able to do anything. That's what happened in Old Charcote. They got credit, it was eaten up, so many of them had to leave, because of the lack of logistics.'

So that's what he was trying to do now, get all the logistics in place.'It's been so slow. The machinery has only just arrived. But there's more seriousness about it now. All of us have a lot of confidence that this will go forward now. And the communal councils are the bodies to get support for this.'

A PROBLEM IN NUMBERS

In August 2007 Venezuela's National Land Institute, INTI, reported on the progress of land reform so far. It said that 1,834,502.6753 hectares (18,345 square kilometres) of land on 658 estates were 'in the process of being recovered' as part of the struggle against the *latifundios*. This represented, according to INTI, 27.2 per cent of the total land held by such large holdings, and benefited some 32,000 peasants, either as members of co-operatives or as individual family farmers. This was in addition to the 3,901,244.8438 hectares (39,012 square kilometres) of land where property rights had been 'put in order', with title deeds or provisional papers being handed out to

88,884 co-operatives or individual peasant farmers, and with a further 80,000 or more families benefiting indirectly. Almost all of this was state land, and more than half of it had been handed over in 2003 and 2004. These figures seem quite impressive. They suggest that the number of families benefiting from Venezuela's land reform is equivalent to between a quarter and a half of the country's rural population.[11]

However, two kinds of reservation are in order. One is that even if these figures are accurate, the indication is that a significant majority of those who have benefited from Venezuela's land reform did so *before* January 2005, when President Chavez launched the 'war on *latifundios*' and promised such a great 'leap forward'. Although the proportion of *latifundios* or large, 'private', land holdings targeted under this new phase of land reform – over a quarter – is also impressive, the vast majority of this is only 'in the process' of recovery. In other words it is still subject to appeal and other legal challenge. A little earlier, in December 2006, INTI could only point to seven cases, including El Charcote, where large areas of land had already been recovered from ostensibly private estates, representing only 4.4 per cent of the total amount of land believed to be in the hands of *latifundistas*.[12]

The other reservation is that it would be wise to take these figures with a large pinch of salt. It is not just that there are disparities. For example, the numbers given by INTI for 2003 and 2004 do not tally with those given by President Chavez in his speech at the Poliedro in January 2005. Nor do they seem to be compatible with other figures mentioned to me by Captain Otaiza in an interview later that year, when he talked about directly involving 1.2 million families. It may well be that INTI's August 2007 figures are as accurate as it has been possible to get. But the truth is that neither INTI, nor President Chavez, nor anyone else is in a position to *know* exactly how much land is involved in the various aspects of Venezuela's land reform, nor even exactly how many people have benefited.

Simón Uzcátegui, one of the leaders of the country's best-organised and most radical peasant movement, the Ezequiel Zamora National Peasant Front (FNCEZ), explained why. In the decades before Chavez came to power, he pointed out, Venezuela's chronic dependence on oil revenues – especially from the mid-1970s – had not only reduced its agricultural production to a spectral condition. It had also stripped bare the modest machinery of agrarian administration that had developed around the time of the previous land reform law of 1960. So the census of all public and private land fit for production, mandated by that law, was never carried out. Budgets were cut. The old Ministry of Agriculture and Livestock and the Agricultural Bank, BANAGRO, were dismantled or run down. The little credit that was available went not to peasant farmers but to big landowners and what agribusiness remained. 'The Ministry stopped producing its Statistical Annuals, which had been the only basis for saying how much beans or sugar we'd produced on how much land, or how much had been spent on what.' In 1996 the authorities did embark on a new agricultural census, but according to Simón Uzcátegui it was carried out with serious imperfections. 'At that time, the public bodies were riddled with corruption. A lot of officials supplied false information. We know this because still you get some report saying that x number of pest controls have been put into such and such settlements, and we are the ones who are there and know for a fact that no one from the ministry has set foot anywhere near there.'

This means, he says, that the data simply is not reliable. So is it really 1.8 million hectares that are 'in the process of being recovered' from the *latifundios*? 'It's impossible to say. It may be right, it may be wrong. It could be less, it could be more. Because the state really hasn't systematically reported and accompanied this.'

Now this was beginning to change. The new administration at the Ministry of Agriculture, under Elías Jaua, ordered a new agrarian census to be carried out in 2007, although the actual collection of data did not get underway until April 2008.

OBSTACLES TO LAND REFORM

This administrative black hole is one of a cluster of obstacles facing Venezuela's land reform. The story of El Charcote illustrates most of the others too. They fall broadly into four groups.

Firstly, as we have seen at some length, there is the difficulty of actually acquiring the land. Contributing to this are a number of separate but related problems. Obviously there is the direct resistance of the old landholding class, including the fact that as many as 200 peasant leaders and activists have been killed since the Bolivarian government came to power, almost certainly by gunmen in the service of large landowners. Even more debilitating are the endless legal delays and roadblocks. Some of these are down to those very elaborate, probably unworkable, mechanisms for the identification and expropriation of *latifundios* laid down in the law, presumably in an attempt to be as fair as possible to the old owners (see above). But they are also a result of open or covert hostility to land reform from much of the judiciary, especially at local level. Sometimes this means obviously partial judgements in favour of the old 'owners'. More often it means simply burying any challenge to the status quo in an endless and incomprehensible paper chase.

This goes hand in hand with similarly surreptitious opposition from some local and regional government officials, even when these have been elected as ostensibly Chavez supporters. This is not just a matter of bad faith or explicit corruption, although sometimes both may be present. It has more to do with the very nature of such administrations, which have changed neither their basic structure, nor often their core personnel, since before the Bolivarian era. Not surprisingly, the machinery of such local government is intricately entwined with the networks of influence – financial, commercial and cultural – that have been dominated for decades by both the local landowners and the many businesses that supply them, provide their services, transport and warehouse their produce, slaughter their cattle and so on. The inability noted earlier, of federal institutions to provide accurate statistics and monitoring, feeds off and back into these mixed loyalties at local level.

The second group of obstacles has to do with the level of support available to peasants once they are on the land, to help them make it productive. We have seen how this was slow to materialise at El Charcote, in spite of the early promises. However the arrival of the agricultural machinery operated by the CVA from later in 2006, the increasing flow of credit, and the support of Cuban and Venezuelan agronomists through the Mission Campo Adentro appear to have made a real difference. We'll see similarly stepped-up levels of government action when we pay a brief visit to a *Fundo Zamorano* collective project shortly. All this pointed towards a wider shift. According to Simón Uzcátegui, in earlier years most of the credit still went to big producers, and what little did reach small, peasant farmers was often tied to the purchase of chemical fertilisers and other, as he puts it, 'agro-toxic' products, from particular agribusiness suppliers, especially those made by major international companies like Monsanto and Bayer.

Since 2006 however, he says, there's been a real advance, not only in increasing the amount of machinery, credit and technical support available to peasants benefiting from land reform. There's also been a change in kind. He points to the development of organic fertilisers and biological pest controls; to the Florentino Socialist Genetic Centre in Barinas, developing seeds and production systems targeted at small producers and co-operatives; to the network of agricultural diagnostic laboratories providing free back-up to peasants across the country; and to the Latin American Agro-ecological Institute, also in Barinas, where a team of experts from the Brazilian Landless Movement are developing and disseminating such techniques to students from around Venezuela and Latin America. It's true, says Simón, that the process of land reform is not going fast enough. '200,000 families benefited, if that's what it is, isn't much for seven or eight years. But at least now the Ministry has an integrated policy. There are new settlements, and with the machinery, the money to plant and harvest, and the technical programmes and institutes that are being developed, they're getting support that never reached the countryside before.'

But state policies are not necessarily coherent. The third group of problems facing land reform has to do with what happens *after* the producers have succeeded in growing their crops or raising their animals. It is here, in the realm of distribution, that Venezuela's land reform has continued to face some of its greatest problems. We've already seen how the lack of usable roads or vehicles caused some of the early harvests in Charcote Viejo to be lost. This is a common enough problem, with a relatively obvious solution that merely requires co-ordinated action and funding by different government entities and credit agencies, in combination with or ideally under the control of the local communities' own organisations. In the case of El Charcote, such a solution is already on the way to being implemented.

But there are bigger, more intractable problems, as you move further along the food chain. The Ministry of Food, which was created at exactly the same time that Captain Otaiza was appointed to breathe new life into the Land Institute and Elías Jaua became the first Minister for the People's Economy,[13] was intended to link up Venezuela's new, reinvigorated capacity for food production, largely through its war on the vast expanses of idle *latifundio* land, with the already expanding network of state-subsidised food stores known as Mercal, to provide a backbone to the whole system of endogenous development and the shift towards a different, 'people's' economy. Its mission statement says it aims to develop an integrated system of production, distribution and consumption, in order to ensure food security, while giving preference to home-grown produce. For the most part, this is not what has happened. 'More or less none of the products sold in Mercal come from land reform settlements,' says Simón Uzcátegui. 'That's certainly our experience. We do not sell direct to Mercal because Mercal will not take our produce.'

There are several reasons for this, and at least two ways of looking at them. Simón Uzcátegui sees it as a failure of conception and commitment. 'Mercal', he says, 'hasn't adjusted to the real conditions of the countryside. The peasants' produce, if it isn't processed, packed and labelled in the right way, cannot be sold to Mercal. But if we're just beginning to produce, how can you expect us to deliver everything perfectly packed and labelled?' But behind this, he adds, there is a problem of design, which has both historical and cultural roots. The long years of dependence on oil revenue and imported food produced a cultural distortion in Venezuela's habits of consumption. For example, Venezuela has one of the highest levels of wheat consumption in the region. Yet it is a tropical country that cannot grow wheat.

The founding documents that preceded the Mercal network of subsidised food stores called for a state food retail system that would allow peasant farmers to deliver their harvest to the population at lower cost. But the crisis provoked by the employers' lockout and oil shutdown in 2002–03 meant they had to import a lot of food from Brazil and Argentina. 'That had to be done. People had to be fed. But it introduced big structural problems right at the start that have never been corrected.' They never built the warehouses or cold stores for animal or vegetable produce that they would have needed. And almost no Mercal store has even a space to store, display and sell fresh vegetables, like potatoes, onions, yucca or tomatoes, freshly picked and delivered. 'What Mercal sells now is either imported or from big Venezuelan agribusiness. So we've made progress in handing over the land, in credit and machinery, but the distribution, warehousing and marketing chains are still very weak.' Simón also suggests that the particular interests of some officials in these areas of administration mean there is little desire to make corrections. 'They are more interested in their own interests than those of the people.'

This, however, may be unfair. It may not be bad faith but simply another logic that is at work here. If the priority is to ensure that as many Venezuelans as possible have access to decent food at affordable prices, it may make sense to import. The huge surge in Venezuela's oil income from 2004 though 2008, combined with a fixed exchange rate that has kept the bolivar strong against the dollar, means that it has been cheaper and easier to buy from abroad than from domestic producers. This indeed is what has happened. Carlos Machado, an agricultural economist at the Institute of Higher Administrative Studies in Caracas, reports that the demand for food in Venezuela rose by 30 per cent in the two years to mid-2007. In the same period, corresponding to the first two years of the renewed 'war on the *latifundios*', the capacity to produce food in Venezuela increased by only 5 per cent. On the one hand, this suggests a positive rise in living standards. Yet it also means that the pressure of the market, at least in the short term, is pushing the country even further away from food security and food sovereignty. Venezuela's entry into Mercosur, and its unshielded exposure to the mass production of Brazilian and Argentinean agribusiness, is only likely to increase this pressure.[14]

At the same time, if the priority is to provide the majority of Venezuelans with safe, quality foodstuffs, could it be that the unevenly handled, haphazardly packed, unlabelled produce of a land reform settlement is simply not acceptable, or at least less suitable than the better-known, more controlled parameters of presentation and quality control adhered to by big established producers from Venezuela's private sector? We come back here to the same question we asked about the Fabricio Ojeda textile factory in Chapter 2. What are the priorities, and which logic takes precedence? Can the economy of co-operation compete with the economy of competition, and should it even try?

This underlying question, of whether or not the beneficiaries of land reform should be tested against the logic of the market, overlaps with another, possibly even more fundamental, one: the question of how far these peasant farmers could or should depend on the state, or how far the relationship might be reversed, with the state increasingly depending on them and their collective organisation?

The three groups of obstacles looked at so far all relate to the extent and quality of state support – for acquiring the land, helping to bring it into production and then distributing its produce. But this is only half the story. The fourth, and perhaps the greatest, obstacle to making Venezuela's land reform into an engine of the new 'people's economy' has been the weakness of any tradition of collective organisation among the Venezuelan peasantry itself, and the consequent difficulty of launching and consolidating genuinely collective forms of co-operative enterprise. Of course it has been true almost everywhere that peasant production has usually gone hand in hand with a fiercely individualist attitude to work and property. But in some Latin American countries there has also been a powerful counter-current of collective concern. More often than not – say in Bolivia, Ecuador or Mexico – this has drawn on deep indigenous traditions of community work and collaboration, the *minga*, the *cayapa* or *convite*.[15] Some other cases, like the Brazilian Landless Movement, have had to generate their own 'mystique' – possibly with an injection of collective spirit from the traditions of liberation theology and its peculiar forms of social communion. The Venezuelan experience has comparatively little of this to draw on. This may be one reason why the tension between individual and collective production – and the dependence of both on state support – remains one of the biggest challenges facing Venezuela's land reform. Take the case of Bella Vista.

BELLA VISTA: LOOKING TOWARDS AGRARIAN SOCIALISM

The Fundo Zamorano Bella Vista, in Yaracuy state, was meant to be the real thing – one of the most complete experiences of land reform leading directly to a collective agricultural enterprise. I'd seen the Vive TV programme about the occupation here too, and it was impressive.

Following a carefully planned, self-organised occupation in July 2005, the peasants had quickly been given a full *Carta Agraria*, or title deed, for 233 hectares of prime land, issued collectively to their co-operative, bringing together over 200 members. After striking out on their own, they'd quickly won comprehensive support from the Ministry of Agriculture, INTI, Campo Adentro and several other public institutions. When I visited over two years later, in addition to the initial training from Vuelvan Caras, they'd received credit for crops, a couple of Iranian-designed tractors, and an array of technical support, including an organic fertiliser production unit, from a team of Cuban agronomists. The government had also chosen their *Fundo* as the site for one of its first 'socialist townships'. A couple of kilometres from the occupation, to replace the self-built shacks of sticks, canvas and zinc that I'd seen in the video, the government had built a complex of 50 smart, three-bedroomed bungalows (and 50 more to follow), with free electricity and water, at least for the initial period. There was a Barrio Adentro doctor's surgery, a *Simoncito* nursery and community centre, a library and Info-centre internet café, even their own community radio station (which insisted on interviewing me and my 13-year-old son about our impressions of the revolution).

The contrast with the halting start at El Charcote appeared to be striking.

For El Charcote represented a particular moment of Venezuela's land reform – one where expectations were set high, then frustrated, only to give way eventually to a more modest but not insignificant achievement. Bella Vista, on the other hand, represented a slightly later phase in the process – one where it was only reasonable to expect a better-balanced, more co-ordinated combination of action from below, by organised groups of peasants, and support from above, by the different organs of state.

Yet appearances can be deceptive. The Bella Vista co-operative had run into problems.

The land looked in good condition. Several different crops seemed to be thriving: onions, peppers, pumpkins, tomatoes and maize. The infrastructure was extensive. But in the main building of this model collective farm – a combination of barn and office – there were few people and little activity. Three men were playing dominoes at one table outside. In the office several more people were watching a disaster movie on the DVD. A tour of the fields was not much different. Of the 200 odd original members of the co-op, no more than 20 turned up on that particular day. Felix Rojas, the new secretary of the co-op, told me that the active membership had shrunk to under 100. Others told me it was not more than 50 or so.

Why?

The short answer was simple. So far, this model co-operative had not been able to provide its members with a sustainable living. But the reasons for this were complex. Some were external, beyond their control. They'd lost their first tomato crop because this top-quality land had been 'poisoned' by the herbicide the previous 'owners' had put on their sugar cane. Just three months earlier, they'd lost another 30,000 kilos of tomatoes, over half their latest crop, because they'd been unable to sell it. 'The market was already taken by people from the plains,' Felix told me. 'In this sense we do need *more* help from the state. We need the state to buy all our produce, because this is for the people to eat. And if the government could build a processing plant next door to turn it into tomato paste, then we'd all benefit.'

But beyond this were deeper problems to do with some of the peasants' own expectations and commitment, and the level of collective organisation needed to carry these through. The critical issue had been whether or not the co-operative would pay its members to work while they were waiting for production to take off and begin to turn a profit. This is not an unfamiliar problem. Simón Uzcátegui had told me that the Ezequiel Zamora Front, which was now insisting on developing all its own land reform settlements as collective enterprises, had found several ways of dealing with it. In some cases, applications for credit had built into them a provision for paying the co-operative members a monthly advance on future income, similar to that paid in most industrial co-operatives like the garment factory at Fabricio Ojeda. But many rural co-ops did not have this included in their credit. In such cases, said Simón, they had to rely on organised solidarity. This might come from some other better established co-operative nearby, or more commonly it meant the co-op itself organising so that each member would have two or three days a week off to seek paid work elsewhere, whilst others covered their duties in the co-op. This would give them a small cash income for immediate family needs, to supplement the free food and other services they drew from the co-op.

This was more or less what the Bella Vista co-op had tried to do. But it had turned out to be chaotic and had generated resentment. Early on, the first president of the co-op had decided to pay out a monthly advance to all members, even though there wasn't a budget for this. It seems a sizable number of them, some of whom had played little part in the occupation and initial development of the farm, simply pocketed the money and disappeared, never to be seen again. Those who stayed had to pick up the debt. That was the first desertion. Subsequently, the same leaders of the co-op used co-operative funds on a discretionary basis, to solve individual members' particular problems as and when these arose. Not unreasonable, perhaps, but it soon generated accusations of favouritism and patronage. At the end of the previous year, the remaining members voted by 60 per cent to sack the co-operative's executive committee and elected a new one.

Felix Rojas and his new committee took over with a commitment to put the co-op's finances back on an organised and transparent track. They decided to ban all advances except strict emergency payments until all of Bella Vista's debts had been repaid. And what income they did get from the last tomato crop was ploughed back into planting the next maize crop. This more rigorous approach was, it seems, what the majority wanted. But in the process, a number of other founding members felt discriminated against or neglected, and began to vote with their feet. The result was a much-reduced core of active members, working without pay, struggling to get the co-op back on track.

The immediate lesson here takes us back to the discussion of co-operatives in Chapter 2. In isolation, co-operative production has to confront a barrage of pressures. These come from without – the pressures of the market economy in which, to varying degrees, it has to operate. But they also come from within – from all the deeply rooted individualist habits and prejudices generated by the age-old struggle for survival. To confront either, or both, requires not just support from the state, or those parts of the state that are committed to this kind of revolutionary change. Above all it requires a powerful culture of collective responsibility. And that demands a level of popular organisation and democratic control that remains perhaps the biggest challenge still facing Venezuela's Bolivarian revolution.

4 DEMOCRACY AT WORK

CONFRONTATIONS OVER CO-MANAGEMENT

It was just after midday, on Friday 10 August 2007, that the end came. Most of the 500 or more workers who for nine months had been occupying the bathroom furniture factory in Maracay had just left, as they had every Friday at this time for the last few weeks. The factory committee had finished handing out the food parcels and small cash allowances – what the general assembly of the workforce had agreed that each worker should receive for keeping the factory open and producing, albeit at only about 30 per cent of capacity.

As the workers drifted away for the weekend, 150 administrative staff, who had not supported or taken part in the occupation, arrived on the scene with a couple of former union leaders. They proceeded to call a lightning assembly. This promptly voted to remove the leadership of both the trade union and the factory committee that had been leading the occupation, and to hand the factory back to its private owners. It was understood that in return the owners would pay off the outstanding benefits they still owed to the employees.

Seeking to avoid a direct confrontation among the workforce, the members of the factory committee and those of their supporters that remained decided to withdraw. They ended up camped out in an annexe of the main factory building, on the other side of the road. The occupation at Sanitarios de Maracay had been hailed by many on the left in Venezuela, and internationally, as one of the most inspiring examples of workers' control to emerge from the Bolivarian revolution. Now it was clear that the workers had lost control, and in the short term it didn't seem they had much chance of retaking it.

The ousted leaders of the occupation accused the Ministry of

Labour of having conspired with the administrative staff and the factory's absentee owners to put an end to their experiment in direct workplace democracy, by mounting a *Carmonazo sindical*, or trade-union coup d'état (in reference to the failed April 2002 coup that briefly installed business leader Pedro Carmona in place of President Hugo Chavez).[1]

Sanitarios de Maracay: taking control and losing it

This was not the first time the workers at Sanitarios de Maracay had found themselves shut out of their own workplace. I had visited the factory exactly a month earlier and José Villegas, Organisation Secretary of the union and a leading figure in the occupation, told me how the owners had tried to get rid of them five times before. The first was in the anti-Chavez, national lockout at the end of 2002, in which the owners of Sanitarios, the Branger-Pocaterra family,[2] had played an active part. When the bosses' stoppage collapsed after 63 days, they tried to reopen the factory under much worse conditions, including paying the workers for only a three-day week. 'We resisted that and formed a new union, to replace the old yellow union, and this became one of the first affiliates of the new UNT (National Workers Union).'[3] Even then, he recalled, they ran into difficulties with the Ministry of Labour, whose inspectors took eight months to recognise their new union.

There followed three years of a cat-and-mouse game. The owners repeatedly threatened to shut up shop or disregard the collective agreement, on the grounds of poor market conditions. The union pointed to the 16 different countries Sanitarios was exporting its bathroom products to, and refused to give up their conditions. In April 2006, the owners left the factory and took all the supervisory staff with them. They said they'd run out of money and there were no investors, but according to José Villegas their aim was to get rid of the new union and the collective agreement by provoking a 'technical closure' (*cierre tecnico*). That produced the first occupation. The workers spent 42 days in the factory. They didn't attempt to restart production, but they'd switch the motors on to stop the cement solidifying in the tubes and thus prevent the owners from claiming a technical closure. In May the bosses returned.

[99]

In November the employers issued another threat: either abandon the union and accept worse conditions under new individual contracts, or the factory would close. This time the workers had a more ambitious alternative. They'd been studying the example of other occupied factories in Venezuela and elsewhere. The union called a general assembly on 14 November which voted in favour of launching another occupation. But this time they would continue production under their own, workers' control. For a week they debated the forms this might take. Then a second assembly elected a factory committee, separate from the union, to organise the occupation and the continuation of production.

The structure adopted was a model of direct democracy in the workplace. The sovereign body was the assembly of all workers, which met every Friday, and had the last word on all matters. The assembly elected a factory committee of 21 members, which became the day-to-day administration of the factory, answerable to and recallable by the assembly. The factory committee also formed six sub-committees for different areas of responsibility – raw materials, production, sales, administration, mobilisation, and legal and security – each including two members of the central factory committee and involving a total of some 60 workers. In parallel, the factory committee nominated, on the basis of perceived ability, some 15 'delegates', one for each department in the factory. These took over the functions of what had been the heads of production in each department, and together they made up the delegate body. At the same time, and separate from these structures, the trade union retained its own autonomous organisation within the factory.

Wednesdays were the main meeting day. First the delegates met and reported to the factory committee. 'First we listen to the delegates, because they are responsible for the production. They raise whatever problems are faced in production, any cases of workers who don't turn up, and so on. We listen and discuss. Then the delegates withdraw and the factory committee begins to make proposals to correct the situation.'

Later on the Wednesday, the seven members of the trade union leadership, who were also members of the factory committee, held a separate meeting to discuss any union business arising from this, as well as other trade union and political issues, national or local. Major decisions and a general report-back then went to the Friday assembly. A few weeks earlier for example, the assembly had decided to award one top-end bathroom suite to every worker, for them to take and sell where they could. This should be worth about 500,000 to 600,000 bolivars each. The aim was to help the already hard-pressed workforce meet the extra expense of sending their children back to school for the new school year. The assembly had also decided earlier to donate free bathroom fittings to a number of local schools whose toilets were in a bad state of repair.

Factories abandoned, factories occupied

The occupation at Sanitarios was an extension of several other experiences that had developed in Venezuela over the previous few years and which came to prominence at the beginning of 2005. That was when the government finally agreed to expropriate the Venepal paper manufacturer, in neighbouring Carabobo state.[4] It was one of a large number of private Venezuelan factories and processing plants that the owners had run down, closed or claimed as bankrupt before, during and since the 2002–03 employers' lockout. The workers at Venepal had been struggling against this for over two years. They had occupied, marched and mounted campaigns. With no solution in sight from Venepal's joint Venezuelan and North American owners, they were now demanding the state intervene.

On 13 January 2005, parliament had taken the first step by declaring the company's large site at Moron, which once had a work-force of 1,600 but which in recent times had been run down to around 600, to be 'of public utility and social interest'. Six days later, on 19 January, the Venezuelan president signed Decree No. 3438 that expropriated the abandoned firm and handed it over to the workers to run themselves. Renamed Invepal, it would become a 'co-managed' enterprise, with the state owning 51 per cent of the shares and 49 per cent being given to a co-operative set up by the workforce.

After six years in office, this was effectively the Bolivarian revolution's first 'expropriation', and it came less than two weeks before that speech in Brazil where Hugo Chavez announced that socialism was the solution. At the time President Chavez insisted that this expropriation of Venepal was an exceptional measure. The government was not about to seize the assets of the private sector around the country. But, somewhat ambiguously, he added that if companies were closed or abandoned by their owners, 'we will come after you'. The aim was to reconstitute Venezuela's industrial fabric. This should not be seen as some sort of state capitalism, but rather 'a process of liberating the workers' through co-management, within the overall project of endogenous development. 'It is essential', he said, 'that we change the relations of production.'

This support seemed to be gathering momentum. One month later, President Chavez broadcast his weekly *Aló Presidente* TV show from the Invepal factory, which he called 'a first step towards a new kind of productive relations'. Sitting in front of a row of giant rolls of newly pressed paper, he took up another of the Bolivarian revolution's new themes. He invited the assembled Invepal workers to form their own military reserve or militia to defend the plant they now controlled – and he added, 'I tie my destiny to that of these workers.'[5]

On 27 April 2005, the government proceeded to expropriate another factory, the smaller National Valve-Making Company, at Los Teques, just outside Caracas. The workers there had been through a similar two-year struggle, and this was now turned over to their control under a similar co-management arrangement.

That weekend, government and unions alike mobilised for a massive May Day march. Again President Chavez talked of the key role of the working class in this new kind of socialism that Venezuela was on the way to building, and he offered 'the government's unqualified support for co-management, but not capitalist co-management'.

In the following months, Chavez and his Minister of Labour at the time – the same Maria Cristina Iglesias I had met at my first *Aló Presidente* back in 2004 – identified some 800 factories that had been closed or run down by their owners and which might therefore be taken over by their workforce. Maria Cristina Iglesias told one meeting on co-management that occupied factories were not part of the problem but part of the solution. In the event, however, there was no move to 'go for' these other factories, and the handful of further occupations did not result in expropriations.

There were already considerable differences between these various experiences in co-management or workers' control, as there were between the many programmes and proposals being put forward for how to organise such workplace democracy and where it should lead. But by the time the majority of the 800 workers at the Sanitarios factory in

Maracay voted to re-launch production under their own direct administration – on 14 November 2006 – there was another, more pressing difference. It seemed the central governmental authorities had either lost interest, or turned openly hostile to the whole idea.

Of course the fact that the Sanitarios workers 'did it on their own' was not necessarily a bad thing. On the contrary, not a few on the left and within the new Venezuelan trade union movement saw this 'independence' and 'autonomy' from the structures of power as one of Sanitarios' biggest pluses. But when not only the owners, but also the authorities, began to throw up roadblocks, deliberate or inadvertent, at every turn, things became a lot more difficult.[6]

So were these external obstacles the only reason for the setback at Sanitarios? Or were there internal weaknesses that also contributed? And what do both these aspects, and the relation between them, tell us about the inner dynamics of the Bolivarian revolution and its vision, or visions, of socialism? Before trying to answer these questions we should consider in greater detail another, bigger and strategically more important, experience with democracy in the workplace – one which has suffered a more gradual series of setbacks.

DAYS OF HOPE: ALCASA IN 2005

In the first half of 2005, Venezuela's second-biggest aluminium plant, ALCASA, in the south-eastern industrial centre of Puerto Ordaz, was the site of one of the most radical extensions of democracy attempted anywhere in recent years.

This may seem like an exaggerated claim. Even if we confine ourselves to Latin America, there have of course been larger outbreaks of direct and participatory democracy, involving larger numbers of people and wider geographical areas. We have mentioned some of them before: the kinds of popular assembly that sprang up in Buenos Aires, Argentina, in 2002, in El Alto, Bolivia, in 2003–05, or Oaxaca, Mexico, in 2006; the remaining, radical forms of participatory budgeting that continued to embrace as many as 10 million people in several cities and the entire state of Rio Grande do Sul in southern Brazil up until at least 2002; the self-organised referendum on free trade initiated by the Nasa people of south-western Colombia in 2004.

But ALCASA was different. It was different from Invepal or Inveval or Sanitarios – or any of the other occupied factories in Argentina, Uruguay or Brazil – for several reasons. Firstly it was bigger. This was a state-owned enterprise with a workforce that oscillated just below the 3,000 mark. Secondly, this was a strategic industry. Of course it doesn't compare with oil, but aluminium remains Venezuela's second most important basic industry, and ALCASA is the country's second-biggest aluminium smelter. Thirdly, it was part of a wider network of basic industries, grouped in the CVG holding company (Corporación Venezolana de Guayana), which includes 17 separate state enterprises in the industrial heartland of south-eastern Venezuela employing over 18,000 people and which has almost endless economic linkages backwards and forwards into other industries, other regions and every corner of local society. Fourthly – and this was arguably both a strength and a weakness – the co-management project at ALCASA was not brought about by the authorities responding to a specific struggle and set of demands made by the workforce. It was conceived and launched by at least a sector of central government. ALCASA was *intended* to be a test bed, and catalyst, for much wider change.

ALCASA was different from those other examples of direct democracy in Latin America for a different reason. In varying degrees and for a variety of shorter or longer periods of time, those other experiences had transformed the existing political structures by giving citizens far greater power to express political preferences and make political decisions than they ever had within the prevailing structures of representative democracy. In some cases, this 'radicalisation of democracy' gave people a real degree of control over the distribution of certain, usually local, economic resources. But it never touched what had always been the Holy Grail for traditional socialists. It never exerted control at the point of production – over the core economic activities that, according to the basic premises of materialist theory, gave shape to all the rest, or at least set the outer limits of all other possibilities. The co-management project at ALCASA was deliberately setting out to do just that, to democratise the relations of production at a nodal point in the Venezuelan economy. By giving the workforce control over decision-making at all levels, it aimed to transform the way production was organised within the workplace, and the ways this connected with the world outside.

ALCASA before co-management

The heat and noise were almost unbearable as we walked down Line 3 towards the casting shed in May 2005. My guides, Alcides Rivero and Marivit Lopez, had already begun to explain to me some of the difficulties ALCASA faced because of its ageing and neglected technology. For the previous decade or more, managers at the 38-year-old state-owned enterprise had deliberately starved it of investment, they told me. They'd been softening it up for privatisation. As I lined up my camera and peered through dripping perspiration into the viewfinder, it did look like something out of a 1960s documentary – the deep, red void within the holding oven, like gazing into the bowels of the earth; the worker in full mask and protective gear, seen through clouds of metallic steam as he stirred and prodded with a giant spatula at a tank of liquid aluminium, like liquid silver. I was reminded of Fernando Solanas' classic film *La Hora de los Hornos* ('The Hour of the Furnaces'), about an earlier experience of workers' control in the Argentinean factory commissions of the 1960s.

Line 3 at ALCASA, dating from 1988, was in fact one of the plant's two newest lines of pots – those large oven-like units where a process of electrolysis extracts molten aluminium from the treated ore. But all the lines were producing at well below capacity. When the new company president arrived and the co-management experiment began, three months earlier, the company had overdue debts of US$258 million, equivalent to a full nine months of production. There was no proper schedule of repairs, Alcides, a maintenance electrician told me, as we emerged back into a blazing, but comparatively cooler, tropical sun. It was a case of running around patching things up as they broke. Much of the servicing and supplies had been farmed out at inflated prices to private contractors. As you looked out over the industrial landscape stretching here along the southern bank of the mighty Orinoco River – Venalum, the other, more modern aluminium smelter, Carbonorca, which made components for both smelters, Sidor, the partly privatised steel works – it was becoming clearer how public and private nestled together in the pre-Bolivarian economy that still prevailed in much of Venezuela. The former was clearly at the service of the latter. ALCASA's losses were the private contractors' gains. Catering and cleaning for the entire plant was also contracted out, on generous terms, to a handful of large, private companies.

Something similar appeared at the end of the production chain too. Sixty-five per cent of the primary aluminium produced went for export, but almost all of it via intermediary traders who picked up most of the profit. Another 30-odd firms dominated domestic sales, selling the ingots and rolled aluminium on to a number of small manufacturers at a mark-up of as much as 400 per cent, according to ALCASA's new president, Carlos Lanz.

The plant's environmental debt was out of control. Only a third of the protection measures promised had ever been implemented. An extra US$40 million was needed to complete even this bare minimum.

At the same time, ALCASA's debts to its own workforce went unpaid. Marivit, who works in Personnel, pointed to the failure to pay agreed wage increases and pension commitments, and the number of workers injured on the job who had still received no compensation. Hardly surprising then, that 2004 had seen 266 hours of work interrupted by industrial action (102 hours of it in December alone), compared with 107 hours in 2003 and 37 hours in 2002.

In spite of all this, there was a strangely buoyant mood among my guides and just about everyone we bumped into – a notable contrast with all the dire statistics of past failure. 'This *is* socialism of the twenty-first century,' commented Alcides, as if he felt a need to justify his good mood. 'It's a new, humanist system. Co-management here has a lot to do with workers' control, because it's really the workers who are taking the decisions – about production, technology, administration – and running the company. For the first time in 40 years, workers have the chance to elect who they want to manage the company.'

The new company president, Carlos Lanz, later put this in a wider context for me. This was not the kind of co-management, he explained, that European social democracy, and even Christian democracy had promoted, especially in West Germany in the post-war period, 'which came down to handing out shares and a few seats for workers' representatives on the board. ... We see co-management as tied to workers' control of the factory, as a proposal for transition towards socialism, towards another system of production.'

The enthusiasm of those involved seemed infectious. Elio

Sayago was a case in point. Another of the key activists in the plant helping to push forward the co-management project, he too had a mischievous twinkle in his eye. 'I know,' he said, 'there's a meeting of one of the *Mesas de Trabajo* (departmental works committee) about to begin in Rodding Shed Number 3. That'll show you what this co-management is all about.'

The works committee at Rodding Shed No. 3

The meeting was already underway when we arrived. In a plain office room there were about 25 men – and one woman – squashed round a large rectangular table, a white board and flip chart at the far end, and in the middle of the table a fist-sized model of a carbon anode. That's the bit that's lowered, on a rod, into the pots or cells to provide an opposite pole and make the electrolysis happen. The workers in the rodding shed were responsible for providing and repairing those rods.

I didn't understand much of what was being discussed. 'Friction welding is clearly cheaper than conventional welding, yet for 80 per cent of the rods we are using those other methods.' One of the workers was gesticulating excitedly with the model anode. There seemed to be a connection between this and the efficiency of the electrolysis itself. Another man started scribbling numbers on the flip chart. 'You have to include in the calculation the materials that ALCASA provides, *plus* how much electrical conductivity we *gain*. That's the purpose after all. How much extra are we spending on energy because of voltage drops in those units we weld by conventional means?'

The key discussion seemed to be about how, where and by whom the repairs would best be carried out. They were talking about technology and costs, but they were also talking about the labour process, about how best to organise their own work. 'The rods arriving at Line 2 are the ones that have had welds repaired, and we're having to go through another whole selection, to see how many have one, two or three bad welds. Three or four times to do the same job! Just because we organised it badly in the first place!' This, it seemed, had an impact on the productivity of the anodes themselves. 'We need to reach a definite conclusion on what to do about this. We need to know where these percentages are located, how much in pod 1, how much in pod 2 and 3, and so on. Then we need to identify the repair method in each case and who is going to carry out that repair.'

Here was another focus of the discussion: how ALCASA's internal production processes should link up with the world beyond. 'At the moment, all this work is contracted out.' One of the reasons for that seemed to be health and safety. 'Remember, this stuff is highly toxic. We need breathing apparatus.' It was because of this danger to the workers and the environment, one of those present reminded the others, that the previous management had to go to outside contractors to get the work done. Now new considerations were coming up: 'How do we know the people working for that contractor won't be subjected to the same dire conditions?'

So what were the options? There seemed to be three or four. They could continue to contract the repair work out to small private companies, or possibly to ALCASA's larger sister aluminium smelter, Venalum, just down the road. 'If Venalum could repair 20–30 rods per shift, then that would work out cheapest for us.' They could give the work to specially formed co-operatives. But didn't that bring a danger of undercutting existing employment rights? 'The union has rightly complained about us forming co-ops that turn out to be sweatshops that just undermine existing terms and conditions. No, the endogenous projects must be sustainable in the long run.' The best option, several argued, would be to bring the repair work back in-house. 'But that would mean buying three or four new machines, because the one we have are fully occupied on the pod lines.' Whatever the choice, everyone seemed to agree with another member of the council when he argued that: 'If we want to advance in terms of technology then we also have to advance in terms of health and safety, and restore the central importance of us as human beings! Because without human beings there *is* no technology.'

Sitting, watching and listening to all this was a remarkable experience. I had of course read about workers' control. I had visited factories where it was happening. I had been to plenty of union meetings of my own in the past where colleagues would complain about the generally useless nature of managers; about how much better our rotas or our programmes would be, if we could just get on with doing them ourselves and didn't have 'suits' flapping about, sticking their noses in and getting in the way. But I'd never actually seen it happen. I hadn't ever witnessed a group of employees, individual workers from different areas and levels of the operation, come together to identify problems, discuss solutions and determine the actions needed to carry these through. In other words, I'd never actually seen workers exercising control.

For that is certainly what appeared to be happening here in Rodding Shed No. 3. In those first few months of the co-management experience at ALCASA, after February 2005, it was these departmental works committees (the Spanish '*Mesas de Trabajo*' doesn't translate well into English) that became the radical centre of this experiment in direct workplace democracy. This was where the day-to-day running of the plant by the workforce took place.

The division of labour

It was a few hours after sitting in on the works committee that I finally met the man who President Chavez had put in charge of ALCASA to introduce this co-management scheme. It wasn't easy to get to see him. But when I was introduced to Carlos Lanz – in the kitchen of the ample but bland company house that served as his *casa presidencial* – he didn't immediately strike me as the fearsome, former guerrilla leader I had heard about.[7] He seemed rather a mild man, probably in his sixties, with grey hair and a goatee beard. He did seem to have an awareness of his own importance, but it was more the manner of an impatient academic than a political potentate. The key thing, he told me, was 'overcoming the division of labour'. In other words, 'we put at the centre of co-management the need to overcome the division between intellectual and manual labour, between those who take the decisions and those who carry them out. That means the whole management structure has to be flattened out, made more collective, *democratised*.'

There was some serious theory behind this. Traditionally, Marxists had seen a transition to socialism as being characterised by a change in the relations of production. But often such a change had been identified mainly with a change in property relations – from private property to public or state property – and to a lesser extent with a change in exchange relations – moving away from the overarching dominance of 'market forces' towards some form of central planning or command. This had certainly been true of most versions of 'actually existing socialism' in the twentieth century. What ALCASA's co-management proposal was trying to do, in Lanz's view, was to restore a third, vital component to its proper place in a socialist transition. This was the indispensable question of overturning any monopoly of knowledge and giving all people, in this case all members of the workforce, the power to discuss and decide. 'As you know,' he said, 'the French philosopher Michel Foucault, quoting others before him, said that knowledge was power. Here we are attacking the hierarchy of knowledge in the factory and in society. If we democratise knowledge, that is the best way, the only way, in my opinion, of genuinely exercising democracy.'

For Lanz there was a link here back to Article 62 of Venezuela's 1999 Bolivarian Constitution – 'for me the most revolutionary article of the constitution' – which challenges the monopoly of knowledge when it talks of the need for 'the participation of the people in the formation, execution and control of public affairs'. There was also a link forwards, to a genuinely democratic socialism for the new century.

'The old pro-capitalist, social-democratic kind of co-management was never intended to affect the relations of production. It was rather intended to reinforce property relations and the system of production for profit, even softening some harsher aspects of exploitation in order to mask the underlying exploitation of labour. It was born as a response by capital to the advance of the workers' movement. It generated a certain form of participation by workers' organisations in the administration of the factory, in order to make the workers complicit in their own exploitation. That for me was a counter-revolutionary proposal. Which is why we talk of "revolutionary co-management". We put the word "revolutionary" in front in order to incorporate elements of workers' control and self-management. We aim to overcome exploitation, to do away with the exploitation of labour. That is why our revolutionary co-management connects directly with socialism of the twenty-first century.'

In his view there was a fundamental ambiguity about co-management, just as there is about other areas of participatory democracy, about co-operatives, endogenous development, land reform and almost all the constituent elements of the Bolivarian process and of any other possible transition to socialism. 'If you go to the roots of the relations of production', Carlos Lanz told me, 'co-management opens the way to socialism of the twenty-first century. If you don't, it reinforces capitalism.'

Under the revolutionary version of co-management, the criteria of quality and efficiency would also have to change. 'To the traditional indicators of efficiency and effectiveness, we have to add other categories, like social and environmental pertinence or appropriateness.' Carlos Lanz put this in the context of the 'people's economy' that Venezuela was trying to develop, 'where profitability and growth *per se* are not the objective, but human development is'. 'You could have a process that was effective and efficient in terms of profitability, in purely technocratic and economic terms, but which wasn't appropriate or desirable for society and its citizens. We want to combine different types of technology. It's not just about cutting-edge technology, but about linking this to human development and a balance with nature, making sure it is appropriate. That doesn't have to mean it's not efficient. But efficiency is not enough.'

Nonetheless, in those first months, Carlos Lanz claimed that even by a conventional yardstick, co-management had proved its worth. In the very first weeks, according to him, 80 idle pots or cells were brought back into production and by the end of March 2005, total output in tons of aluminium had jumped by 11 per cent. 'Democratic planning', said Carlos Lanz, 'putting the workforce consciously in charge of running the company, is such a powerful lever, that in spite of the outdated technology, the lack of investment, the lack of spare parts, the innumerable environmental and other problems, production went up. Why? Because the worker is working with much more awareness than before.'[8]

It was also the case that the 266 hours lost to industrial disputes in 2004, fell to just four hours in 2005, and zero hours in 2006.

The shape of co-management at ALCASA

The departmental works committees were at the centre of a co-management scheme that operated at three main levels. Alcides and Marivit guided me to another part of the plant – Baking Ovens No. 1, at the beginning of the production chain – to explain how each departmental works committee was formed, and how it fitted into the broader structure.

The first level, the basic building block of the whole edifice, was the election of 'spokespeople' (*voceros*) by small work teams in each department of the factory. The work teams were made up of about five to ten workers depending on the particular area. 'For example', said Alcides, 'in this part there are eight workers. They meet and choose a spokesperson.' For all the 201 workers in Baking Ovens, there were 30 elected as spokespeople, and these 30 came together as the departmental works committee, or *Mesa de Trabajo*, like the one I'd attended at Rodding Shed No. 3. In those first months of co-management at ALCASA, 231 spokespeople were elected to works committees in 19 departments or managerial areas. Marivit insisted that these were not elected 'representatives' of the workforce, in the old sense, who could then go off and do what they liked, but genuine spokespeople. Their job was to gather the concerns, problems and suggestions of all the shop floor workers and convey these to the committee. If the people who chose them felt they weren't doing that, they could recall them at any time. A substitute was chosen alongside the main spokesperson and the intention was that these roles should rotate around the members of a given work team.

It was the departmental works committee's job to consider all these problems and come up with solutions. Decisions could be taken by simple majority vote, but usually there was an effort to reach a consensus. For example, part of the Baking Ovens department was slated for closure – the technology was well past its sell-by date and the work could be done better elsewhere. 'So, it's the workers who will decide if that does happen, or suggest technical solutions for keeping it open. And the departmental managers, the company president and the board will be expected to respect their decision.'

If the works committee was unable to decide on any issue, then it would be taken to an assembly of all the workers in that department. Similarly, big issues facing the whole company would be taken to an assembly of the entire workforce, held according to tradition at the main factory gate. These assemblies were the ultimate authority within this scheme of co-management. They were the last level.

Between them and the departmental committees were the elected managers. Under the old system, each of the 19 departments or managerial units had one departmental manager appointed by the company president, the Carlos Lanz figure. Now with co-management, each of these was to be replaced by a team of three elected managers, rotating in their functions. In that first year, 15 of the departments elected 36 new managers. Initially there had been an attempt to hold these elections at the factory gate assemblies, but the old rivalry between trade union currents threatened to derail the process and it was decided to return to a secret paper ballot. In an unprecedented move, Carlos Lanz also put his own job, as company president, up for ratification by ballot.

The three elected managers in each department also took part in the works committee alongside the spokespeople, so in Baking Ovens, for example, there were a total of 33 members of the departmental works committee. Between them, the committee and the management team ran the department, with the elected managers essentially executing on a daily basis the decisions taken by the departmental works committee at their (usually weekly) meetings.

Even apparent opponents seemed to be convinced by some of this. The man assigned by ALCASA's PR office to accompany me on my first tour of the plant was not, it seemed, an enthusiastic supporter of Hugo Chavez. 'He's *escualido* (opposition),' someone had whispered in my ear. Still, he had been there for years and I was thankful for his encyclopaedic knowledge and because he was the only person able to translate into equivalent English terms the technical vocabulary of aluminium processing. I asked him how he felt about ordinary shop-floor workers being in charge of the factory. Didn't many decisions need to be taken by experts? He looked at me for a moment, then said: 'People who have been working for 20 years smelting aluminium *are* experts. We wouldn't choose just anyone to manage our plant. I'm sure they will make very good decisions.'

The final, fourth level of the co-management system was the 'co' bit. For while the assemblies, the works committees and the elected managers had real decision-making power and considerable autonomy over matters within the company, they did not control the external environment. They operated within a framework set by the Bolivarian government. This was *co*-management *with* the state. The essential parameters within which ALCASA had to work – financial, industrial, commercial and political – were set by the Venezuelan government through its Ministry of Basic Industries and Mining, a ministry which largely overlapped with the bureaucracy of the CVG (just as the Ministry of Energy overlaps with the bureaucracy of PDVSA). This was an initial source of strength. Indeed, it was the newly appointed Minister of Basic Industries, Victor Alvarez, himself a strong supporter of the co-management project, who brought in Carlos Lanz and was by his side at the very first factory-gate assembly that launched ALCASA's co-management in February 2005.

More than that, there is a strong argument that some kind of oversight by the state – or some other sort of *external* democratic accountability – is absolutely essential if co-management or workers' control is not to lead individual companies to look inwards and begin competing against each other. This, arguably, is what happened to the experience of self-management in the former Yugoslavia, which had been something of a beacon for the European left in the 1960s and 1970s, and that seems to have played no small part in the later, bloody break-up of that country.[9] But the positive value of such state oversight obviously depends on the nature of the state in question. This is another issue we shall return to.

ALCASA's participatory budget

One of the most ambitious projects in that first year of co-management at ALCASA was to involve the entire workforce in drawing up the company budget for the following year. They called it the Participatory Budget for 2006. This drew in part on one of the classic demands of workers' movements in the earlier part of the twentieth century, the demand that a company 'open its books' to scrutiny by the workers. But the name, and in part the actual design of the project in ALCASA in 2005, came from that much more recent Latin American tradition, started in Porto Alegre, of trying to give citizens control over local government finances.[10]

When I made my first visit to ALCASA in May 2005, the discussions on the budget had just begun and the workers had two more months to complete the first phase. The basic unit for that first phase was again the department and its departmental works committee. Marivit explained: 'At the moment the works committees have received the draft budget for 2006 which already existed. They are now reviewing this and deciding what they think the priorities should be, so that the budget can be restructured in line with the real needs of the company.' For Alcides, this was the first time the workers had a chance to look seriously at the company's numbers. 'There are no more commercial, administrative or technological secrets here. In future we expect to be able to decide how any profits should be used – whether on upgrading technology, preserving the environment or benefiting the whole surrounding community.'

Carlos Lanz told me that everything should be up for discussion by the departments in this first stage: purchasing, investments, tenders, questions of technology as well as improvements in working practices and in efficiency. 'This will be the first time a company in Venezuela has drawn up its budget on the basis of this kind of democratic structure. Of course there are experts who are helping out and will have their input. But the crucial thing is to involve the ordinary shop-floor workers in weighing up what needs to be done and shaping this into a plan of work for the year to come. We have to start from what each department sees as its needs. After that there will be a mechanism for reconciling the proposals coming from each department into one overall budget proposal, for pulling it all together into a single strategic vision for the company. This is all part of a collective process that to some extent we are still making up as we go along.'

One area Carlos Lanz was keen to develop further through this participatory budget was the question of how any overall surplus – once basic operating needs had been covered – should be allocated. His suggestion was for four separate funds for different areas: 1) one for amortisation of debts and improvements in technology; 2) a social fund, to pay back to the community a part of the dividends; 3) another for the remuneration of the workforce, including all wages and other benefits; 4) and a fund for what he called 'emulation', a kind of performance fund to reward exemplary work. Deciding the percentage going to each fund would be one of the main tasks of the participatory budget. But, he pointed out, this would lead to a legal struggle. ALCASA, as a limited company, had statutes in line with existing company law. These would have to be changed – and that might not prove so easy.

Building bridges, upstream and downstream

The other area where ALCASA's co-management entailed radical innovation was in the company's external relations – with the other companies within the CVG state holding company, with the rest of its suppliers and clients, and with the local community.

The question of the CVG was crucial. Carlos Lanz had been made President of ALCASA, but at the same time he was put in charge of co-management and endogenous development for the whole of the CVG. From the beginning there was a conscious effort to spread co-management to the other member companies, starting with those that were closest, both geographically and in production terms. I went with Elio Sayago, Marivit Lopez and Edgar Caldera, another of the ALCASA activists showing me round, to a lunchtime meeting at Carbonorca, a CVG factory just down the road that made many of the anodes used in ALCASA's pot lines. Elio got up and described to the canteen full of workers how co-management was working at ALCASA. He made an impassioned appeal to them to begin electing their own spokespeople and forming their own works committees. He argued that co-management would be unstoppable if it developed right across the CVG and then beyond. But if it didn't, he said, it would be vulnerable. 'We are not used to working as a team,' he told them, 'but we are making a start.' In recognition of the difficulties that surely lay ahead, he noted the resistance coming from several quarters, not just among existing managers but among some in the trade unions too. 'Some fear they will lose power. Yes they will.' Because this was a new power that was emerging, he concluded: '*your* power'.

Carlos Lanz brought onto the board of ALCASA a series of new representatives from the other CVG companies. The idea was that they should transmit the co-management experience back to their home companies – a task that, as we shall see, they never really carried out.[11]

The challenge of spreading co-management was closely tied to a programme of popular education, drawing on Latin American traditions of a pedagogy of the oppressed.[12] I went to a school just opened in Puerto Ordaz city centre – the first of what was intended to become a *Red de Centros de Formación*, or network of training centres – where Marivit and other ALCASA workers, along with some external trainers, were running courses to prepare 'co-management facilitators'. The students were workers from Carbonoraca, Venalum and other CVG companies, as well as a handful from local co-ops and community organisations.

'What is the procedure you should follow to promote co-management in your factory?' asked one of the women trainers. She invited the students, in teams, to work out a proposal and bring it back for discussion, 'so that we can build this knowledge collectively.'

As we chatted after the class, trainer Milagros Cova waxed lyrical about spreading co-management across the country. 'We're starting the real revolution here,' she said. I asked them all if they thought that was a real possibility. For example, what about the state oil company? After an important but brief experience of spontaneous workers' control had kept the oil industry more or less functioning during the opposition-led lockout of 2002–03, the Bolivarian government had ejected the managers and technicians who had supported the lockout. But they had also brought an end to any form of workers' control or significant co-management. They had chosen to rebuild PDVSA along conventional, top-down, managerial lines.

Marivit was guardedly optimistic. 'The experience in the CVG can set an example that will allow PDVSA to take up co-management again. But it'll be with greater awareness this time, because in 2002–03 it wasn't very thought-out.' Still, she recognised that the oil industry, as the backbone of the Venezuelan economy and the bankroller of the Bolivarian revolution, was a more delicate case. 'We probably do have to go more slowly with PDVSA. The international companies that PDVSA works with are really alarmed by this experience of co-management. It's a serious risk for them.'

The presence on these courses of people from co-operatives and community organisations pointed to several different kinds of bridge being built out from the co-management experience in ALCASA. Most of the other CVG companies were in some way upstream suppliers to ALCASA. Bauxilium supplied the raw material bauxite, mostly in its treated form, alumina; Carbonorca supplied anodes; Edelca supplied electricity, and so on. The other big smelter, Venalum, was apparently a direct competitor, but could at least potentially be a collaborator, supplying industrial services, maintenance and so on. As we have seen, some such services had for a number of years been outsourced to private contractors. So one of the first tasks for the new democratised management structure at ALCASA was to review all these tenders. A number were already being transferred to self-managed co-operatives, often formed by the workers previously employed by those contractors. In the case of industrial services that were integral to the production process itself, this was seen as a temporary measure. The aim was to bring these services, and the workers providing them, back in-house and onto the company payroll.

Co-ops were, as we have seen in earlier chapters, an important part of the Bolivarian vision for an alternative, endogenous development. ALCASA's proposals for re-shaping the aluminium industry also gave a strategic role to co-operatives. So it was envisaged that some of the services that had been contracted out – those less integrated into the production process – should be turned over to new co-operative enterprises on a longer-term basis. This could include the hugely lucrative cleaning and catering contracts that had been farmed out across the 17 companies of the CVG, and which made for one of the state sector's most generous contributions to local private business. To begin with, however, it was the manufacture of company uniforms and working clothes that took the lead, with the setting up of the San Buenaventura Textile Co-operative. Rather like the clothing factory at Fabricio Ojeda in Caracas (see Chapter 2), this was made up largely of previously unemployed women workers who received help from ALCASA with training, raw materials and start-up credits.

Another aspect of the co-operative role had to do with the company's clients. After all, what and who should ALCASA be making its primary aluminium for? The fact that most of the output went straight to export meant that little of the potential benefit (in terms of value added) was being realised in Venezuela or by the Venezuelan people. One priority was to turn this situation around. The 35 per cent sold within Venezuela in 2004 climbed to 38 per cent in 2005, 41 per cent in 2006 and 56 per cent in the first quarter of 2007. This also meant beginning to cut out the intermediaries who were taking such a large slice of the profit, and delivering direct to the processors. Thirdly, the aim was to ensure that more of these processors were themselves self-managed co-operatives or otherwise fitted into the then emerging concept of social production enterprises. Clearly this could not happen overnight. But in that first year of co-management ALCASA helped to set up two such 'client' co-ops locally, one making aluminium bodywork for mini-buses to be used in the city's public transport system, another making aluminium cooking utensils. It also began to work with a factory on the other side of the country, making aluminium wheelchairs and medical aids for the public health programmes. As Carlos Lanz pointed out, all this was not going down well with the small group of private trading companies that had come to regard ALCASA's sales as their own private prerogative – nor with sections of the local industrial and political bureaucracy that had been enjoying a cosy and mutually beneficial relationship with those private traders.

Lastly, ALCASA under co-management began discussing ways of directly involving, and benefiting, local communities, backing local development projects that had nothing to do directly with ALCASA or its aluminium business. 'We want workers' co-management', said Carlos Lanz, 'to become also society's co-management. We want to build a network linking co-management in the workplace to co-management in the communities.'

THE BACKWARD MARCH OF CO-MANAGEMENT: ALCASA 2007

When I returned to ALCASA in the second half of 2007, the mood was very different. Carlos Lanz had just been removed as president of the company. Co-management had not spread to any of the other CVG companies. The departmental works committees had stopped functioning. Opposition supporters had been elected to lead the union. Many of the old managers were back in place. Production was threatened by continuing technological failures, financial pressures and serious incidents of apparent sabotage. When I spoke to those who had shown me around with so much spirit before, their judgements varied. Some thought it had all been a terrible failure. Others felt that after some setbacks things were set to move forward again. Most fell somewhere in between.

The first sign of trouble came at the main factory gate. There was a small demonstration taking place, led by a group of mostly women co-operative members. Half a dozen of them were standing in red

Chavista t-shirts on the back of a flat-bed truck with a megaphone and banners, a few dozen more were standing listening and handing out flyers to the passing ALCASA workers. They were denouncing what they said were attempts by some of the old, recently re-elected, departmental managers to do down and do away with the community co-operatives that had been sewing uniforms for the factory. Their leaflet named several managers and administrators whom they accused of lying, presenting false figures and withholding materials in order to undermine the co-operatives and the commitment to endogenous development and a people's economy. 'We are ordinary mothers and fathers who possess nothing. We are not the ones who have bought cars, houses, flats and farms that no one could afford on their company salaries.'

This invective was not reserved for the managers alone. The protestors were also accusing the current leaders of the union, SINTRALCASA, of being involved in these murky attempts to take back supply contracts from the co-operatives and return them to commercial sub-contractors. 'We demand a judicial inspection of all administrative procedures,' they concluded. '*Patria, Socialismo o Muerte, Venceremos!*'

After the speeches had finished, I asked Rosmery Duque of the Confecciones Alexandra garment co-op to explain the particular case they'd been denouncing: 'They claim that we have failed to deliver 5,000 shirts from the 2006 order. But the point is, they never delivered us the fabric for those shirts. Because ALCASA brings all the material ready-cut from Maracay. They also supply us with the buttons, buckles, zippers and so on. All we put in is the thread and the labour to sew it together. So in this case the union demands the uniforms from ALCASA and ALCASA accuses us of failing to deliver and not being competent. But they're the ones who didn't deliver and then they cook the books to conceal the fact. The truth is they'd rather go back to having a capitalist company do the garment-making because under the table they get their kick-back. With us they're losing out because our accounting is transparent.'

Was this just an isolated local conflict? It certainly seemed ironic. For ALCASA's relationship with local communities and co-ops was one area where co-management had achieved and sustained most success. At the Negro Primero Training Centre inside the plant – which had taken over most of the functions of the city-centre training facility I'd visited two years earlier – I met Angel Arevalo with a group of mature students from the local branch of the Venezuelan Bolivarian University (UBV). He was ALCASA's Co-ordinator for EPSs (social production enterprises), which was the name increasingly given to co-ops like these engaged in networks of 'endogenous development'. They were students of social administration doing a placement in ALCASA, helping to strengthen links between the company and a variety of co-operative and community enterprises. Angel explained how by 2006 *all* the ALCASA uniforms were being supplied by a network of 11–16 co-ops, with the exception only of the boots and protective gloves. That meant 18,000 shirts and 180,000 cloths and towels a year just for ALCASA. Venalum had its own network of supply co-ops. 'That's a lot of money,' he pointed out.

At the same time, ALCASA was giving logistical support to a number of local community projects. Together with these UBV students, it was working with the communal councils in four communities in particular to help them carry out their own 'participatory community diagnosis' and come up with production projects – for example to make adobe bricks for housing, or to improve their local agriculture.[13] ALCASA would provide infrastructure and organisational support, including access to credit. It was also working with five of the garment co-ops that were supplying ALCASA's uniforms to try to set up an endogenous development nucleus (NUDE) like the one at Fabricio Ojeda in Caracas.[14] Indeed contacts had already been made with Fabricio Ojeda itself to see if they could supply the boots ALCASA was still having to buy in commercially.

All this sounded positive. But it was clear that a common pattern of resistance had emerged to this, as it had to other aspects of the co-management scheme. The promotion of a 'people's economy' through community projects and community-based supply co-ops was not popular with those who had benefited from the old system. The motives, said Angel Arevalo, were obvious. 'All in all, the CVG needs US$2 billion worth of services every year. The mafia of the old management try their hardest to keep as much as possible for their mates in the private sector.' In spite of all the speeches, decrees and framework agreements in favour of a new co-operative economy, the private sector interests were able to use contradictory principles from other existing statutes – the Law on Tenders for example – to undermine the new co-ops coming out of the Vuelvan Caras training programmes, arguing that that they lacked the requisite competence or experience.

To get a clearer account of what exactly had happened since my visit in May 2005, I moved into a room just across the corridor in the Centro Negro Primero and sat down with the same group of co-management enthusiasts and activists that had shown me round before – Marivit, Alcides, Edgar and Elio. For several hours we talked through what they thought had, or had not, gone wrong, and why. To their accounts I add some remarks made to me later by Carlos Lanz – by then installed in his new office at the Ministry of Higher Education in Caracas, following his removal from ALCASA in August 2007 – and by a couple of former trade union leaders at the plant.

Socialism in one factory

The narrative of setbacks was stark. They all agreed the first, and one of the most serious, had been the failure to spread co-management to the other CVG companies. 'It was difficult for us that only one company implemented this co-management,' mused Alcides. 'I think that has taken a heavy toll on ALCASA. We were left on our own, isolated and blockaded like Cuba, except our *gusanos* [worms[15]] were still on the inside, not outside.' The others laughed, but there was little doubt they felt let down. 'The plan with that first ALCASA company board that Carlos Lanz helped appoint was to spread co-management to the other companies. That's why they were then appointed as presidents of Venalum and the other companies.' But, Edgar went on, 'when they got there, they didn't do it.'

'There was a lack of political will', added Marivit. She recalled how the other CVG presidents had blocked the Negro Primero training programme and the Network of Training Centres – where back in 2005 I had seen her helping to deliver courses on co-management for workers from the other companies. We needed that, she said, because 'you can't impose participation by decree. You have to generate a culture.' But the CVG had just put obstacles in the way. 'The fact is, none of the presidents of the other companies that came from ALCASA's board of directors really believed in co-management.'

Edgar was more categorical. 'In fact they were against it. They went to those companies with the intention of managing them in the same old way, with the same old structures. At the same time, there was not a policy from central government to encourage co-management in any consistent way – I'm not talking about the German, social-democratic kind of co-management, but our Bolivarian co-management.'

This was the second, related setback. The enthusiasm and support of central government seemed to evaporate almost as quickly as it had emerged. As Carlos Lanz recalled, 'certainly co-management underwent a transmutation, because the ministers at national level gave less importance to it. They put a fence around me, a financial, political and ideological one. They treated us "as an experiment".' The impact had been grave. President Chavez also distanced himself. After his fighting speech at the First Latin American Meeting of Occupied and Recovered Factories, on 27 October 2005 – where he called on workers to retake all closed factories – it had been difficult to find even passing references to workers' control or co-management in any of the Venezuelan leader's speeches. There was no mention of either in the series of keynote addresses made at the end of 2006 and the beginning of 2007, following his re-election, in which Chavez presented his scheme for a transition to socialism based on the 'five motors' of the revolution.[16] Just as he began to give much greater emphasis to the need for direct democracy and popular power in the communities, he seemed to have lost interest in these in the workplaces.

Not surprisingly, then, there was even less sign of co-management spreading to other state industries. The backbone of the Venezuelan economy, the state oil company PDVSA, remained completely insulated from any form of workers' participation, much less control. There was little evidence that the companies nationalised at the beginning of 2007, like the telephone company CANTV, would be any different. Venezuela's main state electricity company, Cadafe, *had* been experimenting with a form of co-management since April 2003, just after the employers' lockout. But it had never been as ambitious as that in ALCASA. In Cadafe, Marivit recalled, 'it was capitalist co-management. They were talking about the participation of employees in the productive process, but not in the decisions of the company.' As early as

2005, workers' leaders in Cadafe were denouncing management for deliberately sabotaging even that level of participation, although a more effective form of co-management did survive in the Merida branch of the electricity company, Cadela.[17]

ALCASA's isolation led to a loss of confidence and enthusiasm. For Edgar Caldera it was a reminder that 'if you can't build socialism in a single country, then you certainly can't build it in a single factory'. The first aspect of co-management to suffer was probably the most important, the departmental works committees, or *Mesas de Trabajo*. At the beginning, Marivit remembers, there was real enthusiasm for participating in the *Mesas*. The spokespeople elected to the councils didn't receive any kind of pay. They usually came in to meet on Saturdays, when most of them would have been at home. 'That continued for about a year, but with most dynamism in the first six months.' But when the extension to Venalum in particular failed, Edgar says all this ran out of steam within ALCASA too. The policy lost its coherence and divisions began to appear. By the end of 2005 the works committees has almost entirely ceased functioning.

The return of the right

It was in this situation of lost momentum and mounting division that the ground was prepared for the next big setback, the election of a new, opposition-oriented leadership of the ALCASA union, SINTRAL-CASA, in union elections in January 2006. 'When ALCASA was left isolated, the right began to operate, to buy off our own leaders. If you don't understand that, you can't understand why Henry Arias and his right-wing slate won in the union. In the end, the current was in their favour, we were swimming against the current.' That was Edgar's version. Alcides was more succinct. 'There's no two ways about it. The counter-revolution won the trade union election.'[18]

But there were other interpretations of this setback. For Marivit, it was *not* a vote against co-management. 'At no point did Henry Arias speak against co-management, because the workers, at least the majority of them, had been won over to co-management, they supported it. That is why Henry Arias, from the right, ran a campaign in favour of co-management, in favour of the participatory budget, in favour of the departmental works committees. In fact he still talks about these committees at the factory-gate assemblies, although his conception of course is different. He wants to pack them with his own people and argues that the trade union should control the departmental committees.'

This is also Carlos Lanz's interpretation of the election results. Some of the defeated union leaders accuse him of doing a deal with the right to get rid of them. But he argues that you cannot even call the Henry Arias slate right wing. 'The only ones opposed to co-management', he says, 'were the so-called Chavistas of the Bolivarian Workers' Force' (FBT, later re-baptised FSBT to inject a socialist reference into the name).[19] Other observers have argued cogently that the union elections were less a victory for the right than a vote of protest against the official left.[20] Whatever the rights and wrongs of these various interpretations, two things became clear from these decisive union elections. One was that the organised Bolivarian forces within the ALCASA workforce – and indeed in the wider Venezuelan labour movement – were deeply and damagingly divided, with one or both of the biggest 'pro-Chavez' union currents at ALCASA being at best lukewarm, if not actively hostile to the co-management project. The other was that the new leadership of SINTRALCASA elected in January 2006, while paying at least lip service to co-management, had no intention of developing it in its initial, radically democratic form.

This became clear just a few months later, when the new union leaders proposed and won support for a referendum to reverse part of the co-management system for electing the company's managers. In place of a team of three rotating elected managers for each area, they proposed reverting to a single manager for each area. Edgar's explanation was simple. 'Having three managers in each area meant they would have to divide the pie into smaller slices.' It wasn't just about Henry Arias or any particular individual, he argued. 'It's like a whole structure of complicity in the company. This place is like PDVSA, the state oil company, before they sacked the old managers in 2003. There's this *Adeco* structure that's been there forever and still runs the show.[21] Since no one was sacked, they've taken advantage of this democracy for their own ends.'

This roll-back was completed at the beginning of 2007. Another round of elections for these single managerial posts returned almost a clean sweep of right-wing candidates allied to the new union leadership. Some were the same people who had been removed from these posts in the first co-management elections two years earlier. Many had openly opposed Chavez in the opposition-called recall referendum of August 2004. These in turn ensured that what remained of co-management stayed well within what for them would be acceptable bounds. Marivit recalls that when, in her personnel area, they tried to reactivate the departmental works committee, it was the new elected managers who were the first to block the attempt. 'Of course the Personnel Department manages all the workers' benefits. So it's not something they want to democratise too much, especially not a union leadership like the one we have now.'

The attempts to undermine the garment co-ops that we heard of earlier, like the eventual transfer of Carlos Lanz to a more educational and 'ideological' role in the Ministry of Higher Education, were predictable extensions of this trend.

Within the law or without it

The underlying obstacles that upset that extraordinary honeymoon period of co-management at ALCASA seem to fall into four categories.

Firstly, there was, as we have touched on, a structural mismatch between the aspirations of wholesale democratisation and the still-prevailing regulatory and legal framework. ALCASA's co-management was born out of a convergence of moves from above and below – a synthesis between the demands and mobilisations of some activists in the workforce and the plans developed by the incoming company president Carlos Lanz and his team. But neither of these, nor the resulting structures of decision-making assemblies, departmental works committees and elected management teams, could count on the support of a clear legal or regulatory framework. Even the company's own internal statutes remained at odds with the actual practice of co-management for much of the time and in many areas. The decisions taken by the departmental works council I visited in Rodding Shed No. 3, on where and how to buy in maintenance services, could probably run foul of the existing Law on Tendering. The attempts to shift more sales to 'socially pertinent' endogenous manufacturers of, say, aluminium wheelchairs for the health missions, might well be open to challenge under Venezuela's unchanged Commercial Code.

There was no formal or statutory guidance on what kind of co-management could or should be introduced. As Alcides complained, 'the government doesn't have a clear policy on co-management in the state enterprises. We don't even have a Co-management Law.[22] We only have Article 70 of the Constitution.' But both he and Carlos Lanz had also, from the beginning, warned against placing too much reliance on legal backing. 'Co-management is a process of transition, which means it is a process marked by conflict – between contrary forces, contrary customs, values, habits. For this very reason it unleashes the energy of growing awareness and organisation. It is a process of construction. We are constructivists. It doesn't come as something already given and that is why we say it is not a problem of the law. We need to be careful about this. Before getting hung up on the formal aspects, we first need to develop the process itself, and unleash all its transformational potential.'

This points to one of the central dilemmas posed by the Bolivarian experience in Venezuela, and potentially by almost any other imaginable transition towards socialism in the twenty-first century. It is a dilemma that will come up again when we look at the forms of popular power emerging in local communities in Chapter 5. Put briefly it comes down to this: should these emerging forms of popular power be sanctioned by law? In other words, if co-management and workers' councils, like the communal councils, are to be the beginnings of a new, much more democratic way of administering social and economic life – the seeds of a different kind of state, one that is capable of not just 'representing' but of 'expressing' and 'embodying' the wishes and interests of the great majority – then should they be regulated, institutionalised, even initiated by laws and regulations emanating from the old state machine, either from its bureaucracy (ministries, state enterprises etc.) or from its 'representative' institutions (parliament, executive, local and regional governments, etc.)? The possible answers to this question are complex and we won't attempt to explore them here. But they go to the heart of what any socialist democracy worth the name might really look like.

As Carlos Lanz recognised, this formal or juridical contradiction had a cultural, ideological, even psychological, corollary. Both these overlapping kinds of obstacle to revolutionary co-management are illustrated by an anecdote he tells from his first months at ALCASA and the CVG. Along with Victor Alvarez, then the Minister of Basic Industry and Mining and therefore also the President of the CVG, he had gone to a meeting at the Macagua Conference Centre, next to the monumental Macagua Dam and hydroelectric complex, with all the presidents of the CVG member companies and a raft of other senior managers and technocrats, to discuss the budget for 2005. There ensued, he recalls, a discussion that revealed the deep gulf 'between the logic implanted in our basic industries within the framework of state capitalism, and the new paradigm rooted in the emancipation of labour'.

The technocrats, he recalled, began by blaming ALCASA's serious financial problems on the 'excessive' number of workers on the payroll and the expenses associated with that. Referring to 'international norms' and making comparisons with, for example, Norway, they discreetly suggested that the solution would be a reduction in personnel, along the lines followed by the neighbouring steel plant, Sidor, after its partial privatisation in 1997.[23] They suggested ALCASA could perfectly well make do with a workforce of 1,100 instead of its then 3,000, allowing 1,900 to be laid off.

Carlos Lanz proceeded to counter this view of unfettered capitalism by giving the assembled managers a short lecture on the labour theory of value. He explained to them that reducing the number of workers employed would cut the amount of surplus value, since only living human labour can add fresh value. The labour frozen in machinery and equipment, he continued, could of course only transmit its value as dead labour, as objectified labour. The expulsion of living labour from the production process must therefore lead to a falling rate of profit, by changing the organic composition of capital. This was, he concluded, one of the inherent contradictions of capitalist production – whereby so-called technical progress, by saving labour and reducing employment, would lead to a reduction in the share of profit and force capital to increase exploitation and cut wages in order to obtain more surplus value or unpaid labour. As he patiently delivered his potted explanation to this hall full of people steeped in the logic of capital, he remembered, the technocrats began to look bemused, then exasperated. 'Who is this madman from Mars?' they appeared to ask. By the time he finished they were virtually having heart attacks. 'Fortunately,' he said, 'Victor Alvarez, as a Marxist economist himself, supported my arguments and resisted any moves to lay off part of the workforce.'

Not surprisingly, the old way of doing things had sunk deep roots among the workforce too. 'ALCASA's 40 years have a weight in the culture of the workers,' says Alcides. 'It's not easy to change that into co-management. We have to make a leap from the democracy of the ballot box to the democracy of popular power. Here we had a small experiment with that.' In spite of this weight of a hostile culture, Edgar feels that one of the lessons of the co-management experience at ALCASA is that workers *were* prepared to take on these big structural changes – and to take them on with enthusiasm – as long as they felt they were working. 'We're still reflecting on what happened in that year. A lot of things were left in the air. We wanted to change the structure from below, with the workers, with the workers' councils having maximum authority, even over electing the president of the company. We wanted to turn the pyramid upside down. So we pushed forward the works committees. But when these gathered real strength they didn't get the attention and support they needed. When you start to give democracy and power to working people they start to demand results from you. When they don't get results, when you can't solve their problems, you tend to react by withdrawing support from those committees. So they got marginalised and the workers going to them became disillusioned; they couldn't see the point and stopped going along.'

When that happened, when disappointment set in and momentum was lost, old habits reasserted themselves – and this made it much easier for the right to reposition itself.

These cultural obstacles obviously had a bearing on the third problem area for co-management – the deep divisions within the left and the Bolivarian camp that we have already mentioned. As Alcides put it, 'the revolutionary movement is divided in a thousand pieces. Everyone claims to be Chavista, but everyone defends their own fiefdom.' The former general secretary of the ALCASA union, Trino Silva, who was ousted by the right in 2006, puts it more sharply: 'The problem with the Chavistas is that amongst them there are some who wear the colours of the revolution, who put on their red berets

[129]

and red jackets and take up top jobs in the revolution, but who on the inside are capitalists through and through and still behave like the *Adecos* and *Copeyanos* they were before.'[24]

However, there seems little point in the proponents of co-management simply lamenting such disunity, berating those deemed responsible, or making moralistic appeals for all wings to 'pull together'. For behind such divisions are real, well-grounded differences. They reflect diverse designs and diverging interests. Elio Sayago puts it mildly: 'The thing is there are different concepts and not much clarity. From Chavez to the others, when you speak of socialism everyone has something different in their heads. What socialism? What workers' control?' Some, he says, are prepared to question quite openly the very concept. 'You have people like Ali Rodriguez [another former guerrilla leader who became head of PDVSA, Foreign Minister, Ambassador to Cuba and Minister of Finance] who argue straight up in favour of state capitalism as the way forward. They say, workers have no experience of administration, we'll do the administration, pay them well, and then, as state capitalists, we'll sort out the problems of the rest of the country's poor. Is that a bad position to hold? Well it depends how you look at it. Solving people's problems is not a bad thing.'

One of the more curious aspects of these ideological differences was the role – albeit a minor one – played by some Cuban advisers. The Cubans had, of course played an extraordinarily important part in helping to shape, and to staff, the health and education Missions that had been the Bolivarian revolution's most striking achievements. But I had heard and read several references to Cuban opposition to co-management, so I asked if it was true. It was true, Alcides told me, that some of the other CVG companies like Edelca (the regional electricity company), had invited Cuban advisers to visit. 'One of them spoke out publicly against co-management,[25] and within the government there was a confrontation between some of these, alongside some of the presidents of the other CVG companies, and Carlos Lanz with his very different approach.'

Marivit, citing another instance of Cuban partners' resisting the co-management experience, said: 'They weren't opposed to co-management as such, but to the way we were doing it. The idea of the factory committees and the power of the workers is not something they share. Their idea of industrial organisation is one of a hierarchy in the factory. Factories are there to produce and workers are there to obey. What we are trying to do, passing decision-making downwards, making it collective, for them that is anarchy. It's not part of their revolution, maybe because that came about so violently.' 'The most important thing for us', added Alcides, 'is that in our proposal we are fighting the social division of labour – between those who think and those who do. They don't accept that. They believe in the pyramid, of the party, the bureaucrat, the manager, who commands. They don't believe the workers can do that.' Their other argument against co-management – and in this they were in a sense proved right – was that too much democracy might give the workforce the chance to vote for reaction and a return of the right. It was a similar raft of objections that were to be deployed by the 'official' Chavista current in the unions, the FBT.

But beyond these doctrinal and strategic differences lurks a simpler, starker reality. Very few of those who already exercised power under the old regime, or thought they might under the new one, were prepared to give this up. This was the fourth and most fundamental barrier to co-management – the reluctance or refusal to relinquish control.

This was not just a question of the previous managers or the old-style trade union leaders, who saw their individual spheres of influence under threat. Right from the beginning in 2005, Carlos Lanz was well aware that it was a whole system that was in question. 'We are affecting, encroaching on interests, even within the government. We have a fight with the bureaucracy. Because this state is not the revolutionary state we need. In the public administration in general there are embedded all the values of the old culture. Many of those sectors see us as the enemy. So there is a lot of obstruction and even sabotage. They struggle openly or in secret to ensure we fail. They work through the media to criticise and diminish us, to try to sway public opinion by distorting reality.'

Two and a half years later he was more specific. 'There is an extended front of opposition embedded in the municipal and state governments.' He suggested a link with international industrial lobbies operating in the Guayana region of Venezuela. 'These have their own operators in local politics, in the trade unions and in government. They have roots in society.' Edgar pointed the finger at specific union leaders and the state governor.[26] But, he insisted, it went deeper than that. 'These union currents are just the foot soldiers of a whole capitalist policy and functioning of the state, which is intact. This state, which involves managers, supervisors, analysts, ministers, this whole bureaucracy worked against, and will continue to work against us workers having power.'

He argues that there was a perfect fit between the old, corrupt Venezuelan bureaucracy and the ideological arguments in favour of the need for centralised state control in the strategic industries, 'acting in the interests of society as a whole',[27] of the kind being put forward by some of those Cuban advisers and their Venezuelan co-thinkers. 'In that way the bureaucrats get to keep on exercising power on their own, and doing their own "business" on the side. So there's a coincidence between their interests and the Cuban-type policy, and the workers are the ones who lose out.'

What's left, what's next

Whatever the problems, all of those I talked to who had been centrally involved in developing ALCASA's experience of co-management, felt there had been a lasting legacy. Edgar's was the most pessimistic conclusion. I asked him if he thought such experiences of direct democracy could be the seeds of something else, of another possible future. 'In the mud of capitalism', he replied, 'nothing grows, nothing germinates. But we brought our grain of sand to the experience. We had a rich experience of how workers' councils function at the beginning. We lived that. We didn't read it in a book. We also lived the setback, of course. But even if we come to the conclusion that the ALCASA experience has completely failed, it's still been an enormous advance, because it has allowed us to understand just how powerful the capitalist system is.'

Marivit was a little more positive. 'It's true, of course, that if you compare the co-management that exists now with what we had in those first months of 2005 and what seemed possible at the time, then much of the promise has not been fulfilled. But I don't think we should see this as a purely linear thing. I think we go forward, suffer setbacks, then keep going again. And culturally there have been changes.' She described how much more open the administration was now, how everyone knows what is being discussed by the company board, 'and if they don't like it, they let them know.' Alcides added that even if most works councils no longer operate, they too have left their mark. 'For example, if I go to Industrial Services now, I am amazed to see how, when the managers are making even small purchases, they get everyone to sign to say whether they are in favour or not. That never would have happened before.'

Marivit recalled that before only the unions called assemblies at the factory gate; now the managers do too, including Carlos Lanz' successor as president, Ramón Betancourt. These assemblies hold real discussions and even take some decisions. Some of the participatory budgeting continues. The budgets for 2007 and 2008 were both prepared on the basis of at least partial consultations with the workforce. And of course individual departmental managers are still being elected, even if the outcome has hardly been revolutionary. Elio pointed to the continuing emphasis given to educating the workforce, and alongside them people from the co-ops and the local communities. 'We are trying to implement a workers' university here. We already have 144 workers who, in conjunction with Mission Sucre, have begun their higher education. And that's not something decided by the state, but by us the workers.'

All of them agree that, as Alcides says, 'whether you like it or not, ALCASA has become *the* point of reference for co-management in Venezuela' – a source of hope in the country, just as Venezuela became a source of hope in the world.

For Alcides, and for Carlos Lanz himself, the legacy goes further than that. In fact, at the end of 2007, they believed the tide was turning back in ALCASA's favour. Both pointed to the company's Collective Agreement reached in March and April 2007, which enshrines the principle of direct democracy and the works committees, and incorporates these into the new form of the Factory Council or Workers' Council. 'The departmental works committees were an extraordinary experience,' says Alcides, 'and now they are embodied in Clause 145 of our Collective Agreement. This stipulates the need to elect spokespeople – with two from each departmental works committees making up the Factory Council. No one else in Venezuela has this, nor, I think, does it exist anywhere in Latin America.' For him, the inclusion of such

Factory or Workers' Councils in President Chavez' failed proposal for constitutional reform meant that 'we felt vindicated, because that was already our proposal. It showed what weight our experience of co-management had had.'

For Carlos Lanz, this was a key part of the promised move towards turning all the state industries into socialist enterprises (ESs).[28] 'Even with all the problems and contradictions encountered, ALCASA is the pre-figuration of the ES or socialist enterprise.'

What's different

In conclusion, it is worth summing up what made ALCASA special.

The ALCASA experience of co-management – or 'revolutionary co-management', or 'co-management with workers' control' – is different from almost all older examples in history, and from other examples in Venezuela. It was different from the post-war, European, social-democratic versions of co-management because, as we've seen, at its high point it involved not co-option into existing structures and priorities, but real control by the workforce at several key levels of the company's operations, pointing towards a wholly different set of priorities.

It was different from the classic, revolutionary experiences of workers' control: the Petrograd factory committees in 1905 and 1917, the Turin factory councils of 1920 on which the young Gramsci cut his political teeth, the variety of workers' commissions that sprang up in Spain in 1936, in Bolivia after the 1952 revolution, repeatedly in Argentina through three decades of Peronist rule, and also from the Solidarnosc shipyard and factory occupations of 1980 and 1981 in Poland. Firstly, almost all of these occurred in workplaces that were still being owned or run by the employers or managers, who were themselves *opposed* to any such extension of participation or control by the workforce. Secondly, they emerged within contexts of social upheaval, where the old political structures were being challenged and in some cases were collapsing, but *prior to* any transfer of governmental or state power. While the question of who holds power may still be incompletely resolved in Venezuela – and could evolve in different directions in the future – it is clear that the experience of workers' co-management at ALCASA, like many

THE OUTLINES OF A SOCIALIST ENTERPRISE IN THE TWENTY-FIRST CENTURY

The talk of 'socialist enterprises' that emerged in Venezuela in 2006 and 2007 often seemed more an aspiration than a clearly conceived policy. When, in April 2007, President Chavez invited the assembled heads of the different state companies of the Corporación Venezolana de Guayana (CVG) to move towards transforming these into socialist enterprises, Carlos Lanz responded with a proposal based on the experience of ALCASA.

This included a comparison between the old model of industrial development and this proposed new model.

The old model

The old model, he said, was shaped by the international division of labour, because previous governments, when they promoted the industrialisation of Venezuela's southeastern Guayana region, did so in line with the priorities and conceptions of the transnational companies and their associated local monopolies. It was therefore characterised by:

- the transnationals cashing in on comparative advantages like cheap labour, raw materials and energy
- primary, export-oriented production: the production of commodities and semi-elaborated goods and the import of manufactured goods made out of those same products
- technological control not only of equipment and machinery but also through patents and licences
- the imposition of unfavourable prices and contractual terms
- a high level of contamination and environmental damage in the region
- fragmentation and atomisation of the industry, through a lack of integrated production chains or networks
- the creation of monopolies in various services, like transport, catering and insurance
- corruption and backhanders in state purchases, the awarding of contracts, and so on.

[135]

This resulted in:

- social exclusion and injustice
- economic imbalances, including underdeveloped agriculture, industrial mono-production and an inflated commercial sector
- a distorted demographic occupation of the region, with most of the population concentrated in the single conurbation of San Felix and Puerto Ordaz*
- a 'port economy' based on exports and enclaves
- environmental degradation, with a high level of occupational injuries and sickness
- bureaucracy and inefficiency in the basic state enterprises
- a loss of social and cultural identity.

The new socialist model

The dire legacy of the old model makes it urgent, according to Lanz, to identify the outlines of a new development model that would fit the promised transition to a socialism of the twenty-first century. Based on the experience of ALCASA, he proposes this should be characterised by:

- changes in the relations of production and more humane working conditions (shorter working day, workers' control, factory councils); the overcoming of exploitation and hierarchy in the factory
- going beyond the logic of the market and its 'invisible' guiding hand
- the diversification of production with more value added 'downstream'
- the drawing-up and execution of plans and projects that contribute to a new social structure and raise the quality of life of the local population, including those living in acute poverty
- the use of the basic industries as a motor for endogenous development in the region, promoting integrated production chains and networks
- a reorganisation of the CVG to root out bureaucracy and set up

in each member company work teams dedicated to permanent training in the technical, social and political foundations for endogenous development

- a more balanced spread of population throughout the Guayana region, with production being decentralised and directed towards depressed and neglected areas; the encouragement of endogenous development nuclei and poles on a local and regional level, and the promotion of social production enterprises (EPS) as part of the new social fabric
- the development of co-operatives and different kinds of co-management and self-management, as envisaged in the Bolivarian Constitution, as vehicles for the new production relations being developed in the transition to twenty-first-century socialism
- proposals for continuing education to support these development plans, involving all the professional, technical and academic educational institutions in the region
- the promotion of technological research and development aimed at improving the quality and social appropriateness (or 'pertinence') of production.

* The twin cities of San Felix and Puerto Ordaz, on either side of the Caroni River as it flows into the Orinoco, together make up the conglomeration now called Ciudad Guayana. This has a population of nearly 800,000, about 50 per cent of the entire population of Bolivar state. The region known as Guayana includes the states of Bolivar, Delta Amacuro and Amazonas. They occupy the entire, sparsely inhabited, south-eastern part of Venezuela, accounting for half the area of the whole country, but only 6 per cent of its population.

other experiences of the Bolivarian revolution, would never have happened if the old elite had not *already* been displaced from some of the central sites of governmental and administrative power.

And it was different from other experiences in Venezuela for the reasons we have already discussed. This was a large, strategic, state industry in which co-management, albeit supported from below, had been essentially designed and nurtured from above, by the Lanz–Alvarez top management and ministerial team, as a deliberate test bed for moves towards a socialism of the twenty-first century. Paradoxically, this peculiarity proved both a strength and a weakness.

But there is one thing ALCASA did share with almost all these other examples, historical and contemporary, at home and abroad – the inherent antagonism between any kind of effective democracy in the workplace and the institutions of the old state. This was not a novelty for generations of twentieth-century Marxists. The Argentinean-Mexican writer Adolfo Gilly put it like this in an essay on factory councils written back in the 1970s. 'It is in the despotic control exercised by capital in the factory that resides the central core of the bourgeoisie's dictatorial domination of society, no matter whether this is carried on under the most developed political and constitutional forms of bourgeois democracy. ... In opposing this despotic control by capital, [the factory council] always emerges, whether it knows it or not, as the embryo of another power, even though this duality of power in the factory very seldom reaches the point where it openly expresses or becomes fully aware of its own opposition to the state.'[29]

Venezuela's experience of co-management and workers' control has repeated this opposition in a new form – as a litany of conflict with old institutions largely inhabited by fellow supporters of the Bolivarian revolution. Many of these *chavistsas* also claim to be moving towards a socialism of the twenty-first century. But it is difficult to see how the project can contain both. Maybe that is why the moves towards workplace democracy were put on hold – at least 'for the time being'.[30]

5 WHO'S IN CHARGE HERE? FROM LOCAL DEMOCRACY TO COMMUNAL POWER

PIONEERS AND APOSTLES

'Chavez is like Christ, and we are going to be his apostles. When we've got started here, we're going to spread the word to all those communities down there along the coast, from La Guaira to Caray-aca. We're going to encourage people to make their own projects and to participate, so that his work can be done.'

Seventy-seven-year-old Andres Marin was standing in one of the most beautiful spots I have ever seen – just a few kilometres from the centre of Caracas, on the northern slopes of the Avila mountain, with shreds of white, cotton-wool cloud wafting about our heads and the intense blue of the Caribbean Sea opening up like a chasm a couple of thousand metres below us. We walked past a broken arch and the ruins of a thick stone wall – remains of the eighteenth-century coffee plantation that once stood here. 'On that side we're going to build the guesthouse, and right here will be the restaurant, facing the sea.'

The former peasant leader came to a stop at the edge of a drop, turned and flashed a wide grin. His rugged, weather-beaten face looked like it was hewn out of the same volcanic rock as the mountain on which we were standing. At his side was Hernan Toro, a clean-shaven, 23-year-old canteen manager. An unlikely pair, but these two seemed to be the main architects of the Integrated Plan for Endogenous Development in this tiny hillside community of Gali-pan. More significantly they seemed prime movers in setting up the body that planned and approved it – the Galipan Communal Council for Public Planning. It's difficult to be sure – the history of any revolution tends to be confused and poorly documented – but this may well have been the country's very first communal council. 'It was born out of the need not only to regenerate tourism here, but for us to *emerge* as people' – that word '*surgir*' again from Chapter 1. 'We want to show that we can achieve things for ourselves and run things on our own.'

The engine of twenty-first-century socialism

The communal councils were to become the single most widespread and effective instrument of self-organisation and even self-government in the whole protracted process of the Bolivarian revolution. By the time of the December 2007 Referendum on Constitutional Reform – which would have given these councils increased authority, putting them on a par with the existing bodies of municipal, regional and national power[1] – there were said to be more than 25,000 communal councils set up across Venezuela.

The basic idea was simple. Communities of between 200 and 400 families in urban areas, or 20 plus in rural areas, would meet in an open citizen's assembly and elect a communal council made up of spokespersons for each of the areas of work relevant for that community, for example housing, infrastructure, health, education, agriculture or whatever. They would also elect a finance commission, known as the communal bank, and an oversight commission, to ensure transparency and accountability and to field any complaints that might arise. The citizen's assembly was the sovereign body, discussing and taking all decisions on what projects, development plans or other activities the community wanted to pursue. The communal council itself was the executive body, charged with implementing those decisions. And the communal bank, formed as a co-operative, was the body that would receive and manage the public monies made available to fund these activities, as grants or credits from a variety of municipal, regional and federal sources.[2]

But back in November 2004 – when I made that first visit to Galipan – hardly anyone in Venezuela had heard of communal councils. The people of Galipan had in fact formed *theirs* eleven months earlier, at an assembly of the whole community. But the idea still hadn't caught on. Just a few days before my visit, President Chavez had devoted a large part of his high-level workshop on 'The New Strategic Map' to the parallel objectives of 'rapidly moving towards a new kind of democracy based on popular participation' and 'creating a new set of state institutions'.[3] But there was no mention of communal councils. It was only 16 months later, in April 2006, that the National Assembly would pass the new Law on Communal Councils that would give the go-ahead for these to become the main instrument in a new phase of participatory democracy. And it was only two years later, in January 2007, just after his re-election to a second full term, that President Chavez would identify the communal councils, and the 'explosion of popular power' that they implied, as 'the most important engine' of Venezuela's transition to a socialism of the twenty-first century – as the vehicle for dismantling 'the old bourgeois state' and replacing it with 'a communal state'.[4]

This points us back to a question posed at the end of the first chapter, and one of the most interesting and important raised by the entire Bolivarian experience in Venezuela: who or what is the driving force of this revolutionary process and its promised transition to a new kind of socialism? More specifically, what is the relative importance of territorially based community struggles and forms of organisation, as compared with more traditional forms of struggle and organisation in the workplaces, at the point of production? This is of course part of a much wider debate facing the left in most parts of the world, over the agency of political change in a world where, according to some perceptions, the earlier twentieth-century forms of working-class experience have been 're-structured' and 're-converted' out of existence, or at least beyond recognition. To what extent then does the Venezuelan story so far corroborate or refute hypotheses suggesting that new forms of political identity, based on territory, gender, ethnicity and the like, have replaced the economically grounded identity of class as the cutting edge of social transformation (or indeed of socialism)? We are still not in a position to answer this, but it is worth making one, more or less factual observation, the meaning of which we shall return to later.

It is this: while it may be true that the kind workplace democracy attempted at ALCASA, under the name of 'revolutionary co-management' or 'co-management with workers' control', was Venezuela's most radical innovation yet in terms of building new kinds of democratic power – radical precisely because *for a time* it began to transform the very relations that shaped the way production was organised – it certainly was not the most successful. The kinds of neighbourhood or community-based control pioneered by people like Señor Andres and Hernan with their communal council have proved far more effective and durable. As we began to see in Chapter 1, this story of local democracy and community control goes back much further in the Bolivarian process, and its influence has spread much more widely through Venezuelan society. And as we shall see further, it survived the December 2007 defeat of the constitutional reform more effectively than any other aspect of self-organisation, and managed to remain the most promising 'motor' of any move towards twenty-first-century socialism.

To endogenous development and beyond

Standing above that extraordinary vista in 2004, among the ruins of La Hacienda Vieja, the colonial coffee-farm, Andres Marin and Hernan Toro seemed to have a modest sense of their place in history. They pressed a copy of the project into my hands – a dozen slightly creased sheets, stapled together. Beneath the project title and the full name of the communal council it bore a sub-title: 'Pioneers of council democracy'. As we watched one of Andres' middle-aged sons picking herbs on the terraced slopes below, they explained with pride how it would work. 'In all we aim to have 560 people working or playing an active part in the project.[5] That's 48 per cent of the population of Galipan.' In addition to the two tourism co-ops, each with a guesthouse and a restaurant, there was to be an agricultural co-operative to supply the restaurants and local community with fresh, organically grown fruit and vegetables, as well as flowers – 'we want to restore the traditional agriculture here, which has been lost'. There would also be a transport co-op with its own four-wheel drives to ferry guests up and down the mountain, and an educational co-op that would train up local residents in specialist skills of the tourist trade. 'So the five co-ops mesh together perfectly, each serving each other.'

The shape of this project in Galipan may not seem so different from other endogenous (or 'self-sufficient') development projects which, as we saw in Chapter 2, had been gathering momentum throughout the year 2004. What *was* different here was who was in charge, and how. For this was not a project dreamt up by the state oil company or some other government institution, which then sought to involve the local community, with greater or less success. Here was a project that had been conceived *within* the local community. And although they had received sporadic support from this or that official, the community had had to organise itself and fight, over a long period, to get its project off the ground – in the face of repeated, entrenched opposition from a whole gamut of government departments and bodies.

The experience in Galipan, and the phenomenon of communal councils in general, therefore has a double origin. On the one hand, it was a further expression of the plans and principles of endogenous development. On the other, it was a result of – and an attempt to overcome – the obstacles placed in the path of local communities when they sought to implement such plans for themselves, to put into practice the principles of 'participatory and protagonistic' democracy contained in the 1999 Constitution. The adoption of communal councils on a national scale was at least in part a response to the failure to reproduce in any widespread way the practices of local direct democracy through participatory budgets, which President Chavez in 2004 was trying to persuade his new set of mayors and governors to promote.

We'll come back to this. First let's listen to Andres' and Hernan's story.

The Galipan story

'The Hacienda de Galipan was built by the Spanish in 1714. Here they gathered all the coffee grown in Galipan and San José. This was where they put it out to dry. Then they'd take it down to the port at La Guaira and export it to Germany and England.' Señor Andres was still showing me round. He pointed out where the African slaves, and indigenous people who were also forced to work as slaves, had stripped the pulp from the berries, before the coffee beans themselves could be prepared. 'It belonged to the crown. But it seems the family of Simon Bolivar's wife also had some connection with the place.' By the 1920s the *hacienda* had fallen into disrepair. That's when the dictator Juan Vicente Gomez moved people out of another part of the Avila. Some of them, including a number of families recently arrived from the Canaries, moved here and began renting small plots of land from the owner of the *hacienda*. 'They built their own homes and planted flowers. So Galipan became a flower garden.' 'My mother's family came here then,' Hernan chipped in. 'But my grandfather's side were already here as slaves. So the family was a mix of Spanish and blacks.'

Andres had been born in the plains of central Venezuela, in Guarico state. Orphaned at seven, he'd been shunted from one uncle to another, told he couldn't go to school and sent out to work on the cocoa farms from the age of eight. He left home for Caracas, worked as a conductor and a street vendor, then back to the countryside to work on a coffee farm. He finally moved here to Galipan at the ripe old age of 16, in 1943. In the decades that followed, Andres brought up a large family in Galipan, became a leader of the peasant movement for the whole of Vargas state, and an active supporter of Acción Democrática, the social-democratic party that dominated so much of Venezuela's political history in the second half of the twentieth century. 'I was a member of the National Agrarian Bureau of AD in Romulo Betancourt's time. I remained *Adeco* until Carlos Andres Perez' second term. But when he won he forgot about everyone. He forgot about the peasants. Corruption got worse. I didn't like that so I withdrew.'[6]

Galipan had become the main supplier of flowers for the whole of Caracas and the metropolitan area. But it wasn't to last. 'The flowers died off when Carlos Andres signed the Andean Pact.' That was in 1978, some time before free trade became a universal mantra for mainstream economists and policy makers. 'They started bringing planes full of roses from Colombia and flowers from Ecuador. They didn't pay tax. The flower-growing and agriculture here went bust.' Later, with the reopening of the cable-car on the Caracas side of the mountain, there was a resurgence of tourism in the Avila National Park. But almost without exception, the restaurants, guesthouses, taxi services, pony rides and all belonged to businessmen moving in from Caracas. The local community in Galipan felt completely excluded.

The communal council as solution

Senor Andres had been thinking about this, and what to do about it, for a long time. 'For maybe 20 years I'd been dreaming of developing the Hacienda. At the beginning the idea was just a family project.'

The disaster of the Vargas mudslides, which left thousands dead in 1999 – including some on the upper slopes of the Avila around Galipan – had focused increased official attention on the area. Hernan's brother, who'd always wanted to open a restaurant, went on one of the courses put on to encourage local businesses. It was about that time, Andres recalls, that President Chavez began to talk more about the need for communities to get organised, 'in order to lift themselves out of their situation of disaster and ruin and achieve things for themselves, and not just complain and ask for favours. So I began talking to these lads and we began to get organised.' They brought in a sympathetic architect to draw up plans, taking advantage of the spectacular location and making use of the remaining ruins of the old *hacienda*. At this stage it had become a two-family project, but no more. 'But when we thought about it more, we realised we could involve many more people by including the agricultural co-op and then the transport and education ones. Because the whole community, 500 people or so, obviously couldn't work in two restaurants.' That was how the project took on its eventual form, as an integrated proposal for endogenous development.

At the time there was a project building new homes for some of the victims of the mudslides, run by CORPOVARGAS, the regional development body of Vargas state. Hernan explained: 'So we presented the project to the president of CORPOVARGAS, General Walter. We had big meal, with soup and a barbeque. We invited everyone. This must have been the beginning or middle of 2003. So what happened? The general came down on us like a ton of bricks. He wasn't at all in agreement with the project. He said it couldn't be like that because there was no precedent for such a thing, because there was no co-operative set up, and so on. "You're going to set up a restaurant?" he said. "You know nothing about this." He offered us a vehicle instead, so that we could transport people to one of the other restaurants. And what he wanted to give my mother was a stall to sell fried fish! That is the model these people still wanted.'

But there were two people from FIDES, the government's decentralisation fund, at the presentation.[7] 'After the general's attack, one
of them approached us and said: "Don't worry, we'll find a solution,
something will come out of it."'

Andres and Hernan were called to a meeting at FIDES the
following Monday. Someone explained to them the new idea of
communal councils as a way of organising communities. 'We saw
this as a way of involving more people so we were quickly won over.'
They held various workshops on the subject over the following
months and 'on 9 December 2003 we elected here the first communal council in Venezuela, or at least the first one here in the region of
Caracas and Vargas state.'[8] The communal council was elected at a
big assembly by the five different sectors into which the community
of Galipan was divided. 'FIDES was also present, because they were
supporting this. The law had just been changed to ensure that 20 per
cent of the fund's resources went to organised communities, so Galipan was to be a pilot project for them.' The communal council was
the body that adopted the project as a whole and became its political
backer. 'But legally we needed to establish each of the co-operatives
actually to present and execute the project.' Almost immediately, this
solution ran into problems.

Obstacles and more obstacles

The law had been changed but it still left state governors and local
mayors with the power to decide *who* should get the 20 per cent
reserved for the communities. 'We presented the project to the governor's office on 31 December 2003. They stuck it in a drawer.' Part of
the problem, explained Hernan, was that there simply weren't any
precedents. 'Neither the governor nor anyone else had ever given
resources to the organised communities to manage. And they didn't
agree with that.' So the first block in the path of the new communal
council came from the elected regional government, which was itself
pro-Chavez. Nonetheless, for Hernan, this was the simplest problem
to overcome, because again FIDES offered a solution. 'They said "if
you can't get it with them, come to us," and we started dealing
directly with FIDES.'

Then there was another problem, with the credit laws. 'At that time, if you presented a project as a co-operative, the law applied the same criteria as if you were a private company. For example you needed a guarantee or collateral of two to one. So if the project was for 2.3 billion bolivars, we'd need 4.6 billion as collateral. Obviously we didn't have that kind of money or we wouldn't be asking for a credit. Clearly the law needed changing, to make the guarantee for community projects more of a symbolic one. When it came to interest, we were set a rate of 24 per cent!'

With the help of FIDES, they managed to work around these obstacles. With FIDES' backing they began to travel around to other communities to promote the new combination of co-operatives and communal councils.

Paradoxically, the next problem was with FIDES itself. Six months went by and they discovered the project had been lost. Nobody in FIDES knew anything about it. It had disappeared in the archives. Why? 'Because there were people even within the institution who didn't agree with it, because they couldn't accept that peasant families could develop a project on this scale. It was ridiculous. We'd spent six months going here and there with FIDES promoting the project, everyone knew us, and all of a sudden it was lost!' Everyone passed the buck: Oh no, that's down to the Director of Projects; No it's the Director of Archives, or the Project Specialist. 'Now we've discovered that many of these people are opposed to the whole Bolivarian process. But they're still in post.' In the end they went to the archives themselves, found the box of files and took it straight to the president's office. 'It *was* there. Elias Jaua, who was the head of FIDES at the time, was furious.'

Hernan said the contradiction was dramatic: on the one hand FIDES was calling for everyone to organise co-operatives and communal councils and present projects; on the other, there was the reality within FIDES where projects got lost and just disappeared down the drain. For Señor Andres, it illustrated a wider problem. 'Let me be frank, because this needs to be said loud and clear. Chavez is governing with people from the old system, from the Fourth Republic. Because the truth is here in Venezuela we were all *Adecos* or *Copeyanos* [supporters of the two traditional parties AD and COPEI]. When we saw Chavez really wanted the well-being of the poor communities, really wanted people to get organised, to work, to develop projects, then we got started. But then the same old people, ministers and other government officials, appear and put up road blocks.'

Opposition from within

The fourth big obstacle in the path of the Galipan Communal Council came from within the community. From years earlier there had been a neighbourhood association in Galipan. Like most such organisations, as we saw in Chapter 1, it had long since ceased to be an effective representation of community interests. It was 'run' by one prominent member of the community and became closely aligned, like him, with one of the traditional political parties, COPEI. Now it came out of inactivity and began to campaign against the new communal council. It drew up a letter accusing Andres Marin and Hernan Toro of conspiring to cheat the nation with a supposed endogenous development project, and managed to get about a hundred local signatures. Andres and Hernan claim that most of these people were themselves cheated into signing. But it seems the campaign did connect with the real fears of some in the community that the new endogenous development project and the communal council was designed to benefit the Marin and Toro families, and that they would be left out.

There was an investigation. Andres and Hernan later discovered that their phones had been bugged, and that they had been interviewed for eight hours by investigators posing as journalists. 'The only thing they didn't know about us was what time we went to the toilet.' Hernan was summoned to the Situation Room in the White Palace, an annexe of the Miraflores Presidential Palace. When they realised that some of the president's right-hand people had taken an interest in the Galipan project, they began to row back. 'Not to worry, they told me, it's all been a mistake and we'll write a report to say it's proven as such.'

When I first visited Galipan in November 2004 they had just got over this trauma, but the funds had still not come through. Before they did, there was yet another obstacle to surmount: the environment.

Galipan is part of the Avila National Park, so any development project there requires clearance from the National Parks Institute, INPARQUE. When they went to get this, INPARQUE first came up with a supposed 'owner of Galipan', a descendant of the old *hacienda* owners, who wouldn't allow the community to do anything there. 'Our lawyer soon got that dismissed.' Then INPARQUE pulled something else out of their sleeve. '"Yes, it's a fine project," they told us, "but you have to carry out an environmental impact study." The idiot who told us this said, "Don't worry, boys, this costs 120 million bolivars, but I've got a friend who will do it for you for 100 million. Here's his card." Of course we didn't have that kind of money. We were so frustrated. We thought the project was dead.'

But another member of the community had a friend who was a biologist at the university. They went to look for him, and he had a friend who was a lieutenant in the Environmental Guard section of the National Guard. Together with their supporters in FIDES, they made contact with the Commander of the National Guard. 'He said fine, I'll come and see on Sunday, and that Sunday he landed right here on the patio in his helicopter.' From there on it seemed automatic. 'We did the environmental impact study ourselves, accompanying the technicians and with support from the National Guard. We did the soil perforations, the hydrological study, the morphology, flora and fauna, the social study, at the end of 2004, and presented it. But INPARQUE refused to accept it.'

That unleashed another confrontation. 'We went to the INPARQUE office at 7am and locked ourselves in the President's office. We said neither you nor anyone else is coming in or going out until you sign our environmental study and give us our permission.' Then things really started heating up. The press arrived. 'We made declarations from inside. A row broke out between the employees and the President of the Parks Institute. Some were demanding his resignation. Then the Minister of the Environment, Jaqueline Farias got involved. At 6 pm they agreed to give us our permission.' That was on the Wednesday. On the Saturday, the Galipan Communal Council organised an event. 'The Minister of the Environment came and handed over our permits in person.'

When I returned in February 2005 they had also succeeded in breaking through the remaining logjams on finance. The municipal and state elections the previous October had shifted the political balance among the Chavista forces in Vargas state. The day I went the legislative assembly had decided to transfer one of its sessions out of the assembly building in La Guaira and up into the community of Galipan itself, for a joint meeting with the communal council.

The mountain's changeable weather seemed to be offering its own perverse comment. In place of the spectacular views I had seen before, we were enveloped in thick fog and cloud. Visibility was down to a few metres. Then it began to rain. But with everyone huddled under a large canvas awning, the chairwoman introduced the various local political figures present and moved on to the business of the credit for the community of Galipan. The temperature rose when she mentioned the letter from some members of the community alleging that the project had not been decided in a proper citizens' assembly but designed by a cabal. She invited anyone present to speak in support of that view, but no one stood up. Hernan made an impassioned defence of the people of Galipan and their commitment to, and practice of, 'council democracy'. Then the meeting formally ratified its approval of the credit and closed. The weather had hardly improved, but those who stayed behind were clearly ecstatic. As they played a game of *boule* in the fog, Señor Andres belied his 78 years by dancing a little jig after each throw. The first instalments were released soon after, and a few months later building work began.

Results

It was not until two and a half years later that I finally made another visit to Galipan, and the difference was dramatic. A 200-seat restaurant, with a large wooden balcony overlooking the Caribbean Sea far below, a three-course menu and waiters standing around polishing glasses now occupied what had been the abandoned courtyard area where we had huddled beneath that awning. The remaining ruins of the old *hacienda* walls were tastefully integrated into the design, and under-lit for effect when night fell. The guesthouse itself for the 'Posada La Hacienda Vieja' was still under construction, but the cooperative here already included 18 members of the Marin extended family, with five or six outsiders, including the chef, working alongside them. Just below, the Toro family co-op had its 'Posada Miradas' open, with ten double rooms, each a separate cabin with its own balcony overlooking the spectacular view, and another smaller, but smart, restaurant with an international menu. Hernan's brother was the chef here, and there were four other family members in this co-op, with six or seven other people from the community working alongside them.

Further down the hill the educational co-op, with a small auditorium and study-cum-conference facilities, was just getting going. There were nine members here, but only four from the community, with the rest brought in from Caracas for their professional skills. A small fleet of shiny, white Land Cruisers was parked up on the side. This was the transport co-op, with eight members and eight vehicles. 'Each has a vehicle assigned to them, but the vehicles belong to the co-op.' These offered all-in packages, picking up and returning guests and diners from Caracas or from the airport for less than the usual single fare of an airport taxi into the city. The agricultural co-op, with 48 members, was slightly different, because each member owned their own plot of land and would come together for marketing and services. They'd had one joint credit to promote the recovery of traditional varieties like strawberries, plums, apricots and roses. 'Most of the strawberries consumed in Galipan are produced here now, which wasn't the case before, and the roses are doing well in the market place too, because they are good quality, so all that helps the project as a whole.'

There might be many fewer people working here at the moment than foreseen in the over-optimistic projections back in 2004. But Hernan told me they were proud of what they'd achieved, and they felt they could hold high the banner of being a co-operative with state funding. 'Unfortunately most people associate co-operatives with doing things badly. But here you can get quality, a good meal with good presentation for example, that compares with any Swiss restaurant higher up in Galipan where the owners are from Caracas. Only here the owners are the ordinary people from Galipan.'

But hadn't it just become a group of successful family businesses, I asked? No, said Hernan, because the agreements they signed were very strict. They would have to begin repaying their credits right away, and that money would have to be reinvested in the community, sector by sector – transport to transport, tourism to tourism, education to education – and of course it would be with interest. And it will be the communal council that decides what goes where, according to the projects that people in the community present. 'So you can say that out of the 350 to 400 families in the whole of Galipan, only 60 or so are directly involved now. But this multiplication process is precisely what endogenous development is about. At the moment the lungs of the project may be in our sector, San Antonio, but already through the transport and agricultural co-ops people from the other four sectors of Galipan are directly benefiting, and that will spread. That's what we were saying back in 2004, and that's what we patiently try to explain to those people who still say, "Well if you've got a guesthouse, we want one too." The fact is, somebody has to start, and with a lot of hard work, it was us.'

So was there still opposition within the community? In the wealthier San Isidro sector, where the old neighbourhood association was based, yes, they told me, there was still quiet hostility, 'but down here most people are solidly behind it'. Some people had argued that the Galipan Communal Council was illegal, because it had been set up before the Law on Communal Councils was passed in April 2006. So they agreed to elect new communal councils, one for each of the five sectors of Galipan, in line with the new law. The San Antonio Communal Council was elected in January 2007. 'There was a secret, direct ballot, which was actually organised by some of the opposition people who took part in the organising commission, as set out in the law. I think they were hoping to control the vote. But who got elected? Basically the same people as before, those of us who are involved in the project. There were at least five candidates, including opposition people, for each of the six committees: infrastructure, housing, sport and culture, education, oversight and finances. And everyone voted for us. We elected a communal council of 20 people and they were all people who supported the project.'

Hernan's view of twenty-first-century socialism seemed to be quite pragmatic. 'Of course you can be critical,' he insisted. 'That's part of our democratic society. And it's true that in socialism maybe all this should be some kind of collective property, although I have my doubts about that. But the fact is, if you want a tourism project you have to work to develop a tourism project. If you don't participate in the communal council, if you don't get organised and work, then you can't come along later and complain about those who did.'

Lessons of Galipan

There are several reasons why it has seemed worth telling the story of Galipan at length. One is simply that it is an inspiring tale of what ordinary people – 'those from below' in the Spanish expression, *los de abajo* – can achieve: a small epic in the David and Goliath tradition, of common people's persistence prevailing over the endless obstacles put in their way. There is also the fact that it was one of the first, maybe even the very first, communal council in Venezuela. Given the importance these have since acquired in the Bolivarian revolution, it is therefore an experience with a certain historical value in its own right. To my knowledge, apart from one or two passing newspaper stories and TV interviews, it is one that remains almost untold even inside Venezuela.

The details of the Galipan story – like any such story – are particular. In some respects they are atypical, partly because the community was ahead of its time and navigating in uncharted waters. As an example of direct democracy at work it also has limitations. This is after all the story of one very small community, led by a few determined individuals, organising to implement a comparatively small community development plan. Many issues of control and accountability still hang in the air. But even these particularities of Galipan illustrate more general questions – issues that in different forms in different places repeat themselves as the communal councils multiply and become the chosen instrument for Venezuela's promised move towards socialism of the twenty-first century.

The most important of these is the relation between such local experiences of direct democracy and the existing machinery of government, the old 'state apparatus' of Marxist parlance. This was the constant subtext of the litany of obstacles placed in the path of the Galipan Communal Council. It was the rock on which earlier attempts by Chavez to introduce forms of participatory democracy had foundered, and it would become arguably the single most important and under-reported challenge that the proposed Constitutional Reform of 2007 failed to surmount.

On a more micro level, there is the extent to which democratic control within the communal councils is real, how far it can deal with the conflicts that emerge within any community, and what kind of regulation, if any, this requires. There are plenty of examples of where domination of a communal council and its projects by a particular group in the community has shaded into downright abuse and corruption. This was not the case in Galipan. But this challenge has been a constant theme in even the most robust examples of direct democracy that have developed in recent years, and we shall see it in action when we visit some of the communal councils in Carora and La Victoria later in this chapter.

A less developed theme, but one with huge potential implications, is the extent to which direct democracy and community control in the localities can engage with plans for endogenous development and other forms of economic activity and production, both locally and in society more widely. This has been a missing link in almost all forms of local participatory democracy of recent decades, both internationally, in the participatory budgets in Brazil for example,[9] as well as in most of the early experiences of communal councils in Venezuela. What the vast majority of these organs of popular power actually discussed, in the first couple of years of their existence (2006–07), was how to spend the $10–15,000 grants made available from central government for improvements in community infrastructure – drains, houses, leisure facilities and so on. In this respect, Galipan was doubly ahead of its time, because the communal council there actually emerged *out of* a plan for economic production and development.

This leads back into the discussion over the primacy of direct democracy in the communities or at the point of production, and the possible combinations between the two. It also flags up some real tensions that can develop when communal councils do engage in productive activity, and the business logic of economic efficiency begins to pull against the logic of democratic participation and control. This does seem to have emerged as at least a potential problem in Galipan. In the context of what remains essentially a market economy, is there a danger that as the community's economic activity is consolidated, the need for widespread involvement and democratic control will come to be seen as a dispensable add-on?

All of these questions have come up and will continue to come up as thousands of other communal councils across Venezuela follow, even without realising it, the path blazed by Galipan and a handful of other communities – the path of conceiving, developing and putting into practice their own projects, as the work of the community, for the community, as an experiment in self-government.

THE EMERGING FRAMEWORK FOR DIRECT DEMOCRACY

At this point we need to look at the framework within which the communal councils and related forms of direct democracy moved from being a handful of scattered, ad hoc experiments, to becoming a nationwide project for socialist transformation.

As early as 1999, the new Constitution of the Bolivarian Republic of Venezuela outlined the core principles of a new kind of democracy in the country, in which the people should become the protagonists of a participatory democracy (the phrase in Spanish most widely used to refer to this, *'una democracia participativa y protagonica'*, does not translate directly into English).[10] It also spoke, in general terms, of the possibility of 'municipalities and states decentralising and transferring services to organised communities and neighbourhood groups for them to manage' on the basis of 'co-responsibility' and of these taking part 'in the formulation of investment proposals' for local and regional governments (Article 184). It also mentioned the 'assembly of citizens, whose decisions will be binding' as one of the one of the mechanisms through which the people could participate, become protagonists and exercise their sovereignty. These formulations are mostly quite moderate. The practice of participatory democracy is generally presented as a complement to, or even just a supplement to, the established institutions of representative democracy. It does not appear as a challenge to the existing state, and hardly constitutes a blueprint for self-government. There is however room for ambiguity, and potential for a more radical interpretation.

Either way, the practical expression of these principles in the first few years of the Bolivarian process was limited. As we saw in Chapter 1, it was not until after February 2002, with the emergence of the urban land committees (CTUs), and then the Missions from the first half of 2003, that there was a real explosion of self-organisation and popular 'protagonism', driven in part by the semi-insurrectionary experience of April 2002, when the people came down from the *barrios* to defeat the coup against Chavez. This explosion of self-organisation went beyond the letter of the constitution. The self-organised communities began to tackle many of their most pressing specific problems directly. It is true there was a symbiotic relationship with both the leadership of President Chavez himself and some sections of the public administration, including in the case of the Missions some sections of the armed forces. But in general this was less an exercise in 'co-responsibility' than in beginning to replace or circumvent some of the functions of the old state, for example in the delivery of education and health care, where the existing public administration seemed hopelessly inoperative.

Nonetheless, it is doubtful how far this can be described as an expression of popular *power*, much less self-government, most critically because at this stage these community organisations had no sovereign control over economic resources of their own. Largely for that reason, they did not develop any systematic, democratic mechanisms for drawing up and deciding on plans or projects for the community.

The first move in this direction came, in theory at least, in June 2002 with the passing of the Law on Local Public Planning Councils, or CLPPs, which included the first formal mention of communal councils, albeit very much in passing. The idea of the CLPPs was to bring together organised communities and municipal governments in a joint effort at local planning. The key functions of a CLPP would include: identifying the needs of the municipality; prioritising and processing the proposals coming from the organised communities; developing and shaping the investment policies of the municipal budget; promoting and planning the transfer of responsibilities and resources from the municipal government to the organised communities; and overseeing and evaluating the implementation of these plans and projects. Communal councils were mentioned as one of the bodies through which organised communities could feed into the CLPP. But there was no detail. One of the main mechanisms for the CLPP to achieve all this was to be a process of participatory budgeting inspired by the experience pioneered in the 1990s in the Brazilian city of Porto Alegre, which later spread to many other local and regional governments in Brazil and beyond.[11]

For the next two and a half years, however, the Law on CLPPs bore few if any practical fruits. Problems of conception seemed to combine with a singular lack of political will. One way of explaining this is to compare the shape of the CLPP proposal with that of the Brazilian participatory budget (PB), at least in its more radical forms.[12]

One problem was that of size. The CLPP was designed in considerable detail at the level of a municipality, which might have a population of several hundred thousand (or many more in the case of Caracas). That was clearly too large a unit to take detailed, democratic discussion and decisions on which drains or which streets should get which repairs at what cost and in which order. The CLPP proposal made only passing mention of the smaller-scale units of the parish public planning councils and, smaller still, the communal public planning councils, with little indication of how these would feed into the larger scheme.[13] The Porto Alegre participatory budget, meanwhile, had developed very elaborate mechanisms for dividing and sub-dividing the municipality into more micro units, and then prioritising and recombining the multitude of investment demands and decisions taken by the communities at these different levels.

Another fundamental difference – and this is a wider feature of the Bolivarian process that we will come back to in the Conclusion – is that the CLPP Law was a law. That is, its form was set in stone by the National Assembly, in other words by the existing machinery of representative democracy. By contrast, the Porto Alegre PB was never set down in law. Its promoters took advantage of a generic clause in Brazil's liberal post-dictatorship constitution to develop a process in which the community set its own rules and could modify them on its own initiative, in a process of direct democracy that did not depend on the elected representatives of the representative democracy. In other words, it was self-regulating.

Thirdly and alongside this, the Porto Alegre PB was autonomous. The mayor or some other representatives of the local government had a voice in the PB, but no vote. The traditional, elected municipal assembly played no part in the process at all and found itself more or less obliged, by the political balance of forces, to rubber stamp the PB's conclusions. The right to participate in the PB was individual and universal for all citizens. Venezuela's CLPP Law, on the other hand, determined from the outset that, alongside the representatives of the neighbourhood and other community organisations, the traditionally elected members of the municipal assembly, as well as the presidents of the old parish boards, would also be full members of the CLPP, and the mayor would be its president. Although the community representatives were to have an inbuilt majority of one, it is clear that this structure would make it quite unlikely for any decisions to be taken against the will of the local government machine. In this respect, the CLPP proposal was much more moderate than the lived experience of the urban land committees and Missions, and much more tied to and ultimately subordinate to the institutions of the existing state.

Finally, although the CLPP Law said that mayors were obliged to carry out the projects presented by the organised communities, it left unclear exactly what part of the budget would be dedicated to these, and who exactly would decide between conflicting priorities and how. This was somewhat different from at least the theory of the PB in Porto Alegre, which declared that the PB process should have decision-making powers over 100 per cent of the municipal budget.

But just as important as any such design faults, there was, as we have seen in Galipan, an almost complete absence on the part of pro-Chavez mayors and governors of any will to make these plans work. For the most part, they were happy to occupy their position in the old state structure. They had little interest in structures of popular power that might challenge the prerogatives which this granted them. This raises another major issue facing the Bolivarian process – the absence of a political organisation or party capable of conceiving, developing and implementing policies of change, policies that inevitably run into conflict with the status quo. In Brazil it had been the Workers' Party in its most radical phase, and particularly its left wing, that had pushed for the participatory budget and used its election to mayoral office to transfer at least parcels of power out of the city hall and into the communities.[14]

After more than two years of inaction – during which so much of Venezuela's political energy was absorbed in the battles over the opposition-led lockout and then the recall referendum – President Chavez tried to breathe life back into these plans for direct democracy. Having swept the board in the October 2004 local and regional elections, he urged municipal and state governments to implement participatory budgets. An entire session of that two-day November

2004 high-level workshop on strategy was given over to the president's then close adviser, Marta Harnecker, giving a presentation and leading a discussion on the PB experience in Porto Alegre. Again the results were extremely limited. Marta Harnecker reports just ten experiences with participatory budgets across Venezuela's 24 states and 335 municipalities, and most of these have not survived.

Nonetheless, it was out of these failures, and out of the few more positive experiments – an attempt to develop 'communitarian governments' in the eastern state of Sucre, the development of local works cabinets (GOLs) in Libertador, Caracas, the experience of Carora with its municipal constituent assembly, as well as smaller isolated struggles like the one we've seen in Galipan – that a change of priorities developed and a new emphasis was put on the development of direct democracy on the smaller scale of the communal council. As Marta Harnecker puts it, Chavez had an intuition that something needed to be done quickly to get some resources into the hands of local communities, so that they would feel they *could* do things. In the end, with some input from Brazilian advisers from Porto Alegre, the Law on Communal Councils was thrown together in a hurry and passed in April 2006.

But it was not until the beginning of 2007, when Chavez took up the banner of the communal councils in earnest, that they really took off. As Felicia Hidalgo or 'Licha', the emblematic community leader we met at Fabricio Ojeda in Chapter 2, put it: 'until Chavez said it, people didn't really believe it'.

There's no doubt the growth was sharp and swift, although the figures available may be misleading. In February 2006, two months before the Law on Communal Councils was passed, General Carneiro at the head of the newly created Ministry of Popular Participation reported the existence of 3,700 communal planning councils with 635 projects across the country. A year later, just after Chavez's key remarks, the new minister, David Velasquez, said he wanted to evaluate the real state of 18,000 reported communal councils. By the end of July 2007, Dario Vivas, a member of the Presidential Commission for Popular Power, said 28,000 communal councils had already been legalised of the 50,000 they hoped to register by 2008. All of these numbers seem improbably high.[15] But it is also likely that relatively more of the first reported communal councils, or even earlier communal planning councils, were in fact phantom organisations, set up on paper if at all, in the hope of future benefits for the group or individuals involved. Certainly the empirical evidence in the communities I have visited is that, with the exception of pioneers like Galipan, a certain number of communal councils began to function after the passing of the law in 2006 but that their expansion on a massive scale came from the beginning of 2007. This rapid growth was only possible because in many places, especially the poor *barrios* of Caracas, the urban land committees and their various spin-offs provided a template for the new communal councils to slip into.

So was this the 'explosion of popular power' that President Chavez had called for in that speech on 8 January as he swore in his new cabinet? Already, in his acceptance speech after winning a second full presidential term on 3 December 2006, Chavez had declared that the people had voted for socialism and that this would be the priority of the coming period. Late that night, under torrential rain, he had joined his supporters from the balcony of the Miraflores Palace, sung with them the national anthem and shouted 'Long live socialism!' 'Nobody should be afraid of socialism,' he told them. 'Socialism is humane, socialism is love. ... Venezuela is red, red right through.' A fortnight later he had called for the formation of a new Venezuelan United Socialist Party to lead the transformation. In the January speech, he spelt out the mechanisms.

There were to be five motors of Venezuela's move towards a socialist society. First was an enabling law whose immediate job would be to renationalise the main telecommunications company, CANTV and the Caracas electricity utility, and then to re-establish sovereign control over the super-heavy crude oil operations in the Orinoco Belt.[16] Second would be a constitutional reform to lay the basis for Venezuela as a socialist, Bolivarian republic. Third came a campaign of socialist education and ideological debate to overcome the values and prejudices of capitalism. Fourth was what Chavez called 'a new geometry of power', a complex series of provisions to overcome existing territorial and administrative barriers, which as we shall see overlapped with the plans for the communal councils. But 'the fifth and most important motor' of Venezuela's transition to a socialism of the twenty-first century was to be the extension of communal councils in a 'revolutionary explosion of communal power'.

And it was this emphasis on popular power, with the communal councils as its basic building block, which underpinned the most radical elements of the constitutional reforms put to a referendum on 2 December 2007 – the referendum that of course turned out to be the Bolivarian revolution's very first electoral defeat.

AN EXPLOSION OF COMMUNAL POWER

One place that took President Chavez at his word was Carora, a medium-sized provincial town in the central-western state of Lara. In fact they'd been taking him at his word since October 2004. That was when a group of local activists around Julio Chavez (no relation of the president) had won the municipal elections and began to implement a programme for direct democracy and popular power that they had been preparing for several years, and which they now hitched onto the priorities set out in the national government's 'New Strategic Map' and the emerging debate over socialism in the twenty-first century.

When, in August 2007, I sat in on one of the weekly assemblies of a communal council in Carora – this one in a neighbourhood appropriately called Brasil Parte Abajo, something like 'Lower Brazil' – it wasn't difficult to discern the different stages of this process, embedded like archaeological strata into the foundations of the emerging edifice.

It was a clammy, rainy Thursday night and there were only about 40 people sitting on white plastic chairs on the covered concrete patio of the communal council's own hall, which housed a small library and a study room with computers. They told me they usually had 60 to 80 turn up.[17] This had been the first communal council in the municipality of Torres, which includes the town of Carora and a large, impoverished rural hinterland, and has a total population of roughly 200,000. In fact this had been the first communal council in the whole of Lara state.

One of the *voceros* or spokespeople, Mario Querales, opened the meeting by announcing that a third communal council had been set up in their neighbourhood the previous Sunday. He reminded everyone that when they had first formed in February 2006, two months before the Law on Communal Councils, they had taken in the whole community of 730 families. 'That was too much for us to cover,' he said.

So the new communal council was 'an important development for our community'. With three communal councils they could work together and get more resources to attend to more problems.

The meeting moved on to housing. They'd already built or refurbished eight homes with money from the last visit of the president's 'mobile cabinet'. Doña Ramona stood up and told everyone how pleased she was with her tiles and the door. They were applying for three more homes through the next of the president's roving ministerial meetings, which went out to different parts of the country and allocated resources to a variety of housing and infrastructure projects, most of them through communal councils.

Earlier that day, a visit to two rural communities in the same municipality of Torres had shown the same thing. The 48 peasant families in La Colonia had already built 13 houses and were applying for 15 more – trim block buildings with three bedrooms, a living room and a kitchen to replace the mud and wattle huts most had lived in before. 'The communal council in assembly decided who needed them most,' Martin Parra told me. 'We didn't know anything but we hired in a foreman to show us and we learnt how to build them ourselves.' It was the same story in Los Uvedales. The 70 families there had built twelve houses so far, with the money they'd been given for seven. This was another story I heard repeated time and again. Because they did it themselves, the money went much further. And success bred success. 'At the first assembly to elect our communal council, we didn't have a quorum,' Teresita Camacaro remembered. 'People didn't believe it was for real. At the second, we just managed to elect 20 spokespeople. Now we get 70 or more at each assembly and the numbers are rising.'

Later the mayor, Julio Chavez, explained to me how housing remained one of the biggest practical challenges facing the Bolivarian revolution and its nascent bodies of popular power. In Torres they had inherited a housing deficit of some 18,000 units. In the previous year and a half they had managed to build almost 2,000, with 85 per cent of these being undertaken by the communal councils and only 15 per cent by the various national and regional public housing bodies. In fact in the first round, the communal councils had built 1,310 homes with the money they'd been given for 947.

This was the bread and butter of most of Venezuela's communal councils – the discussion, selection and execution of a number of one-off infrastructure projects, most of them financed with money coming direct from central, national, presidential funds.[18] There is little doubt that it was access to these kinds of projects and this kind of finance that had done so much to fuel the rapid spread of communal councils across Venezuela. There was also little doubt that it had had a major impact on the quality of life of many thousands. What I had seen in the dirt-poor, semi-arid rural communities of La Colonia and Los Uvedales made that glaringly obvious. But it was also a form of community participation and control that had been sharply criticised from both the moderate and the radical left. In the former case because, it was argued, it made the communal councils heavily dependent on unilateral, centralised decisions by the president and his staff about how much money to disburse where and how. In the latter because, it was suggested, it turned them into simple planners and executors of small-scale public works and neutralised their political potential as instruments to build a new society and a new, communal state.[19]

But there was more going on here than these criticisms allow for. At that meeting in Brasil Parte Abajo they also talked about the mobilisation the communal council was organising to get people vaccinated against dengue. And somebody else stood up to explain that a third list was on its way for people to register for their two-monthly old age pensions. So in addition to the 130 people the communal council had already registered they needed to make sure that anyone about to turn 60 also put their names down. Nothing particularly radical about this perhaps, but it did suggest that the communal council was beginning to take on administrative functions normally carried out by governmental bodies. Then there were the musical instruments. Mario announced that tomorrow they should receive a cheque for 3 million bolivars to buy ten *cuatros* (the small, four-string guitar used in much Venezuelan traditional music) as well as drums and maracas. This was money the communal council's culture committee had got from the town hall for a music programme with the neighbourhood's children. 'I think they'll hand it over at Julio's weekly radio programme so one of us needs to go along and collect it.'

And not all the infrastructure projects came through central government grants. Apart from housing, most came from the municipality's participatory budget which had been running since 2005, but which had acquired more power in the last couple of years. Mario reminded the meeting that Julio was the only mayor in Venezuela to have handed 100 per cent of the town hall's investment funds over to the participatory budget for the organised communities to decide on, as well as almost 35 per cent of the local government's direct block grant. 'So the next assembly is where we have to decide our priorities for where we want the next lot of investment money to go.' They'd already made a diagnosis of the needs. They'd identified several streets that needed paving, other roads that needed repairing, a number of alleyways where the houses still weren't connected to running water, and so on. 'But the assembly will decide.' Those decisions would then go to the assembly of the parish public planning council, made up of spokespeople from all the different communal councils in the parish and from a number of other organised social and cultural sectors, and this would reconcile the various priorities and projects and ultimately decide how much money should go to what. This would then be ratified by the local public planning council, which took in all 17 parishes of Torres municipality, one of the few places in Venezuela where this body has ever really functioned. In other words, one very important slab of local power, the power to control 43 per cent of total local government expenditure, was already in the hands of the organised communities. As Julio Chavez put it to me later, 'This set of decisions from the parishes is then our investment budget for that year. Once it's been approved by the CLPP, I cannot change it.'[20]

But there was another area where the communal council was beginning to test its power, potentially even more far reaching. It came out in the most dramatic moment of the meeting. Mario read out a letter that they and other communal councils had received from the regional office of Fondacomun, an agency of the Ministry for Popular Participation, now renamed the Ministry for Participation and Social Protection. It referred to a spate of recent land occupations, 'often just for personal advantage', and drew the meeting's attention to Article 115 of the 1999 Bolivarian Constitution, which says the right to private property is guaranteed. That meant, the letter continued, that no state institution or body of communal government could approve – much

THE BUDGET IN TORRES

The total budget in Torres Municipality for 2007 was 44 billion bolivars (or US$20.47 million). As in other Venezuelan municipalities, this came from four sources:

- block grant from central government (*Situado Constitucional*) Bs. 24 bn
- Intergovernmental Fund for Decentralisation (FIDES) Bs. 6.8 bn
- Special Economic Allocations Law (LAEE) Bs. 7.3 bn
- local taxes Bs. 5.6 bn.

FIDES and LAEE are both funds intended for investment. It was 100 per cent of these that Mayor Julio Chavez handed over to communal councils to control through the participatory budget. But the law at that time specified that this expenditure had to be put out to tender to registered contractors, building companies etc. At least in theory, it could not be handed over to direct administration by the communities themselves. A change to this was proposed for the Constitutional Reform in December 2008, but after its defeat Julio Chavez told me he was aiming to find a way round this requirement anyway.

In 2007 the municipality also handed a part of the block grant over to the communities – money which could be administered directly by the communal councils. This brought to 43 per cent the share of the total budget discussed in the participatory budget. The rest, almost 60 per cent, went on fixed costs for the municipality's own staff and running costs.

less encourage – invasions or violations of private property. Then, in a barely veiled threat, it warned that the law would punish such behaviour, which was dangerous to the community and could lead to anarchy, and those involved would cease to benefit from any state support. 'Remember', it concluded sententiously, 'you are a new form of government, the government of the commune, and exert control over public policy in your community and area. But, beware, this must always be within the framework of the Constitution and the law.'

Mario was inclined to accept the argument of the letter. He referred to the dispute they currently faced between Yolanda Nieves, who was living in a property that wasn't hers, and the owner, who lived in Caracas and had also written to the communal council to ask them to approve her removal, with an offer to accept just three months rent from her even though she'd been living there much longer for free. Both Yolanda and the owner's mother, Doña Esperanza, were present, and there followed an impassioned and sometimes acrimonious series of exchanges, that amounted to a kind of open court hearing. The two women gave different accounts of who had said and done what. Other neighbours got up and suggested that Señora Yolanda had been doing the owner a favour by looking after a house that had been abandoned and falling into ruin for years, or that the place had become a hazard for the community because it had become a hang-out for all sorts of criminal activity and vice, or that what the owner really wanted to do was turn it into a liquor store, and so on. Mario kept coming back to the law and the owner's right to do what he wanted with his property, but a couple of others present stood up and said they disagreed. They wanted to know how many other cases there were like this, because they shouldn't allow private property to damage the community as a whole. They said there were other bits of the Constitution that took a different approach. 'Private property cannot be above the collective interest of the community.' In the end it was agreed that the following week the housing committee of the communal council should sit down with both women and try to find a solution.[21]

Such disputes are commonplace, of course. But the way it came up at this meeting seemed to reveal three more potential functions of these forms of popular power. Firstly, it showed the communal council could begin to take on a micro judicial role, acting as arbiter in local disputes, somewhat in the manner of justices of the peace, but now in a collective form. Secondly, it provoked an intensely political discussion about one of the most important and controversial issues facing the Bolivarian revolution, the question of private property, its prerogatives and its limits, in the process of moving towards a new kind of socialism. This suggests the importance the communal councils could have in developing political education and confidence among an extremely wide swathe of the population, far beyond the already committed activists. Thirdly it at least poses, though it does not resolve, the thorny question of just how autonomous the communal councils and other emerging bodies of popular power (what it has become common to call in Venezuela the *constituent* power) could or should be from the established institutions (the *constituted* power), both their particular directives and the whole legal scaffolding that supports them. For example, should they care what some bureaucrat in a ministry wrote to them? Or, how acceptable is it for them to break a law that they didn't make, in what they see as the interests of the community?

Not surprisingly, in such a novel process there was plenty of room to make mistakes.

I witnessed another, in some ways similar, dispute at a communal council outside La Victoria – it's another provincial town, more industrial than Carora, of 170,000 inhabitants, in Aragua state, just an hour west of Caracas. The community in Sector 3 of Guacamaya parish was discussing whether or not to revoke the mandate of a young woman who had been elected as a spokesperson to the communal council but had been missing meetings because she had a new job. The case was put against her. She defended her right to continue. It seemed probable that there was some subtext to the immediate dispute – old scores or group rivalries within the community. It began to turn into a bit of shouting match. I'd gone with two of the local mayor's staff and somebody got up and said it was a disgrace that they were putting on such a bad display for the foreign visitor. The chair tried to cut through the uproar, called for a show of hands and the woman was voted out. At which a woman member of the traditionally elected local municipal assembly, who happened to be present, stood up and started telling the meeting it couldn't do what it had just done because it violated article number this, that and the other of I can't remember which regulations. The uproar got worse and we decided it would be politic to leave. As we drove away one of the mayor's aides began to say that she had to agree with the assembly member because that was no way to run a meeting and it really wasn't fair to summarily dismiss the young woman like that. The other replied, 'formally you may be right, but these things happen when you hand people power to run their own affairs. It's a learning process; they have to have the right to make mistakes.'

[167]

Like Carora, La Victoria – or the municipality which includes it, José Felix Ribas – has one of the few local governments in Venezuela that has made serious efforts not only to promote the communal councils, but to extend their reach and power by transferring resources and control out of the town hall and into the hands of the community. Here too they had practised a participatory budget since 2005, albeit in a less developed form than in Torres. This was mostly money from the national investment funds, FIDES and LAEE, mentioned earlier. And by 2007 they also calculated they were transferring 22 per cent of their direct block grant income to the almost 80 communal councils formed so far in the municipality.

This was the novelty in La Victoria – the way the town hall was encouraging the communal councils to join together and take over complete responsibility for some public services. From May 2007, groups of 15 or more communal councils in a particular sector began to band together in *mancomunidades* or federations. The town hall would provide a building with basic facilities, tables, chairs, a computer and so on – what they called the *casa de integración* (integration centre). The federations would then get a monthly cheque to run for themselves the services in question. So far ten social programmes previously run by the town hall's social development department had been transferred, including things like a public dispensary for medicines, the provision of wheelchairs and prosthetic limbs for the disabled, a free school uniform programme and a free funeral service. The communal councils would decide who needed what, and the federation or *mancomunidad* would see they got it.

In the *casa de integración* for the Northern Zone, I met 32-year-old Rafael Vasquez; with severe inflammation in his legs, he needed crutches which it would have taken at least month to get through the old town hall social department. He'd presented his request to the communal council the previous Thursday. Now it was Wednesday and he was getting what he needed.

The mayor of Ribas, a passionate young woman called Rosa Leon, told me this was exactly how they needed to get round the bureaucracy. I heard her tell a gathering of communal councils that the programme was proving so effective that she had just agreed to close down the old social development department. 'The communities have shown in deeds that they are running it better, so why do we need this department?' She looked and sounded more like a student leader agitating on campus – which is what she had been until a few years earlier – than a mayor. This, she said, was what had to be done: the 'implosion' of the old bureaucracy to replace it with a new, communal administration. Next, she said, they were aiming to 'implode' the maintenance department and hand the town hall's basic repair and maintenance work over the to the federated communal councils. When I returned in 2008, she recognised this was proving more difficult, because of the debts and lack of equipment that bedevilled the existing works department. But they held to this aim, and she told me her next big hope was that she could transfer over to the communal councils and their communal banks complete responsibility for collecting local taxation.

Beyond communal councils

So what was special about Carora and La Victoria, compared with most of Venezuela's local and regional governments? In part, at least, it was a question of leadership, of the political will of those elected mayors. In the case of Carora, for example, Julio Chavez and those around him had a very different history from the majority of Chavista mayors and governors. He and his team had been active builders of the social movements in Carora since the end of the 1980s. Several had their roots in liberation theology and Christian youth movements led by Jesuits. They'd been involved in student struggles, peasant struggles and the co-operative movement. They'd tried to get the neighbourhood associations to organise their own street cleaning service. In 1993, Julio had been arrested for his part in building civilian support for the two failed military coups of 1992.[22] Although they'd had no party affiliation, in 2000 they linked up with one of the minority parties supporting Chavez, the PPT, to launch an electoral alternative.[23] 'The main Chavista candidate for mayor came from the oligarchy, from COPEI (the traditional Christian Democrat party). We didn't expect to win, but to launch a project, for a municipal constituent assembly, to rethink the concept of the city.'

Four years later that project won, in the 2004 local elections, 'against both the opposition and the imposition' as Julio Chavez puts it, because again they had been marginalised by the main Chavista forces locally and he was forced to stand for mayor against the official candidate. They promptly launched their local constituent assembly, elected by secret ballot in 58 local assemblies. It sat for five months in 2005 and drew up the blueprint for this new concept of the city, based on the organised communities, including the communal councils and the whole system of participatory budgets described above. For Julio Chavez, this was already some way ahead of the national project for communal councils, because it included plans for a complete system of powers based on community control, including an executive, elected by the communal councils, a legislature based on citizens' assemblies, structures of communal justices of the peace, communal electoral powers and so on. 'The Law on Communal Councils, when it came in 2006, did not include any of these things.' What they were bringing together in their local constitution was 'a package for moving from a neoliberal, capitalist, bourgeois state, to something that is still capitalist, but on the way to creating a communal state'.

The strategic challenge posed here was precisely that which has faced the Bolivarian revolution on a national scale throughout the period covered by this book, and potentially any other left-wing government elected in Bolivia, Ecuador or elsewhere – namely how a project for social transformation, or socialism of the twenty-first century, which is elected into office through the mechanisms of the *old* state, can move beyond these institutions to build the structures of a *new* kind of public administration, based on direct democracy and the power of the organised population.

Consequently, another key difference in Carora – and to a lesser degree in La Victoria – was that when the boom of communal councils did come in 2007, there was already a wider structure of direct democracy for them to slot into. The fact that here the local government had taken seriously both the CLPP and the participatory budget was key to this.

However, the objective for Mayor Julio Chavez and his team went beyond this. The framework laid out in that municipal constitution prefigured, even exceeded, many of the most radical reforms to the national constitution that would be put to referendum in December 2007. Not surprising, perhaps, for Julio Chavez had become part of the Presidential Commission on Popular Power that helped to draft those reforms. There were three main aspects to this. Firstly, an increasing shift from representative to direct forms of democracy. So for example, from 2007 the community representatives on the Torres CLPP ceased to be representatives from a variety of community organisations and became all spokespeople directly elected from the communal councils, now with a clear majority over the representatives of local government that the law still required to be included in the CLPP. Secondly, there was an increasing shift from the communities merely *deciding* what the money should be spent on to the communities also *administering* that expenditure. Thirdly, there was an increasing tendency for groups of communal councils to join together to propose, decide and administer some *joint* projects. This was similar to the experience of federations of communal councils in La Victoria.

All of this pointed towards the idea of *comunas*, or communes, contained in the constitutional reform. Bringing together four or five communal councils, these would replace the parishes and become the basic cell of a whole new structure of communal power, moving from communal cities to communal zones and so on upwards to a whole national structure of communal power. These proposals overlapped with those for a new geometry of power. Perhaps deliberately, the details of both remained hazy, as did, crucially, the relationship between these new structures and the existing municipal and state governments. The opposition accused President Chavez of seeking to do away with the institutions of local democracy in order to centralise his own power. He vigorously denied this. But it seems clear that any successful development of such communal power would indeed strip away the traditional functions and powers of local and regional administrations. Many on the left of the Bolivarian movement have accused numerous Chavista mayors and governors of quietly sabotaging the constitutional referendum for precisely this reason. Certainly, Julio Chavez' objectives as mayor were unambiguous. 'We believe that people can govern themselves,' he told me in the middle of 2007. 'I consider myself an infiltrator in this old state. And from within I'm destroying it, getting rid of all the power I can!'

Six months later, after the defeat of the constitutional reforms, he told me his objectives had not changed. He hoped to press on with many of the same plans regardless of whether they were in the constitution or not. Rosa Leon in La Victoria told me the same thing: in the end, transferring power to the communities did not depend on the constitution but on the will of those in government. President Chavez seemed intent on continuing too. Julio was lobbying for the Tocuyo Medio area of Torres, which included those impoverished rural communities of La Colonia and Los Uvedales that I'd visited, to be made one of a number of pilot experiences with 'communal territories'. The idea would be to use the existing enabling law to suspend in those areas any existing legislation that hindered the transfer of power to the people. The bodies of communal power would then set about resolving the problems of basic services and infrastructure in that territory, launch a series of endogenous development projects and nuclei, as well as 'socialist production enterprises', and, if Julio Chavez had his way, apply what he called 'the principles of the French revolution' which had been included in the Torres municipal constitution: namely that system of five communal powers, including an executive and a legislature, as well as judicial, electoral and moral (oversight and ombudsman) powers. The aim, he told me, would be 'to show in one year what could be the achievements of this new state that we want to emerge, and compare them with the old state and the old form of territorial domination'.

President Chavez' announcement a month later of a new 13 April Mission[24] indicated that this was one of the main policies he wanted to finance with a new tax on excess profits from the high price of oil.[25] The promotion of communes was back on the agenda, in order to build what he called, a new kind of 'democracy from below'.

Back to the *barrios*

It has to be said that the poor neighbourhoods on the hillsides of Caracas – where we began this journey in Chapter 1 and which continue to provide the densest mass of self-organisation and popular support for the Bolivarian revolution – are a long way behind Carora and La Victoria when it comes to any formal transfer of power to the people. Here, the skeleton of an alternative, communal administration is much less complete. The forms of self-government are cruder and more uneven. On the other hand, they are often more autonomous, and in that sense arguably more robust.

In some cases there has been positive resistance from well-organised communities – the case of La Vega for instance – because local activists feared the communal councils could absorb and dissolve the existing organisations they had built up. There were concerns that they might be manipulated from above, by one of the Caracas mayors or members of their governmental teams.[26]

Back in Carapita, in Antimano parish, 50 metres up an alleyway from the school where we first met Greydaris Motta and José Gregorio Falcon, completing their secondary education in Mission Ribas, I ran into Teófilo Avilés, who had shown me round on my first visit. He gave me a taste of the problem. 'The communal councils are meant to be autonomous. But many of them only have three of their four legs. The fourth leg is retained by people in local government so they can control it as theirs, so they can show they have mass support. They call out "their" communal councils, "their" health committees and what have you, to stand behind a banner saying "Libertador City Hall" or "Government of Miranda". This leads to clashes with the community. We have this situation with my own communal council. We presented a project to rebuild a pathway. We got 30 million bolivars and the executive spent it all on contracting workers they chose, to build the retaining wall, without any oversight and without even consulting the community. Now we're calling on the community to meet and revoke the current finance committee or communal bank.'

For Teófilo, the few existing communal councils in his part of Carapita were not working well. Mission Ribas had declined and the other educational missions had ceased. Only the health committee was still thriving. But he knew things were better elsewhere. He himself had been helping out some other communal councils that had got together to try to tackle the serious shortages of some basic foodstuffs that had emerged since the end of 2007 as a result of hoarding, speculation and corruption in both the private and public sectors of the supply chain.[27]

Higher up in Carapita, in the Calle San José, I found he was right. I went back to visit Sofia Lashley, the woman who had explained to me in such eloquent detail the history and sociology of the Caracas *barrios* and their community organisations. After a difficult pregnancy, Sofia was now just a couple of days away from giving birth to her second son.[28] She was beached, whale-like as she described it, on a precarious wooden armchair in her neighbour's house. (I wondered how she managed to negotiate her way around the minute space of her own two-room home, down the steep stone stairway at the back.) But she hadn't lost her voice, or her delight in detail, statistics and sharp political analysis.

She explained to me how that very house had become the first PDVAL store in Antimano parish, run entirely by the food committee of their communal council. I took a look in the next room which was full of bags of rice and milk powder, with a window onto the narrow street serving as the shop front. PDVAL was a new initiative to tackle the food shortages. PDVSA provided the stock. As a short term, emergency measure, the state oil company had imported large quantities from other Latin American countries. For the whole of Caracas, this was being housed at the Fabricio Ojeda nucleus, and from there shipped out to the individual PDVALs. Unlike the Mercal network, foodstuffs from PDVAL were not subsidised but sold at the full government-regulated price.[29] However, the communal council had carried out a census to identify those most in need in the community, and was using its small surplus income from the main PDVAL sales to pay for free food parcels for them. So far there were three PDVALs in the parish, but in the next few weeks this should rise to 18. In her familiar style, Sofia rattled off the number of existing and planned PDVALs for all the other parishes of Caracas, the value of the stock delivered, the prices here compared with Mercal, and so on. 'There are four communal councils in our sector, organising 2,216 families out of the 3,116 total number of families in our *barrio*. At the moment we're supplying the others until they get their own PDVAL.'

Three of these communal councils had formed a *mancomunidad* or federation to put forward some joint socio-productive projects – a sewing co-op and another to make mattresses – as well as one to improve the roads. They had joint assemblies most Sundays and usually got 50 or 60 people turning up, but twice that number if there was a big decision to be made on allocating resources. Sofia's own communal council also had a 1.4 billion bolivar project for 67 homes to be rebuilt and another of 300 million bolivars for rainwater collection. In theory all these had been approved but so far they'd had no money through. 'There are two kinds of communal council,' she told me. Some were just in it for what they could get. 'If they don't get any finance they fold up.' That was the case with the fourth council in their *barrio*. 'Others, like the three of us who are federated, keep working regardless because we believe in what we are doing.' She thought the defeat of the constitutional reforms wouldn't produce any fundamental change of direction. But it should give them pause for reflection. Part of the problem had been that the National Assembly had added a number of reforms to President Chavez' original proposals 'We don't believe in the National Assembly. If it had been just his proposals, they would have won. Because when Chavez speaks, we listen. But we don't listen to those around him.'

CONCLUSION:
MAKING SOCIALISM IN THE
TWENTY-FIRST CENTURY

On 15 August 2007, President Chavez revealed his proposal to reform 33 articles of the 1999 Bolivarian Constitution – which had been drawn up, debated and passed by a large majority in a referendum at the end of his first year in government. This was to be the second of the five motors of the revolution that Chavez had promised at the beginning of the year, just after his re-election to a second full term. In September and October, the National Assembly discussed the proposal and added changes to 36 more articles. The aim of the reform was meant to be to open up 'the Venezuelan road to socialism' – although as Sofia Lashley told us at the end of the last chapter, many of Chavez' most loyal grassroots supporters did not trust the National Assembly proposals. On 2 December 2007 the 69 proposals, divided into two blocks, were put to another national referendum. They lost.

The margin was not great – roughly 51 per cent to 49 per cent – but the result resonated like an earthquake through the Bolivarian movement. This was Chavez' first defeat at the ballot box. Why had he lost? What would happen now? Had the possibility of a new kind of socialism been struck down even before it got on its feet?

Much was written on this inside and outside Venezuela, from every angle. But what exactly had been defeated? Was it the socialist project itself – as it had emerged and developed since August 2004 – that had been overturned? This is an obvious question, but not an easy one. Any adequate answer will have to retrace the contours not only of the Bolivarian proposal for socialism but also of the current state of debate, inside and outside Venezuela, on what a revival of socialism in the twenty-first century might amount to.

In the run-up to the December referendum, the opposition, and almost all the international media, had fixed their attention on the proposal to remove the two-term limit for presidential candidates, implying this would allow Chavez to remain 'president for life', as well as to a lesser extent on some other proposals that seemed to strengthen the powers of the executive. There was plenty of wilful distortion here. Removing presidential term-limits may not be the perfect expression of a commitment to overturn the existing system and build socialism from the bottom up. But this was hardly dictatorship. Numerous bourgeois democracies, both presidential and parliamentary, have no term limits. France and Britain are just two. But the sleight of hand enabled the anti-Chavez camp to play on an association that had become deeply embedded not only in the dominant ideology but in the collective consciousness of most of the oppressed and exploited too, since well before the collapse of the Soviet Union. That was the association between socialism and authoritarianism.

In fact the radical core of the constitutional reform proposal, and therefore of the Bolivarian socialist project – which was scarcely mentioned in the mainstream media – pointed in exactly the opposite direction. This was the promotion and constitutional enshrinement of popular power as the basis of a new Bolivarian, socialist republic in Venezuela. In other words, while the opposition railed against Chavez' 'centralising' and authoritarian plans, the substance of the most important of these reforms was a vision of socialism in which democracy – direct, bottom-up, substantive democracy – was not just a desirable adjunct but a necessary condition, indeed the constitutive principle.

The original text from the presidency motivating the reforms talked of the 'progressive dismantling of the political, economic and institutional obstacles that have made it impossible to meet social needs'. It recalled that the 1999 Constitution had set this as its goal, but had not been able to achieve it fully. Therefore it was necessary to adapt that constitution 'and add the elements that can reinforce the move towards a break with the bourgeois, capitalist model'. Two of the main instruments to achieve this were identified as: first, 'Leaving behind representative democracy in order to consolidate the leading role of participatory democracy, where the eruption of popular power becomes the essential historical development needed to build a socialist society in the twenty-first century'; and second, 'Laying the foundations for a new mode of production based on new relations of production, new forms of property, and the democratisation of capital, which allow control by popular power over the production and distribution of goods and services'.

The latter was the second area on which the opposition, inside and outside Venezuela, focused its fire. Again, the attack centred on a wilful misrepresentation – that of a putative attack on private property. The old spectre of nationalisation, equated with authoritarian state control, which in turn was equated with inefficiency, corruption and bureaucracy, extended into hysterical suggestions that the revolution might confiscate the homes of the poor, or even their children. Both the reality and the programme of the Bolivarian revolution were far from this. In almost a decade there had been only a tiny handful of state take-overs. In almost all of these the old owners put up little or no resistance. Either they had no interest in holding on to their old property or they were more than satisfied with the generous terms on which the Venezuelan state bought them out. And even in the text of the constitutional reforms, the proposal for a Venezuelan road to socialism deliberately avoided any suggestion of wholesale state control of the economy. Instead it emphasised a variety of 'new forms of social property', co-operative, communal and mixed, alongside the traditional state and private sectors, and new forms of popular control over these different forms of property.

These two areas – the social economy and popular power – are of course the aspects of the Bolivarian experience whose stories we have listened to in some detail in the preceding chapters. In so far as it is possible to identify a specific Bolivarian strategy for moving towards a socialism of twenty-first century, I would suggest that these would be its two central pillars – always understanding that the first includes both co-management *and* the promotion of a co-operative, social economy as such, and also that over the last few years the different components have fallen in and out of favour with different sections of the Bolivarian leadership, and with Chavez himself. Together these two areas suggest a vision of socialism that is strikingly different from either of the two visions that dominated most twentieth-century socialist theory and practice – those of the post-Stalin communist parties in the east, and of the social democratic parties in the industrialised west.

In spite of their very significant differences, both of these relied on a central, bureaucratic state to either command or regulate the economy. Both justified this in the name of greater equality. Neither involved a significant extension of direct democratic control (in the former case of course there was a grave curtailment of even the basic democratic rights that existed in representative democracies). The Bolivarian project offered, at least in theory, something else – the vision of a transition to socialism based on grassroots control, on direct democracy in the communities and workplaces, and on a variety of decentralised, co-operative, socialised forms of economic activity; and all of this within a framework of political pluralism and basic constitutional guarantees.[1]

The fact that all this coexisted with, and was promoted by, a single, omnipresent, charismatic leader is another of the Venezuelan experience's striking paradoxes.

The third pillar of the Bolivarian strategy would be the launching of a new Venezuelan United Socialist Party (PSUV) from the end of 2006, as the instrument for organising this transition to a new kind of socialism – a party which in its embryonic state was given the job of leading the campaign for the constitutional reform referendum, a first task in which it spectacularly failed.

So was it this Bolivarian strategy for a transition to twenty-first century socialism that was defeated on 2 December 2007?

A TENSION AT THE HEART OF THE BOLIVARIAN REVOLUTION

The question takes us back to a tension at the heart of the Bolivarian revolution. It's one that had been there for several years, but it came to the fore after Chavez' re-election in December 2006, with those ever more explicit plans for the country's passage towards socialism. This is the tension between the revolution's anti-neoliberal and anti-imperialist achievements – which are undeniable – and its socialist promise, which for the time being remained just that: a promise.

It was of course the depth of Venezuela's structural reforms – its often noisy but nonetheless real break with the market-driven priorities of the Washington Consensus, its achievements in providing basic health care and education to millions previously excluded –

that first established the process as a beacon for the global justice movement and the international left. It was this clear, anti-neoliberal stance that lay behind the welcome given to Hugo Chavez at the World Social Forum in Porto Alegre in January 2005, even before the Venezuelan leader had made any commitment to the 'S' word.

That impact reached well beyond Latin America and the traditional solidarity circles of Europe and North America. A couple of examples are illustrative. I came across one in Indonesia in 2006, where efforts to form a new, broad party of the left, PAPERNAS, made repeated reference to the Venezuelan example to explain and justify their platform for reasserting national sovereignty over Indonesian natural resources and economic development. A more striking one comes from Egypt, where there is a tradition in the Cairo bazaar of giving the names of public figures to the dates on sale, as a measure of the quality of each batch of this dried fruit. In the aftermath of the 2006 war in Lebanon, it was no surprise that the poorest, bitterest varieties were called 'Bush', 'Blair' and 'Olmert'. Nor was it much surprise to find that the very finest, sweetest dates were called 'Nasrallah', after the leader of Hezbollah. But among the group of other tasty varieties, following up a little way behind, was one called 'Chavez'. The Venezuelan leader had of course withdrawn his ambassador from Israel in protest at the aggression.

All this illustrates the extraordinary resonance that Venezuela's bold opposition to empire has had among tens of millions of those Fanon once called 'the damned of the earth' – a resonance that began to be felt after the defeat of the anti-Chavez coup in April 2002 and the development of the health, literacy and food 'Missions' from 2003, and which was unlike anything the world had seen for a couple of decades.

But then emerged the 'new phase of the revolution' – precisely the period from August 2004 that we have been following in this book – which gave the Venezuelan process a bigger, more profound impact still. Many of its core ideas were sketched out in the high-level workshop on 'The New Strategic Map' of November 2004 that has come up repeatedly in the preceding pages. It acquired a more explicit, public form with Chavez' invitation in 2005 to begin discussing 'socialism of the twenty-first century'. The discussion became more urgent after the commitment he made in December

2006 that this was now the main challenge for the next period in Venezuela. And it remained very much alive after the defeat in the constitutional referendum – even if for a time the tone became more cautious and self-critical. Of course this 'promise of socialism' had critical importance for those directly involved in the process inside Venezuela. But it also transformed its international potential.

Firstly, for those of us in countries where the word 'socialism' had been erased from most people's political vocabulary since 1989 (and at the very least that means all of the industrialised English-speaking world), it suddenly became possible again to talk about socialism without appearing to have just flown in from another galaxy. More than that, Venezuela provided a special opportunity and challenge. For this was the first living laboratory – at least since Nicaragua in the 1980s – to test out what exactly socialist democracy might look like in the twenty-first century, and what strategies might be available to get to it. These were discussions that almost no one had had since at least that far back. The loss of confidence and the loss of credibility had spread wide and deep after the fall of the wall, affecting even those who had been most critical of the authoritarian, 'really existing socialism' in the east. There were still plenty of well-grounded, powerful critiques of the obvious inadequacies of capitalism as a means of achieving even modest well-being and fulfilment for the majority of human beings. These grew in volume and substance as the global justice movement spread its wings after 1998. But even among those on the left who still held on to some notion that a revolutionary way out of this situation might be possible, there was almost no discussion of what that meant or how it might come about. If anything, there was a tacit, barely mumbled assumption that somehow, in the end, one or another variant of the old shibboleths would prove its worth again.

Venezuela has made it possible for these kinds of discussion to re-emerge and unfold in the light of day. And although it is early days yet, one of the first and most obvious conclusions is that none of the old models fits very well – which is not to say they are useless, or do not remain necessary points of departure. The challenge, which has only begun to be taken up, was not to try to judge how well or not the Bolivarian process shaped up to the old frameworks of the left, but to see how examining and accompanying this process could help to test, refine, reinvent (or indeed simply junk) these old frameworks. A simple example: where exactly was the 'revolution' in the Bolivarian revolution? Did it happen when Chavez was elected in 1998? Did it happen when the people descended from their *ranchos* above Caracas in April 2002 and sent the military and business leaders of the coup packing? Is it still waiting to happen? Maybe there never was any real prospect of a revolution (an easy solution for conservatives and a few doctrinaire radicals). Or maybe it has been and remains a combination of several of these moments. Either way, it doesn't look or feel much like the storming of the Winter Palace, the liberated zones of the Red Army, or Fidel and Che with long beards riding into Havana on jeeps.

It is true that some of these big strategic questions had begun to reappear, in a tentative theoretical form, around the turn of the new century. The Zapatistas in Mexico sparked a crucial debate about the relation between social transformation and power, and whether the latter had to be 'taken' or 'built from below'. The upsurge of the global justice movement after Seattle, and then the international mobilisations against the war in Iraq, fed into new discussions about the agency of change, and the relative importance of social class. These discussions drew on, among others, Toni Negri's writings in Italy about 'empire' and 'multitude' – although the brute reality of 'coalition' (that is, US and British) troops invading Iraq tended to wrench the debate back from Negri's ideas to a more concrete recognition that behind the 'empire' there were still specific imperialist states and imperialist armies, with names and addresses and ID tags.[2] From about 2003, intellectuals writing in the French journal *Critique Communiste* began to re-examine the writings of Marx and other classics on questions of democracy and the state, and on the role of different forms of social appropriation, including co-operatives and public ownership, in any transition to a socialist economy. Some of this echoed earlier or parallel discussions in Latin America, especially Brazil, about participatory democracy, the 'social economy' (*economía solidária*) and new social subjects. From about 2006, this developed into a more specifically strategic debate about the challenges facing any project for radical social change, with contributions from Daniel Bensaid, Antoine Artous, Alex Callinicos and many others. Most of this was concerned with rethinking the conditions for socialism in Europe, but it was clear that the experience in Venezuela hovered in the background as the one real reference point available.

One of the core questions raised had a very direct connection with the Venezuelan process. Under current, twenty-first-century conditions, they asked, does a socialist revolution and the building of a new kind of state necessarily entail one crucial, explosive moment when the old state apparatus collapses, some kind of 'October moment', the result of an insurrectionary general strike or maybe a prolonged popular, military struggle? Alternatively, is it possible to envisage the emergence of new state structures defending a new set of social interests, alongside or even within the old state which defends the old class interests?

For almost a decade, this has been probably the most decisive question facing the Bolivarian movement in Venezuela. For, at the risk of simplification, the political process in Venezuela can be described as a nationalist, anti-neoliberal, anti-imperialist revolution, within which there is a socialist revolution struggling to get out. Paradoxically, the figure of Chavez himself straddles both these aspects. The socialist revolution is struggling to get out because this is a process which first developed out of a conventional (that is, bourgeois representative) electoral victory in 1998, with the backing of quite a broad cross-class alliance, and which at least up until the failed coup of April 2002, did little to step beyond that institutional framework. Certainly the new Bolivarian Constitution of 1999 overhauled those institutions, and had many radical things to say about popular participation and the centrality of human needs and human potential. But it did not challenge the basic premises (either of delegated, representative democracy, or of private property relations).[3] And to some extent it entrenched the class alliance that had backed it.

THE QUESTION OF THE STATE

The individual stories told throughout this book repeat over and over one of the clearest trends since the uprising against the coup in 2002, and especially since the struggle to resist the employers' lockout at the end of that year. Time and time again, the women and men involved in the Missions, the urban land committees, the initial and sporadic

experiences of workers' control, some of the rural and urban co-operatives, most recently in the explosion of communal councils, have run
into the brick wall of the old institutions, the old ways of doing things,
the old interests, in other words the old state. Time and again, they
have also begun to move beyond this old framework and even to 'defy'
it, sometimes deliberately, sometimes less consciously. But so far none
of these initiatives seems to have succeeded in throwing up a viable,
lasting alternative.

The central levers of power in Venezuela – including the office
of the presidency itself – remain institutionally located, even
'trapped', within the old administrative structures. This has been part
of Chavez' own paradox. He promotes, sometimes more sometimes
less, these revolutionary initiatives – the possible seeds of an alternative state – from his office in the Miraflores Palace, the emblematic
edifice of the old one. The central problem for the Bolivarian movement – and perhaps for most conceivable revolutionary processes in
today's world – is right here: how do you get around the existing
apparatus, when you first came to power *through* it (that is, you were
elected into office)? This is not an abstract question. As the Bolivarian project has radicalised since 2004, and pushed its aims further
leftwards, it has also become increasingly clear that a number of
those inhabiting the old edifice alongside Chavez, who helped him
move in and who arguably help to ensure he doesn't get evicted, have
absolutely no wish to move out. They are very happy with their new
home and are quietly inclined to thwart anyone who suggests it
should be torn down and replaced with a wholly different kind of
construction. This is what so many of those in the communities and
workplaces we have visited, and on the left of the Bolivarian process
call the bureaucracy, or the 'endogenous right'. Some of these occupants will be motivated by self-interest, some no doubt of dubious
legality. But some are also driven by an ideological conviction that,
at least here and now, it is simply not possible to design, much less
erect, a completely different kind of building. There are of course
many in the government who are only too aware of these difficulties.
But they too are often bound by the same institutional constraints.

In the case of Venezuela, this problem is connected to another: how
can the movement develop a real collective leadership and free itself

from the overarching dominance of one revolutionary *caudillo*, however honest and able, as Chavez himself seems to recognise it must?

The best hope for tackling both these challenges has seemed to lie in precisely those three most important recent initiatives of the revolution, which we identified above as the central pillars of a Bolivarian strategy for twenty-first-century socialism: local direct democracy or popular power, workplace co-management or workers' control, and a new socialist party built from the bottom up.

WHAT KIND OF PARTICIPATORY DEMOCRACY?

The first pillar is the extension and deepening of that 'revolutionary explosion of communal power', based on the communal councils, which Chavez identified as the fifth and most important motor of Venezuela's transition to a socialism of the twenty-first century.

This is how he described the challenge of communal power in that speech on 8 January 2007, as he swore in his new government: 'This year with the communal councils we need to go beyond the local. We need to begin to create, by law in the first instance, a kind of regional, local and national confederation of communal councils. We have to move towards the creation of a communal state. And the old bourgeois state, which is still there, still alive and kicking, we have to begin dismantling it bit by bit, as we build up the communal state, the socialist state, the Bolivarian state – a state that is capable of carrying through a revolution. Almost all states have been born to prevent revolutions. So we have quite a task: to convert a counter-revolutionary state into a revolutionary state.'

This is indeed a far-reaching vision. The Venezuelan revolutionary and former minister Roland Denis – now often a sharp critic of Chavez from the left – was surely right when he said the communal councils offered a historic opportunity to do away with the bourgeois state.

But there have been several problems with the communal councils as presently conceived that limit their potential in this direction. A couple of them we looked at in the last chapter. One is that they are not entirely autonomous. They were created and are regulated by law, a law drawn up and passed by the 'old state', even if an old state inhabited by Chavistas. A second is that the communal councils do not have sovereign decision-making power over 100 per cent of local budgets. In fact, most of them had no control over, and little if any input into, existing public budgets at municipal or state level, much less on a national scale. In this sense they hardly even began to replace, or displace, the authority of the old state structures. And they only represented a challenge to these old structures in an indirect and latent sense – in the sense that 'more money for you' might soon mean 'less money for me'.

The proposals in the failed constitutional reform, and more practically the concrete experiences developed in towns like Carora and La Victoria, suggested that there was nothing inevitable about either of these limitations, if the political will to go further was present. This raises one of the most interesting aspects of the strategic dilemma mentioned above. Some on the revolutionary left, both inside and outside Venezuela, have argued that the communal councils, like the participatory budgets before them and indeed the entire notion of participatory democracy, are inherently incapable of becoming vehicles for building a new kind of state, a new kind of 'socialist' democracy, because their conception is by definition reformist – it assumes that you can use the existing institutions to begin to build, bit by bit, a whole new set of institutions. In fact, according to this line of argument, any initiative that starts with the existing state machine will inevitably remain subordinate to it. It cannot be the start of something else. We would suggest that one of the key lessons of the Venezuelan experience so far has been that this is itself a limited and limiting notion of the difference between reform and revolution – one that any plausible project for socialism in the twenty-first century will probably have to find its way around. From such a stance, the problem cannot be reduced to where you begin. Even more important is what direction you are heading in, and how far you are prepared to go.

This is how Julio Chavez, Mayor of Carora and Torres municipality, described his view of the Bolivarian strategy: 'We don't know how long the Bolivarian revolution will take. But we don't think you can go straight from capitalism to socialism. There has to be a transition between the two, sociologically speaking. We call it state capitalism, only because the state needs to recover the capacity that neoliberalism privatised, so that we can prepare our people and begin to build on more solid foundations this communal state, which is what in the long run will provide the foundation for a socialist state.'

We may quibble about the terminology, but the need for some kind of transition seems evident. Writing in one of the earlier contributions to the strategic debate mentioned before, French Marxist writer Catherine Samary poses a criterion for judging whether or not a given experience of participatory democracy is indeed pointing in this direction or not. 'All the mistakes over the notion of participatory democracy come down to this: is it or is it not a participation that leaves intact in the long term the parliamentary forms of political domination? A participatory democracy that presents itself, not provisionally but definitively, as the means for breathing life back into parliamentary democracy, is setting itself up as a mere supplement to the soul of domination.'

Such an approach certainly does not exclude the possibility of major confrontations, struggles and ruptures along the way. In fact it probably makes them inevitable. But it does not reduce them to one great, cathartic moment, before which nothing of any real significance can be achieved. This is not so different from the so-called 'pincer' strategy developed by some on the left of the Brazilian Workers' Party back in the 1980s, when they first proposed working both from within the existing institutions (such as elected national and local bodies) and from without, in the social movements and struggles, to mobilise a combined assault on the bastions of established power. The problem in Brazil was that most of those who conceived this strategy ended up caught in the claws of one side of the pincer, the institutional side, and unable or unwilling to engage with the other.

FROM COMMUNAL POWER TO WORKPLACE POWER

Another problem with the communal councils in their initial phase was the disconnection of most of these councils from any kind of continuing economic activity, and the separation of just about all of them from the main workplaces and centres of economic production. As we noted, Galipan was an exception before its time in this respect, because there the communal council was born out of a project for endogenous economic development. This had become more common by 2008, with more and more communal councils moving beyond just building houses and repairing drains towards managing a whole range of small economic production and service activities. There was a growing convergence between the communal councils and some aspects of the 'people's economy' and co-operative production that we looked at in Chapter 2.[4] In some cases, as we saw in Carora, there were ambitious plans to extend this through the joining together of communal councils in communes and then into communal territories, with larger-scale endogenous development plans and even 'socialist enterprises' (for example food processing plants) coming under their remit. In this, Venezuela has already gone further than other experiences of participatory democracy in Latin America, where the lack of any extension into economic democracy was often recognised as a crucial weakness, even by some of its own architects.

However, this still falls some way short of introducing citizen control over the core centres of economic production and services – for example the heavy industries in Ciudad Guayana, PDVSA and the oil industry, or indeed the major banks and financial services. This points towards the second area of potential for the Bolivarian process to break out of its 'entrapment' in the old institutions: the possibility of combining and linking territorial forms of direct democracy based on communal councils with that most radical innovation to date in the area of direct democracy – the experiences of co-management and workers' control in major workplaces like the ALCASA aluminium plant. As we saw in Chapter 4, this inspiring experience had been all but abandoned by the middle of 2007. Its significance therefore remained, for the time being, mostly symbolic. The promise that its hour might return with the inclusion of 'workers' councils', as well as 'peasant councils' and 'student councils', alongside the existing communal councils, in the proposals for constitutional reform, seemed to have been dashed with the defeat in the referendum that December.

But the victory of the workers at the giant Sidor steel mill – just a kilometre or two along the banks of the Orinoco from ALCASA – on 9 April 2008, changed the climate again. After 15 months of struggle they succeeded in persuading the government to step in and renationalise the mill. Chavez had responded to their demands and over-ruled other sections of his administration, including the local state governor and the Minister of Labour, both of whom had actively opposed the co-management experience at ALCASA. Initially, there was little if any talk of workers' councils, co-management, workers' control or workplace democracy. But it was a sign that there was a new mood for addressing the role of the working class in the Venezuela's Bolivarian revolution. And within a couple of months the workers themselves had begun to relaunch the discussion about what a socialist company should look like, and how the employees could exercise democratic control within it.[5] The strategic challenge of how to combine territorial democracy with workplace democracy, community and workforce, as the dynamic forces of this Bolivarian process, was at least potentially posed again.

The need for this kind of combination had been obvious to many of those at ALCASA – and elsewhere in the Bolivarian movement – for some time.

It was increasingly clear that however radical the practice of direct democracy in the communities – however much the communal councils, the communes and other emerging bodies of communal power might be ready or able to challenge and displace the old structures of municipal and state government, even if at some point they were able to come together on a national scale to control, replace or reshape the existing institutions of federal political power – this would not be enough. It would not be enough, and it almost certainly wouldn't survive for very long, unless there was also a way of exerting control over fundamental aspects of how people had to live their lives, make a living, sustain their families, over how society as a whole produced and reproduced. In other words, socialism in the twenty-first century, as in any other century, had to find a way of exerting control over the economy and changing the relations that governed the operation of economic life. So long as it tried to survive in the shadow of an economy that was governed by an alien logic, by the hidden hand of market forces, it would be vulnerable. As likely as not, it would be torn apart, or decay from the inside out, just as so many of Venezuela's co-operatives had already done.

The question was how this could be changed.

There was resistance here from some of those most committed to radical change. I recall listening to a conversation at Sanitarios de Maracay, the bathroom factory that had been occupied under workers' control, between José Villegas, one of the occupation leaders, and Stalin Perez Borges from the UNT union confederation. Villegas said he was suspicious of the communal councils, because so many of them served particular group interests and because he thought the government might be using the communal councils to try to control or muzzle the workers' movement. For him it was the workers who should be organising the communities and not the other way round. Stalin Perez disagreed. The fact that there was corruption in many communal councils, or that governors, mayors or others might be trying to control and manipulate them, did not change the fact that they were revolutionary bodies that workers needed to get involved in and fight for. Inside the company, of course, the workers needed to push to exert their control. But, he argued, the company and all the other ten or so factories nearby were also part of the community, where the community as a whole had to exert control. And of course the workers were part of that community. Carlos Lanz and others involved in co-management had made similar arguments: for example that co-management in the nationalised industries should not just be between workers' control inside the factory and the state setting the wider parameters; it should also be co-management with the organised communities, making the factory in some way answerable to the communities through their communal councils and broader bodies.

It's impossible to say in detail how this might work. So far there have been a few voices talking about it, but to my knowledge only a handful of tentative moves in this direction: at ALCASA at its height, and at Inveval, the small valve factory outside Caracas, which was the only experience of workers' control to survive from that first wave begun in 2005.

But whatever the details, the basic point is clear. The solution can only be democracy – the radical extension of democracy into and across every area of social life – because that, in the end, is what socialism is. Looked at in this way, the question about who or what is the driving force of the Bolivarian revolution, of whether class or territory takes precedence, begins to look like a false dilemma.

A NEW PARTY AND THE QUESTION OF LEADERSHIP

Nonetheless, the difficulty of actually meeting these twin challenges is partly a result of another dilemma. That is the question of leadership or, to put it in other terms, how to develop a collective political force or will capable both of achieving a synthesis between these different demands and of generating an ideological momentum, a mystique if you like, that can resist the disintegrating, competitive pressures of the surrounding, market economy (both domestic and international). The Bolivarian revolution has a particular strength and weakness here. For, in spite of the explosion of all kinds of local mobilisation in recent years, Venezuela has no tradition either of strongly organised social movements or of mass, militant, political parties which can organise such initiatives. On the other hand, to some degree the very potent 'Chavez phenomenon' stands in for both.

This is why the call to build a new United Socialist Party (PSUV) was potentially such an important step. It might just be the best way of moving beyond the reliance on one central leader. But only on the condition that it became a genuinely open and democratic party, and not some monolithic instrument for relaying decisions that have already been taken somewhere else. This was the aim of a number of the more radical individuals, groups and currents that immediately signed up to the new party in 2007, and it seemed to correspond to the mood in at least some of the communities we have visited in the course of this book, fed up with the delays and diversions thrown up by so many officials and bureaucrats, and hungry for an effective expression of their own power and interests.

Here too, the immediate challenges were democratic. Could the new party, the PSUV, become a really big, pluralist, democratic space for organising and co-ordinating the activity of all sectors and currents of the Bolivarian movement, in the communities, in the workplaces, in the countryside, among students and intellectuals, across all the oppressed, exploited and excluded sections of Venezuelan society? It was one part of the bigger challenge: how to push for the radical extension of participatory democracy into every nook and cranny of the social edifice. How to ensure the communal councils became real centres of popular power, with sovereign decision-making power over local and regional budgets and development plans, and how to link them up regionally and nationally to build a new kind of state that defended popular interests. How to revive and extend right through the public and private sectors the exemplary experiences of workers' co-management with workers' control, begun in ALCASA and elsewhere.

Wasn't this, after all, what socialism – before, during and after the twenty-first century – was always meant to look like? An unprecedented deepening of democratic rights which, once they spread beyond the strictly political sphere and started to encroach on the unfettered rule of the market, would begin to dismantle the very logic of the capitalist economy itself. For as soon as capital ceased to be controlled by capitalists, but rather was submitted to the democratic decisions of the workforce and the community, locally and nationally, then it would cease to function as private capital and begin to obey a very different logic – that of human needs and potential, and just as urgently now, that of environmental survival. Was this what socialism in the twenty-first century might look like? Was this where Venezuela was heading?

An important part of the answer depends on something barely mentioned in this book – the wider Latin American and international situation within which the Bolivarian revolution has developed. The reason for not dealing with this is not because we minimise its importance. On the contrary, it is precisely because the international context and ramifications of the Bolivarian process are *so* important, that they would require a wholly different book to do them justice. Nonetheless, it *is* obvious, and important to underline, that this surprisingly prolonged Venezuelan experience would have been unthinkable without three potent international factors: the boom in world oil prices, the overstretch of imperial power in the Middle East, and the erosion of US hegemony in parts of Latin America. All three of these, to an extent, can be subsumed into another: the collapsing legitimacy of neoliberalism, even while neoliberal policies continue to dominate the agendas of most governments. It is also important, though less obvious, to underline that any future for the revolutionary process in Venezuela, and especially any future for its promise of a new kind of socialism, will depend in some measure on these external factors too. In particular, it will depend on how far the winds of change continue to blow across Bolivia, Ecuador, Paraguay and other parts of the region.

The immediate and critical questions, however, remain specific to Venezuela's own experience. Will co-management and workers' control make a return? Will the communal councils and the new party assert their autonomy and push towards a radical extension of democracy, or will they fall back into some kind of subordination to existing powers? At the time of writing, in mid-2008, there were contradictory signs. There were forces pulling both ways. Sometimes the pull seemed to be stronger in one direction, sometimes in the other. It looked as if it could go either way.

NOTES

INTRODUCTION

1. The semi-military vocabulary of the Bolivarian movement has also deployed 'electoral battle units', 'patrols' and 'commands', 'operations', 'platoons' and more recently 'battalions' as the basic branch unit of its new party, the Venezuelan United Socialist Party

2. The Recall Referendum was the last of three major attempts by Venezuela's traditional establishment to get rid of President Chavez – with both overt and covert encouragement from the US administration in Washington. See below in this chapter for more details.

3. *Vuelvan Caras*, meaning 'about turn', was another semi-military phrase taken from Venezuela's nineteenth-century independence wars, where after a series of defeats the independence forces were called upon to turn around, face and defeat their enemies. Launched earlier in 2004, the Vuelvan Caras Mission was intended to turn around and fight unemployment, by providing skills training and support in setting up co-operatives to some 360,000 *lanceros* (from the mestizo lancers of the independence wars) in its first year. Many of the trainees were graduates of the Robinson and Ribas educational missions – see Chapter 1.

4. Twenty-six months later, as President Chavez faced re-election, there was little sign that anyone had seriously tried to implement this particular proposal for people's power. But in a different format, the same idea was to become one of the central objectives of his second full term, beginning in January 2007, when he promised 'an explosion of communal power' to replace what he now explicitly called 'the bourgeois state'. We shall return to this in Chapter 5.

5. This is the case, I would argue, in Chapter 4, with Carlos Lanz, the former guerrilla leader appointed by Chavez to oversee the introduction of co-management at the ALCASA aluminium plant – and who has become one of the most thoughtful theorists of Venezuela's revolution – as well as with Julio Chavez, the community activist who became arguably Venezuela's most revolutionary mayor in the town of Carora, who appears in Chapter 5.

6. See for example the debates between Daniel Bensaid, Antoine Artous and

Alex Callinicos in the pages of *Critique Communiste*, especially No. 179, and *International Socialism*.

7. Michael A. Lebowitz, *Build It Now: Socialism for the Twenty-First Century*, New York: Monthly Review Press, 2006.

1. OIL FOR FOOD, HEALTH, EDUCATION ...

1. In April 2008 the price of the Venezuelan basket of crude hit US$100 pb – three times as much again.

2. The Missions – seven of them initially – were social programmes launched in the course of 2003 as Venezuela's public finances began to recover after the defeat of the opposition-led oil industry shutdown at the beginning of that year. The most important were in health, Mission Barrio Adentro, and education, Missions Robinson, Ribas and Sucre. At least at the beginning, they were financed directly from Venezuela's oil income and administered by ad hoc presidential commissions, often led by military officers, operating outside the traditional health and education ministries, in an attempt to circumvent bureaucratic inertia and indifference.

3. Both the method and the teaching aids for Mission Robinson were another Cuban contribution.

4. General Marcos Fernández Fernández, Secretary of the Presidential Commission for Literacy, speech in Teresa Carreno Theatre on 1 October 2004 at the Award Ceremony for the Seventh Graduation of Mission Robinson I.

5. Greg Wilpert, 'Mission Impossible? Venezuela's Mission to Fight Poverty', Venezuelanalysis.com, 11 November 2003.

6. This is the way Venezuela's ranking in world oil production is usually described. However, the exact figures for Venezuelan oil production and its reserves are a hotly contested political issue, with the state oil company PDVSA, opposition sources and international oil industry bodies all deploying different figures and disputing each other's.

7. See Timeline.

8. Most of the information that follows comes from the oral testimony of a group of community activists in the El Manguito neighbourhood of Carapita: Sofia Lashley from the Calle San José sector; Avelino Montilla, from La Chinita sector; Antonio Briceno, from the Fatima sector; and Benjamin Marquez.

9. In Chapter 5 we shall return to this particular difference when we look at the forms of direct democracy and popular power developing within the Venezuelan process. For example, it is arguably the absence of such structures, as well as the absence of a party like the PT in its early years, that has made it so much more difficult to develop forms of participatory budgeting and other direct community control over the body politic.

10. These comparisons may seem tendentious to some. After all, Venezuela's

urban poor certainly were at the forefront of most of the major political confrontations in the country's recent history, from the Caracazo revolt of February 1989 to the popular uprising that defeated the April 2002 coup against President Chavez – events on at least a par of political importance with many of those others mentioned. But my point is slightly different: that the urban movement in Venezuela, at its strongest, has been much more localised and fragmented than the others mentioned. Its repeated eruptions onto the national political stage have not been the deliberate interventions of one, or even several, structured social movements. Either they have been largely spontaneous, or they have responded to the very peculiar relationship that exists between such a mass of local activism and the charismatic, personalised leadership of Hugo Chavez. There has been little or no mediation by either social movements or political party structures in between.

11. Again we shall return to this in Chapter 5 when we look at some of the difficulties confronting the development of Communal Councils and other forms of popular power.

12. Ronco is a popular pasta brand in Venezuela. It is owned by US grain multinational, Cargill.

13. Venezuela's traditional trade union movement was led by the CTV (Confederación de Trabajadores de Venezuela). This accompanied AD in becoming increasingly a pillar of the establishment. It played a leading part in the early years of opposition to Chavez, but almost completely disintegrated after supporting the failed lockout of 2002–03.

14. These figures are not based on any reliable, systematic study, but on the subjective observations of some of those living and working in the *barrios* – for example the breakdown given to me by one Cuban doctor of the economic situation of his patients in Mission Barrio Adentro.

15. Although the CEBs were never so widespread or well implanted in Venezuela as in some other countries of Latin America.

16. Other forms of organisation came and went in the *barrios*, with more or less impact – more in the case of the Electoral Battle Units (UBEs) of 2004, less in the case of the Bolivarian Circles a couple of years earlier – but these tended to be ephemeral initiatives, usually promoted by the Bolivarian leadership around the priorities of a particular conjuncture. None were rooted in the same way as the CTUs.

17. The new law in 2006 increased this to 'up to 400 homes'. In fact, according to figures for 2006 from the National Urban Land Office, the national average size of a CTU was 147 homes or 220.5 families, based on the calculation that each plot housed on average 1.5 families. In the vast Caracas neighbourhood of Petare, for example, many of the dwellings are on three levels, with a different family living on each level.

18. Libertador Municipality is the largest in Caracas, accounting for about half the city and most of the poor neighbourhoods.

19. In Chapter 3 we shall look at similar problems over the mechanisms for 'expropriation' that have confronted Venezuela's agrarian land reform. But the far tinier sizes of the land involved means that the problems for urban land reform are all the greater.

20. Neither Chavez nor any other senior government figure seems to have ever addressed this issue directly, except to make rather vague references to the slowness of the legislative process. Some more radical voices have specifically identified the National Assembly with the 'bureaucracy' or the institutions of the 'bourgeois state' that block the advance of the Bolivarian process, but these voices generally come from the outer edges of the Bolivarian movement and few even of these question the legislative process itself.

21. We shall return to this early experiment in bypassing established state machinery in Chapter 5.

2. THE PEOPLE'S ECONOMY

1. 'Intervenciones del Presidente de la República, Hugo Chávez Friás, Taller de Alto Nivel "El nuevo mapa estratégico", 12 y 13 de Noviembre de 2004', pp.18, 32; text edited by Marta Harnecker and published by the Ministerio de Comunicación y Información, Caracas.

2. See Introduction

3. 'Lineas Generales del Plan de Desarrollo Económico y Social de la Nación 2001–2007', Ministry for Planning and Development, Caracas, September 2001.

4. Super-heavy crude is a non-conventional oil, once classified as bitumen, and not internationally recognised when calculating a country's oil reserves. However, Venezuela claims its vast store of this super-heavy crude in the Orinoco Belt gives it the world's largest oil reserves. For some years it has been using modern refining techniques, in association with several transnational oil companies, to extract high-grade fuel from this super-heavy crude, mainly at the José refinery complex. In mid-2007 the Venezuelan government obliged these foreign companies to enter into new contracts that gave the Venezuelan state oil company PDVSA majority control. This so-called nationalisation led to a protracted legal battle with Exxon Mobil, which was one of two international majors that refused to agree the new terms..

5. This in turn raises another, vital question, which we shall return to in Chapter 4: 'Who controls PDVSA, how, and for what?'

6. This is a huge simplification, but seems to capture the main drift of what have been multiple and complex, overlapping discussions.

7. This debate is not only about profit margins and bottom lines. It is also about the quality of the product and whether anyone wants it. One journalist colleague, who was not unsympathetic, put his finger on the issue when interviewing one

of the officials at Fabricio Ojeda. As the man was describing with enthusiasm the workings and achievements of the textile co-operative, my colleague noticed he was wearing an Yves Lacoste polo shirt. He asked him when and if he would be happy to swap this shirt for one produced at Fabricio Ojeda. Not surprisingly, the man seemed nonplussed.

8. See, for example, Henri Maler, *Les Figures de l'Appropriation Sociale chez Marx*, and Jacques Texier, *Le Question de l'Appropriation Sociale*, both in Les Cahiers de Critique Communiste, Paris 2003.

9. This debate spread over a series of texts and seminars from 1997 to 2000, including Paul Singer, 'Mercado e cooperação: um caminho para o socialismo' in *Teoria e Debate*, No. 35, 1997; Paul Singer, *Uma Utopia Militante. Repensando o Socialismo*. Petrópolis, Editora Vozes, 1998; João Machado Borges Neto, *Co-operativas e Socialismo*, 1999

10. That is, based on the theories and policies promoted by CEPAL, the UN's Economic Commission on Latin America, based in Chile, from the 1950s onwards. See the mention earlier in this chapter of Osvaldo Sunkel and endogenous development.

3. WAR ON THE *LATIFUNDIOS*

1. For two decades or more the Brazilian MST (Movimento dos Sem Terra) has been an icon for social movements around Latin America and beyond. Its combination of militant struggle for land with sophisticated schemes of alternative production and a broader political platform have made it much more than just a peasant movement. It quickly became one of the biggest and most resilient social movements in the continent, the key initiator of a new worldwide peasant movement, Via Campesina, and one of the linchpins of the World Social Forums that first developed in the MST's home state of Rio Grande do Sul. It is noteworthy that after providing inspiration to many on the international left for a number of years, especially to currents of a libertarian or more or less anarchist persuasion, the MST became something of a reference point for Venezuela's President Chavez (who is anything but an anarchist), mainly after his visit to the Third World Social Forum in Porto Alegre in January 2003.

2. It may come as a surprise to hear a woman like Maria Herrera use language like this, especially to many of us in the Anglo-Saxon world, where there is a cultivated aversion to anything that sounds like intellectual terminology. But anyone who has spent much time with the grassroots activists of Latin America's social movements will tell you how easy it is to find men and women with little or no formal education who have taught themselves to speak at length and often in highly abstract or conceptual language about the economic, social and political issues that concern them.

3. Hugo Chavez has referred to Mariátegui on a number of occasions in his reflections on socialism of the twenty-first century. One of his favourite references cites the Peruvian – who had learnt much of his Marxism in the Italy of Antonio Gramsci – on the need for socialism in Latin America to be an original creation and not a copy of some imported model. See, for example, Chavez' speech to the World Student and Youth Festival, ABN, 14 August 2005.

4. Very approximately, these three views of land reform correspond to the traditional approach of Latin American communist parties, to the scheme of orthodox Trotskyism, and in somewhat different ways to the strategies of both Maoist and Guevarist guerrilla movements. In practice they often overlapped or deliberately combined.

5. Some of the peasants' stories about the English company – 'Lord Beefsteak' was how they referred to Lord Vestey – were exaggerated myths. But they were myths that made some sense. They had obviously heard that some of the Vesteys were close friends of the British royal family, and from there they became 'cousins' of the Queen. Some believed that the farm had really belonged to the Queen herself and that the Vesteys were just providing a public cover for the monarch. More common was the belief that all the meat from El Charcote went to be cooked at Buckingham Palace for the royal table, whereas Agroflora, like all beef producers in Venezuela, was forbidden from exporting any meat because the country has endemic foot and mouth. But the point of this particular myth was probably that the meat might as well have gone to Buckingham Palace, because they were sure they and the local community never saw any of it.

6. Ezequiel Zamora was a Venezuelan agrarian leader of the nineteenth century who was shot dead in Cojedes in 1860. On 9 December 2004, Governor Yánez Rangel, following a lead suggested by President Chavez at his strategy meeting in November, issued a decree for the 'intervention' of 16 large farms in Cojedes state so as to 'establish order' in the countryside 'while respecting private property and the law'. The 16 estates were to be investigated to see whether the land was idle, if it should be regarded as *latifundio* in the terms of the law, or if its title was in dispute. El Charcote was the first on the list.

7. INTI is the only body legally charged with ruling on these matters, before they go to the courts.

8. The original land reform law in 2001 defined a *latifundio* as anything over 5,000 hectares of low-quality land, and less for several classes of better-quality land. This was reformed early in 2005 to give the Land Institute, INTI, more flexibility in setting the limits. INTI reduced the threshold of low-quality land to 3,000 hectares. See Greg Wilpert, 'Land for People not for Profit in Venezuela', *Venezuelanalysis.com*, 23 August 2005.

9. These procedures are similar to those relating to other expropriations which, as we saw in Chapter 1, have rendered all but impossible the regularisation of urban land titles in areas claimed to be 'private' land.

10. According to Reuters, 23 March 2006, Agroflora's lawyers said they'd had sharply varying valuations of El Charcote at US$6.9 and 21 million, which would suggest the government 'bought' the improvements made to the land for around 20–60 per cent of the ranch's market value.

11. This is a very rough estimate, because in the second category INTI's figures do not indicate how many of the title deeds went to co-ops and how many to individual families, nor the average size of the co-ops involved. It should also be noted that a significant number of land reform beneficiaries have come from the towns and cities, so would not themselves count as part of the rural population.

12. See *Ultimas Noticias* newspaper, 12 December 2006.

13. See the account of *Aló Presidente*, September 2004, at Tacagua Vieja in the Introduction.

14. Venezuela's full membership of the South American common market, Mercosur, dominated by set up by Brazil, Argentina, Uruguay and Paraguay, saw its ratification temporarily blocked in the Brazilian senate in 2007.

15. There are a variety of mainly indigenous names for essentially the same practice where communities come together, sometimes on fixed days or for fixed periods, to pool their labour on some collective, community work. The same names and principles have been reproduced by many social movements around the region, even in countries where little indigenous influence remains.

4. DEMOCRACY AT WORK

1. This is a perplexing issue which will come up repeatedly in this chapter. Throughout 2007 and into 2008, a series of sharp conflicts developed between the new Minster of Labour, José Ramon Rivera, along with the trade union current close to him (FSBT), and the most combative sections of the Venezuelan workers' movement, including all the other currents that made up the new trade union confederation, the UNT. Curiously, when he was sworn in by President Chavez in January 2007, Rivera presented himself as a 'Trotskyist', and indeed he had been a member years before of the old Trotskyist PST (Socialist Workers Party), aligned with the largest Latin American Trotskyist current of the Argentinean MAS. But they include many of his former comrades, accused him of adopting policies in defence of the state bureaucracy and the private employers, including systematic opposition to co-management and workers' control. As we shall see, these differences go back to at least 2005 and the disputes over co-management at the ALCASA aluminium plant in Guayana state.

2. This is a branch of the Brangers, a prominent landowning family, two of whose ranches in Cojedes state were 'intervened' by the government at the same time as the Vestey family's El Carcote (see Chapter 3).

3. The National Workers Union (UNT) was formed in 2003 after the employers' lockout to replace the old CTV, whose leaders had sided with the opposition to Chavez. It brought together almost all the trade union sectors that identified in one way or another with the Bolivarian process and quickly displaced the discredited CTV. However, problems soon emerged between its six different currents and the UNT spent most of the next few years divided and unable to hold democratic elections for a national leadership.

4. Excluding the oil industry, the two main areas for Venezuela's limited industrial base are Ciudad Guayana, in the southeast, for heavy industry, and the adjoining states of Carabobo and Aragua, in the centre-west, for manufacturing and light industry.

5. Throughout the first half of 2005, and in parallel with the beginnings of a discussion about socialism in the twenty-first century, President Chavez promoted the idea of a new military reserve up to 2 million strong, to be formed in communities and workplaces across the country, and outside the existing military command structure. Groups did begin some basic training in many places, but this never developed in the form or on the scale that was first envisaged, and in the end it became absorbed into a conventional if somewhat augmented army reserve. To my knowledge the full story of this has never been told. There were indications that part of the Venezuelan military hierarchy was alarmed by the idea and may have quietly made sure it never went anywhere.

6. Detailed accounts of the obstacles put in the way of the workers at Sanitarios, and of their efforts to build local, national and international support, can be found in a series of articles in English at venezuelanalysis.com (e.g. http://www.venezuelanalysis.com/news/2365; http://www.venezuelanalysis. com/analysis/2523; http://www.venezuelanalysis.com/news/2149; http:// www.venezuelanalysis.com/analysis/2555), and in Spanish at aporrea.org (e.g. www.aporrea.org/trabajadores/a28283; www.aporrea.org/trabajad ores/n89867; www.aporrea.org/endogeno/n90208; www.aporrea. org/traba jadores/n93755; www.aporrea.org/trabajadores/n95349; www.aporrea. org/poderpopular/n99473).

7. Carlos Lanz became a legendary figure of Venezuela's revolutionary left after he led the kidnapping of a US businessman, William Niehous, from his Caracas home in February 1976. Lanz's guerrilla group held Niehous in a number of remote locations for 40 months until he was freed in June 1979. That same year Lanz was jailed for seven years for his part in the kidnapping.

8. For reasons we shall see later, this spike in production for March 2005 was not sustained. Over the rest of the year, production levels were no more than stabilised. Many proponents of co-management later argued that this in itself was a major achievement, given the level of technical, financial and political problems faced by ALCASA. But the truth is, by the time Carlos Lanz left in August 2007, ALCASA was again fighting for its economic survival.

9. Michael Lebowitz makes this comparison in *Build it Now: Socialism for the Twenty-first Century*, New York, 2006, chapter 6, pp.73–84. For a detailed account of co-management in Yugoslavia, see Catherine Samary, *Le Marché Contre L'Autogestion: L'Expérience Yougoslave*, Paris, 1988; *Market, Plan and Democracy: The Experience of the So-Called Socialist Countries*, IIRE, Amsterdam; *The Fragmentation of Yugoslavia*, IIRE, Amsterdam.

10. We shall look more closely at this tradition in Chapter 5.

11. One of these figures was José Ramon Rivero, from Venalum, who later replaced Maria Cristina Iglesias as Minister of Labour, in January 2007, and whose controversial role in relation to the Sanitarios occupation we have already mentioned.

12. Most famously, this was associated with the adult literacy work of the Brazilian Paulo Freire from the 1960s onwards. Carlos Lanz and his collaborators had themselves in earlier years developed a version of popular education they called INVEDECOR – for 'Investigate, educate, communicate, organise'.

13. See Chapter 5 on communal councils and they way they tie into such economic development projects.

14. See Chapter 2.

15. A common term in Cuba for the dissident community base in Miami.

16. See Chapter 5.

17. See *Los Desafíos de la Co-gestión, las experiencias de Cadafe y Cadela*, Marta Harnecker, Colección Testimonios, Caracas, April 2005, which reproduces a number of interviews by herself and her co-researchers, Michael Lebowitz, Luis Bonilla, etc. Also texts by union leader in Cadafe Joaquin Osorio at aporrea.com.

18. The divisions within the trade union movement in Guayana, this bastion of Venezuela's heavy industry, are even more confusing than elsewhere in the country. For a detailed analysis of these union election results, with an explanation of currents involved, see Hermann Albrecht, *Aporrea*, 4 February 2006.

19. The Bolivarian Workers' Force (FBT), later the Socialist Bolivarian Workers' Force (FSBT), has been the trade union current presenting itself as most unconditionally supportive of President Chavez. However, it has generally opposed the kind of co-management described in this chapter, especially in 'strategic' industries. It has also proved the least inclined to build the UNT as a unitary confederation, leading to its move in early 2008 to create a new union confederation. Its critics in the other currents accused it of having limited support among rank and file trade unionists and relying on its links with government to maintain its positions in the leadership of a number of union federations.

20. This is the conclusion of Hermann Albrecht in his very thorough analysis mentioned above.

21. He is referring to the structures of patronage and graft that developed during the

decades of government by the two main traditional parties, AD (Democratic Action) and COPEI (Christian Democratic Party).

22. In 2005 there was a Draft Law on Co-management circulating. Chavez referred to it in his May Day speech. But it was a confused and hybrid proposal, including many aspects closer to the 'capitalist' co-management of post-war West Germany than the 'revolutionary' co-management explored in ALCASA. In the end the draft law satisfied nobody and quietly disappeared.

23. Sidor, one of the largest steel mills in Latin America, was privatised in 1997. Sixty per cent of its shares were then controlled by the Ternium consortium, which in turn was controlled by the Italian-Argentinean company Techint (with close ties to the Kirchner presidential family), but there were also minority stakes for Brazil's Usiminas and some Mexican and Venezuelan private capital. A 20 per cent share remained with the Venezuelan state, while the last 20 per cent of shares were distributed among the workforce. This form of workers' participation did not stop Ternium from slashing Sidor's workforce. From around 15,000 at the time of privatisation, this fell to just 4,500 full-time workers, plus 2,500 white-collar employees, plus up to 9,000 occasional contract workers, in April 2008. That's when Chavez renationalised Sidor (see note 30 below).

24. *Copeyanos* are adherents of COPEI, one of Venezuela's two traditional parties.

25. This is apparently a reference to Orlando Borrego, who fought under Che Guevara in the Cuban revolution and worked with him in his subsequent ministerial posts. He later studied economics himself, became an adviser to the Cuban government and wrote a biography of Che that concentrated on his economic theories and the economic debates in Cuba in the 1960s. It was to Borrego that Che sent from Prague, shortly before his final journey to Bolivia, his comments on the Soviet Academy of Science's *Manual of Political Economy*, a critical text that remained unpublished until 2006. However, his interpretation of Che has been questioned by some who argue that he plays down Che's differences with soviet orthodoxy (see e.g. 'Revolución socialista o caricatura de revolución' Mercedes Petit, http://www.aporrea.org, 04 October 2007).

26. General Francisco Rangel Gomez, elected as the pro-Chavez Governor of Bolivar state in 2004, was a former president of the CVG who had come close to deserting Chavez during the April 2002 coup, calling for dialogue with the opposition at the height of the conflict and reassurance for foreign investors. He pulled back as the coup unravelled.

27. Orlando Borrego, *Rumbo al socialismo*, Venezuela, MRE, 2006, quoted and analysed in Luis Vargas, *La Propiedad Social*, Aporrea, 26 October 2006.

28. See box below.

29. Adolfo Gilly, 'Los Consejos de Fabrica: Argentina, Bolivia, Italia', in *Coyoacan No 2. 5*, México, October–December 1978.

30. 'For the time being', or '*por ahora*', is the phrase Chavez famously used in the

brief television address he was allowed in exchange for recognising the defeat of his attempted coup in 1992. It came to symbolise the popular belief that neither Chavez nor his Bolivarian project were finished, that their hour would come. After a long silence on workers' issues, a series of new nationalisations announced in March and April 2008, and a return to repeated references in his speeches to the role of workers in the Bolivarian revolution, suggested these might be back on President Chavez' agenda. By far the most important move came in the early hours of 9 April, when, after final fruitless negotiations with the company, Vice-President Ramón Carrizales announced the president's decision to renationalise the Sidor steel mill in Puerto Ordaz. By taking this action, Chavez was not only responding to a long and militant struggle by the Sidor workforce but directly over-ruling his Minister of Labour, José Ramón Rivera, and the Governor of Bolivar sate, Francisco Rangel Gomez, both of whom had defended the position of the Argentinean company. A few days later, Chavez sacked Rivera as minister. There was, however, no mention from the government of any imme-diate plans for co-management in Sidor.

5. WHO'S IN CHARGE HERE? FROM LOCAL DEMOCRACY TO COMMUNAL POWER

1. Some of the provisions in the Constitutional Reform, the reform of Article 16 for example, indicated that the 'communities', expressed through their communal councils and joining together in 'communes', would actually take precedence and become 'the basic and indivisible unit of the Venezuelan Socialist State'. However, as we shall see, the exact relationship between these and the existing municipal and regional governments remained ambiguous.
2. This is the organisational structure laid out in the April 2006 Law on Commu-nal Councils. The original communal council in Galipan, like other pioneers in this area, preceded the law and developed in a more ad hoc form.
3. See Chapter 2, Note 1. These were numbers three and four of the ten objec-tives identified in the new strategy. As we shall see, much emphasis was placed at this high-level workshop on Brazilian-style participatory budgets.
4. Chavez' speech on 8 January 2007 as he swore in his new government. We shall come back to this vision in the Conclusion.
5. This figure is slightly different from those outlined in the written project Hernan and Andres gave me at that time, which projects 125 direct permanent jobs, 495 indirect permanent jobs and 350 seasonal jobs for three months each year. The reality, as we shall see, fell some way short of both.
6. Romulo Betancourt was the first AD President of Venezuela from 1959 to 1964 and one of the architects of the pact for civilian government, known as the Pacto Punto Fijo, which dominated the country's politics in the second half of the twentieth century and grew increasingly corrupt. Carlos Andres

Perez was president from 1974 to 1979 and 1989 to 1994. His second term was dominated from the start by a draconian IMF-inspired programme of structural adjustment that sparked the *Caracazo* uprising of February 1989 and a failed coup attempt led by a colonel in the parachute regiment, Hugo Chavez Frias. See the Timeline for more details.

7. FIDES, the Intergovernmental Fund for Decentralisation, was set up a decade earlier, but has been adapted by the Chavez administration to support a variety of community organisations, including more recently the communal councils.

8. As mentioned before, this claim may or may not be true, but the communal council in Galipan was certainly one of the first.

9. See Notes 3, 11 and 12 of this chapter, plus the section following Note 12 comparing Venezuela's CLPPs with the Porto Alegre participatory budget. See also the part of the Conclusion dealing with direct democracy based on territorial divisions and the challenge of exerting popular control over production.

10. Article 62 says: 'The participation of the people in the formulation, execution and control of public administration is the means required for them to establish their role as protagonists and guarantee their full development, both as individuals and collectively.'

11. For a detailed account of this see *The Porto Alegre Alternative: Direct Democracy in Action*, ed. Iain Bruce, Pluto Press, London, 2004.

12. This should not be seen as an idealisation of the Brazilian participatory budgets. Many of them were far from radical and not especially participatory. Some suffered from limitations similar to those of the Venezuelan CLPP proposal. Even the most radical in conception, like that in Porto Alegre, failed in important ways to live up to their own aspirations and eventually ran out of steam.

13. Venezuela's municipalities have traditionally been divided into anything between 4–5 and 40 plus parishes.

14. This leaves open, of course, the extent to which this participation of the Brazilian Workers' Party in the institutions of local government over a prolonged period, outside of any broader revolutionary mobilization, ended up blunting its radical edge and reshaping it into another party of the existing order.

15. If 28,000 councils were really functioning according to the law (at least 200 families in urban areas and at least 20 in rural areas, etc.), the arithmetic would suggest that at least 5.06 million families (comprising 25.3 million people, or some 90 per cent of the Venezuelan population) were 'organised' in communal councils.

16. These had been run as 'strategic associations' between a number of international oil companies and the Venezuelan state oil company, PDVSA, with the latter as a minority partner. The so-called 'nationalisation' of 2007 – which was agreed by most but led to a high-profile clash with Exxon Mobil –

involved obliging these international partners to renegotiate contracts that gave PDVSA a majority stake of at least 60 per cent. This was similar to what the Venezuelan government had done in 2005, obliging partners in its 'operating agreements' to 'migrate' to new contracts giving PDVSA majority control.

17. When I returned six months later, after the referendum defeat, they told me the numbers had increased to 120 or more a week, 'because people can see the results'.

18. These funds take various forms, but are in general a result of Venezuela's oil revenues rising to some three times the amount predicted in the 2008 national budget.

19. For the former, see Margarita Lopez Maya, '*Communal Councils: Let's Learn from Ourselves and Others*', in *Aporrea*, 4 February 2007: 'According to the law, the councils depend for everything on central government. That is where they get registered and that is where at different levels the resources they get are reviewed and approved. In effect, it is the president who decides who gets the money. How much bargaining power can a group of 400 poor families have with central government? To be empowering, participation must be from the bottom up. The way the law is conceived, it is the other way round. It encourages dependence on the President and could easily lead to clientelism. Today I finance you, tomorrow you vote for me.'

   For the latter, see the Manifesto of the 1st National Meeting of Communal Councils, called on 23–24 February 2007 by the Frente Comunal Simon Bolivar (an initiative launched by the Ezequiel Zamora National Peasant Front, FNCEZ, which we met in Chapter 3), which includes the following paragraph: 'We agree with President Hugo Chavez that for the first time in the entire history of the republic real power is being put into the hands of the people through the explosion of communal power. At the same time, we warn against the dangerous tendency to treat the communal councils as mere planners and executors of public works, neutralising their real potential as the builders of a new society and a new communal state.' http://www.aporrea.org/poderpopular/a31946.html, 15 March 2007.

20. Both the principles and detailed mechanisms of Carora's participatory budget were strikingly similar to those of Porto Alegre at its best, although both Mayor Julio Chavez and Zoila Vasquez, one of his key aides for the participatory budget, told me they had read about Porto Alegre but received no direct influence.

21. When I returned in 2008 they told me things had calmed down. The woman, Yolanda, was still in the house, they'd managed to find her a job so she could pay some rent, she was on the list to receive one of the next lot of houses and the owner had agreed to wait until then.

22. See Timeline.

23. Patria Para Todos (PPT) was the part of the old Causa R – the main party of

the Venezuelan left in the 1990s – that supported Chavez. The other part, which kept the name Causa R, joined the opposition to Chavez.

24. In his speech at the rally to mark the sixth anniversary of the defeat of the April 2002 coup.

25. The average price for the basket of Venezuelan crude was then at about US$90 a barrel.

26. Most agree that the local government structure in the Venezuelan capital is a complicated mess, with overlapping jurisdictions of a metropolitan mayor and several municipal mayors, some of whom come under the regional government of Miranda state but the most important of which – Libertador, accounting for more than half of the metropolis – is independent of any state administration.

27. I heard many accusations that these food shortages were part of a deliberate campaign by the private sector to undermine the referendum on constitutional reform. If they were, they were probably one of the most effective instruments of that campaign, as the discontent generated undoubtedly played a part in the referendum defeat. However, naked self-interest may have been reason enough for the private suppliers to refuse to sell at regulated prices and prefer to hoard their stock or divert it for export to Colombia, etc.

28. I called her later – it was a boy, his name was Jeffery, he weighed seven and three-quarter pounds and both were blooming.

29. Mercal was targeted mainly at low-income groups and sold its products at 30 per cent of the full regulated price.

CONCLUSION: MAKING SOCIALISM IN THE TWENTY-FIRST CENTURY

1. There had of course been currents of socialist thought and organisation that were radically opposed to both these variants of twentieth-century socialism. Usually their opposition was in the name of some or other version of 'socialist democracy'. But after the first quarter of the twentieth century, these had been marginalised, often violently. The Bolivarian project seemed to hold out the possibility of some reconvergence with these critical strands, which is partly why Chavez' repeated if somewhat eclectic references to Leon Trotsky, Rosa Luxemburg and Antonio Gramsci, all names associated with these alternative conceptions, sounded like music to the ears of many of his listeners.

2. John Rees made this argument in *Internationalist Socialist Journal* and his later book, *Imperialism...* Hugo Chavez' own abundant jibes and railings against the 'empire' and its leading inhabitants, 'the devil', 'Mr Danger', 'Condolences Rice', etc. are much closer to this view than the post-Marxist versions that were fashionable a few years ago.

3. Michael A, Lebowitz's excellent analysis of the Bolivarian revolution in the

final chapter of his *Build it Now: Socialism for the Twenty-first Century*, identifies this humanist imperative in the 2000 Constitution and rightly points to it as the starting point for any credible socialist project. However, in our view he slightly exaggerates the positive aspects of this Constitution and underplays its limited and limiting aspects.

4. It should be noted, however, that co-operatives as a whole were not seen to be doing very well. Early in 2008, one of the government's own estimates indicated that only about 2 per cent of the 80,000 odd co-operatives were functioning well. This figure may be based on questionable criteria for 'doing well'. Foe example, what of the thousands of communal banks set up as co-operatives to receive and manage the resources going to the communal councils? But either way the mixed record of the co-operatives certainly had something to do with the extraordinary explosion in the number of co-ops registered. Many of the smaller ones were not much more than wishful thinking, and many of the larger ones were no more than traditional capitalist subcontractors going under a new name.

5. It is worth noting that one or two of the workers who had done most to develop the co-management experience at ALCASA, like Elio Sayago whom we met in Chapter 4, later played a leading part in the struggle for renationalisation at SIdor and the subsequent discussions on workplace democracy there.

Index

(The interviewees who contributed so much to this book are shown in italic font.)

Accion Democratica (AD), 28, 29, 144, 147, 196n13, 203n21, 204n6
adeco support, 28, 32, 125, 130, 144, 147
Agroflora *see* Vestey
Albarran, Antonio, 80, 81
ALCASA, 103–138
achievements and prospects, 111, 132–4
co-management, 11–12, 111–14, 141–2, 188, 189, 190, 192, 200n1, 201n8, 203n22, 208n5
co-management, decline of, 119–26, 133, 201n8
communal councils, 121
co-operatives, 108, 117, 118–19, 120, 121
days of hope, 103–4
democratic system, 112–13
division of labour, 109–11
experts, 108–9, 113
importance of, 103–4
legal/administrative anomalies, 126–32
participatory budget, 103, 114–15, 133
relations with other companies, 115–19, 122–4
underinvestment, 105

unions, 108, 113, 116, 119, 120, 129, 133
unions' rightward turn, 120, 122, 124–6
uniqueness, 134–8
works committees, 107–9, 112, 113, 190
see also Lanz, Carlos
Aló Presidente, 7–9, 42, 48, 55, 102
alternative media, 14, 29
community radio, 45, 95
community TV, 64
Vive TV, 64, 68, 69, 94
Amaro, Leonza, 54, 55, 56
Arias, Henry, 124–5
Arevalo, Angel, 121
army in civil projects, 43
Avilés, Teófilo, 173

barrios, 33, 37, 43, 160, 172–5
and 2002 coup, 22, 156
assumed temporary, 30
empowerment of poor, 22, 25, 29, 32–3, 36, 156
land ownership, 23, 30–3
urban explosion, 30
see also Caracas, Carapita, urban land committees
Bauxilium, 117
Bella Vista, 94–7

Belmont, Yanira, 54–5, 57
Berlin wall, 15, 181
Betancourt, President Romulo, 24, 66, 133, 144, 204n6
Betancourt, Ramon, 133
Blair, Tony, 2, 180
Blanco, Alvaro, 40
Bolivar, Simon, 4, 74, 143
Bolivar state, 23, 137, 203n26
Bolivarian revolution, 11, 21–2, 29, 35, 40, 52, 97, 103, 130, 137, 142, 157, 158, 162, 171, 178, 179, 185, 190, 192, 194n1, 196n16, 201n3, 207n1
challenge to neoliberalism, 3, 4, 5, 11, 38, 46, 170, 179–80, 183
central elements, 12, 27, 29–30, 37, 38, 141, 153, 160, 177, 185
changing focus, 2, 6, 7, 10, 63, 72, 155–6, 170, 178, 184, 186, 189
and Chavez, 22–3
Constitution, 10, 33, 110, 137, 155, 164, 176
divisions within, 125, 129–30, 131, 138, 158, 169–70, 171

interpretations of, 13–14, 26, 38, 61–2
and land/company ownership reform, 20, 33, 67, 72, 75, 81–2, 101–2, 166, 178
and oil industry, 19, 26, 117
phases of, 62, 63
and self-organisation/ organised communities, 30, 32, 40–1, 46, 59, 98, 123, 127, 140, 172, 179
and socialist revolution, 4–5, 12
tension/contradictions within, 8, 33, 35, 52, 75, 90, 125, 127, 129, 138, 141, 147, 158, 170, 179–83, 184, 188, 191, 197n20
violent resistance to, 90
see also co-management, constitutional reform, endogenous development
Bolivarian Workers' Force (FBT/FSBT), 125, 131, 200n1, 202n19
Brazil, 2, 26, 61, 159, 182
exports to Venezuela, 83, 92, 93
land law/reform, 34, 67
participatory budgets, 103, 154, 156, 157, 158, 204n3, 205n12
see also Brazilian Workers' Party, Landless Workers' Movement
Brazilan Landless Movement *see* Landless Workers' Movement
Brazilian Workers' Party (PT), 1, 4, 26, 60, 158, 187, 195n9, 205n14

Briceno, Antonia, 25–6, 195n8
bureaucracy/official discouragement, 43–4, 51, 72, 86, 89, 90, 93, 103, 122, 131–2, 145, 146, 147, 158, 159, 184
lack of co-ordination of different bodies, 75

Cabimas, 48–52
co-operatives, 50, 51
Cadafe, 123, 124
Caigua, 51–2
Caldera, Edgar, 116, 122, 123, 124, 125, 129, 132
Caldera, Rafael, 24
Camacaro, Teresita, 162
CANTV, 123, 160
Caracas, 17, 22, 52, 151, 196n18, 201n7
23 Enero, 24, 27, 29, 30, 32, 37, 52
barrio population, 33
building boom, 24–5
CTUs, 31–2
food, 47, 93
health centres, 44
importance, 22–3
land ownership in, 33, 34, 35, 37
organisations in, 28, 29, 30, 31, 33, 47, 146, 157, 159, 160, 166, 172–3, 174, 196n17
reaction to coup attempt, 3, 172, 182
urban land committees, 31–2
work available in, 29, 54–5, 144
see also Carapita, Fabricio Ojeda
Caracazo, 2, 22, 196n10, 205n6

Carapita, 17–19, 23–8, 173–4
building boom, 24
co-operatives, 174
CTUs, 31, 32, 33, 35, 173
industry and infrastructure, 24, 27–8, 37
land ownership, 33–5
squatters, 23–4, 24–5, 28
support for Bolivarian revolution, 21
urban land committees, 31, 32, 33, 35, 173
Carbonorca, 105, 116, 117
Carmona, Pedro, 99
Carneiro, General, 159
Carora, 154, 159, 161, 163, 167, 169, 170, 172, 186, 188, 194n5, 206n20
Catholic Church, 29
church communities (CEBs), 26, 29, 196n15
Cecilia, 19, 20, 21
Chavez, Hugo
and capitalism, 4, 5, 6
control of PDVSA, 20, 42–3
constitutional reform *see* constitutional reform
establishes site of Fabricio Ojeda, 41
failed coup attempt of (1992), 2, 204n30, 205n6
goal of socialism, 1, 41, 160
land reform, 73–4
military background distrusted, 3
moderate policies of, 2, 6, 9, 10, 13, 72, 178
popularity/trust in, 11, 18, 21, 22, 55, 86, 139, 159, 175

'power to the poor', 7, 8, 42, 63
and private property, 6, 41, 74, 101
rhetoric of, 10
and socialism, 5, 199n3
speech at Porto Alegre, 1, 4–5, 11, 180
and US administration, 3
wins 1998 election, 2, 182, 183
Chavez, Julio, 162, 163, 164, 165, 169, 170, 171, 172, 186, 194n5, 206n20
Christian Democratic Party (COPEI), 147, 148, 169, 203n21
Ciudad Guayana, 11, 137, 188, 201n4
CLPPs see Local Public Planning Councils
Coba, Andrea, 25
Cojedes, 64, 73, 75, 77, 79, 83, 85, 199n6, 200n2
colonial history, 23, 143
co-management, 6, 12, 48, 130, 132, 178, 185, 193, 202n19
capitalist, 123–4
confrontations over, 98–103
draft law on, 203n22
see also ALCASA
communal banks, 169, 208n4
communal councils, 32, 37, 137, 1141–2, 42, 143, 145–55, 156, 157, 159–60, 161, 169–75, 184, 185–6, 187–90, 191, 193, 194n4, 204n1, 206n19
crucial role of, 141
dangers, 154

dispute resolution, 166, 167
expanding functions, 188
federations, 168, 171, 174, 188
resistance to, 148, 173
scale of, 140, 159, 174, 205n15
and workers, 190
see also ALCASA, El Charcote, Fabricio Ojeda, Galipan, Carora, La Victoria
Compania Venezolana Agraria, 83, 87, 90
constituent assembly, 2
Constitution of 1999, 33, 110, 143, 155, 164, 177, 183
constitutional reform, 140, 153, 160–1, 165, 171, 177, 178–9, 186, 204n1
and National Assembly changes, 175, 176
rejection of, 13, 134, 142, 161, 175, 176–7, 188, 207n27
co-operatives, 9, 41, 46, 50, 59–62, 67, 81, 93, 110, 118, 133, 137, 182, 188
agricultural/peasant, 7, 9, 47, 91, 94, 96, 200n11
and competition, 58, 59, 60, 61, 93, 114, 191
and Marxism, 60
numbers/scale of, 88, 95, 194n3
problems of establishing/maintaining, 32, 86, 91, 94, 95–7, 122, 146–7, 184, 189, 208n4
'socialist implants within capitalism', 60–1

vulnerability, 61, 116
see also ALCASA, Bella Vista, Cabimas, Carapita, El Charcote, Fabricio Ojeda, Fundos Zamoranos, Galipan, Venepal
Contreras, Ender, 50
co-ordination, lack of, 27, 30
COPEI see Christian Democratic Party
Corporación Venezolana de Guayana (CVG), 104, 114, 116, 117, 118, 119, 121, 122, 128, 130, 135, 136
corruption, political, 154
in Brazil, 2
citizens' oversight of, 86
in Venezuela, 2, 77, 89, 90, 132, 135, 144, 154, 173, 178, 190, 204n6
coup of 2002, 3, 10, 20, 22, 30, 42, 72, 99, 156, 180, 182, 183, 196n10, 203n26
see also oil, lockout
Cova, Milagros, 117
CTUs see urban land committees
Cuba, 3, 6, 15, 66, 122, 182
Cuban aid, 195n3
advisers views on co-management, 130, 132
agronomists/vets, 85, 90, 95
medical staff, 11, 18, 19, 36, 44
CVG see Corporación Venezolana de Guayana

direct democracy, 123, 132, 143, 154, 155–61,

170, 179, 185, 188, 189, 195n9
in the workplace, 100, 104, 133, 153
see also participatory democracy, self-management
Duque, Rosmery, 120
Duran, Moises, 46

Economist, 2
Edelca, 117, 130
education, 11, 37, 44–5, 53, 85, 101, 116, 180
achievements, 19
adult, 17, 18, 20–1
grants for, 18
literacy levels, 11, 19
training *see* Mission Vuelvan Caras
university, 11, 18, 21, 121, 133
see also Mission Robinson I/II, Mission Ribas, Mission Sucre
El Charcote, 11, 64, 65, 89, 199n5
community councils, 85, 87
co-operatives, 64, 71, 83–4, 85, 86, 87, 95–6
'intervened', 73, 75–6
land use, 68, 69, 70, 76, 77, 78–9, 84, 87
legal title to, 77–8, 81, 82, 199n6
New Charcote, 69, 80, 85, 86–7
settlements on, 64, 68, 69–72, 76, 79–81, 83–7, 90, 91, 95
size of, 68
surrendered, 82
Enabling Law, 35, 160, 172
endogenous development,

9, 42, 44, 62, 67, 75, 79, 92, 102, 110, 116, 127, 136–7, 152, 154, 188
Chavez' description of, 8
contrasted with neo-liberal development, 46
fruits of, 52–8
projects, 7, 11, 41, 45, 64, 80, 81, 108, 118, 139, 142–3, 145, 172
as second phase of process, 62
sites identified for, 48
undermining of, 120, 148
see also Fabricio Ojeda, Las Salinas, nucleus for endogenous development
environmental damage, 24, 70, 106
EPS *see* social production enterprises
Ezequiel Zamora National Peasant Front (FNCEZ), 88, 96, 206n19

Fabricio Ojeda, 40–2, 48, 52–7, 58, 62–3, 159, 174
assemblies, 43
communal councils, 53, 63
co-operatives, 40, 43, 44, 45, 47, 48, 53–5, 56, 58, 63, 96, 97, 198n7
co-operatives, working conditions, 56–7, 58
disputes, 56
forerunner of people's economy, 62
showcase, 48
social/economic development centre, 44–6
training, 47–8, 55–6
workshops/factories, 45, 53–4, 55–6, 56–8, 93,

96, 118, 121, 198n7
Falcon, José Gregorio, 17, 18, 37, 173
family structure, 28, 29, 57
and emancipation of women, 57
FBT/FSBT *see* Bolivarian Workers' Force
FIDES, 146, 147, 149, 165, 168, 205n7
fishing, 49–51
five motors of revolution, 13, 123, 160, 176
Flores, Pablo José, 71–2, 80
FONDAFA, 87
food security, 47, 74, 75, 84, 92, 93
see also Mercal, PDVALs
Fundos Zamoranos, 64, 76, 80, 81, 83, 85, 90, 94

Galipan, 12, 63, 139–40, 142–55, 160, 187, 204, 205n8
authorities' lack of support, 158, 159
communal councils, 139–40, 142, 143, 145–55, 152, 154, 204n2, 205n8
co-operatives, 142, 145, 146, 150–1
dirty tricks, 148
scale of, 205n15
Garcia, Marta, 32, 37
global justice movement, 1, 11, 180, 181, 182
globalisation, movement against, 1, 15, 59
Gomez, President Juan Vincente, 77, 144
Goulart, President João, 67
Guaikirima, Rosa, 54, 57
Guevara, Che, 4, 68, 69

Haiti, intervention in, 2, 3
health provision, 11, 19,
    36, 53, 163, 168, 180
    see also Mission Barrio
    Adentro, Cuban aid
Herrera, Maria, 64, 65,
    68–72, 76, 79–80, 83,
    84, 85, 86, 198n2
Hidalgo, Felicia (Licha),
    43, 45, 159
high-level workshop, 6, 41,
    141, 159, 204n3

Iglesias, Maria Cristina,
    7–8, 102, 202n11
indigenous groups
    in Latin America, 8,
    59–60, 66, 68, 94, 103,
    200n14
    in Venezuela, 23, 51–2,
    54, 68, 143
INPARQUE, 149
Institutional Revolutionary
    Party (PRI), Mexico, 27
International Monetary
    Fund (IMF), 3, 8, 17,
    22, 205n6
INTI *see* National Land
    Institute
Invepal *see* Venepal
Inveval, 104, 190
Iraq, 17, 182

Jaua, Elias, 82, 89, 92, 147

La Colonia, 162, 163, 172
La Vega, 24, 27, 173
La Victoria, 167, 168, 169,
    1700, 171, 172, 186
LAEE, 165, 168
Land Institute *see* National
    Land Institute
land reform, 47
    anarchy of ownership, 78
    barriers to, 89–94

and Bolivarian Constitu-
    tion, 33
in Brazil, 2, 67
Chavez' announcement
    of, 3
conservative resistance
    to, 3, 72, 74, 90
failure in 1960s, 70, 89
percentage ownership, 74
prescripción (caducity),
    33–4
'squatters rights', 33–4
stages of, 72–6
state/private property, 65,
    72
statistics, 65, 87–8, 89
and twenty-first-century
    socialism, 65–8
unifying issue, 30
urban, 23
voluntary cessions, 9
see also Caracas,
    Carapita, El Charcote,
    urban land committees,
    latifundios, law
Landless Workers' Move-
    ment (MST), 4, 14, 59,
    61, 64, 91, 94, 198n1
Lanz, Carlos, 106, 110,
    113, 114, 115, 116,
    119, 122, 126, 127,
    128, 130, 133, 134,
    137, 190, 201n7
    interviews, 106, 109,
    110, 111, 115, 119,
    122, 123, 125, 128,
    131, 134
    proposal for socialist
    enterprise, 135–6
Las Salinas, 48–52, 63
Lashley, Sofia, 23, 24, 25,
    26, 27, 28, 31, 32, 35,
    36, 37, 173–4, 176
latifundios, 199n6, 199n8
avales, 71

'idle' land, 9, 41, 65, 72,
    76, 81, 82, 92, 111,
    199n6
right to remain, 64, 71,
    76, 80, 86, 95
war on, 3, 9, 64–97
    see also El Charcote
Latin America
    agro-ecological Institute,
    91
    clientalism, 8
    integration, 2, 5
    guerrilla movements, 15
    land reform, 65–6
    literacy/education, 19,
    116, 198n2
    measures to strengthen,
    42
    resistance to neoliberal-
    ism, 1, 2, 5, 59
law
    complexity impeding
    reform, 33–4, 75, 81,
    90, 115, 126–32,
    146–7, 165, 185
    Enabling Law, 35, 72,
    172
    Land and Agrarian
    Development Law, 72,
    74, 76, 78, 81
    Land Law 1960, 66
    Land Law 2001, 3, 65,
    72, 73, 74, 76, 78,
    199n8
    Law on Communal
    Councils/CLPPs, 141,
    152, 156–8, 159, 160,
    162, 170, 171
    Law on Expropriation,
    33
    reform within or outside,
    127, 172
    Special Law on … Land
    Tenure, 34–5

Lebowitz, M., 16, 195n7, 202n9, 207n3
Leon, Rosa, 168, 172
Local Public Planning Councils, 156–7, 158, 164, 170, 171, 205n9, 205n12
Lopez, Marivit, 105, 106, 111, 112, 114, 116, 117, 122, 123, 124, 126, 130, 132, 133
Los Uvedales, 162, 163, 172
Loyo, Juan Carlos, 56
Lugo, Leopoldo, 76–8, 79, 84
Lula da Silva, 3, 60
  Chavez' praise for, 5
  left's disappointment with, 1–2, 4

Machado, Carlos, 93
Machado, João, 61
Magdalia, 19, 20
Maracay, 70, 98, 120
  Sanitarios de Maracay, 98–101
  unions; 98, 99, 100
Mariátegui, José Carlos, 66, 199n3
Maribel, 20, 21
Marin, Andres, 63, 139, 142, 143, 144, 145, 148, 150, 204n5
Martinez, Ivan, 29, 30, 31, 32, 34, 35, 36, 70
Marx/Marxism, 60–1, 109, 129, 138, 153, 182, 187, 199n3
Mercal, 63, 174, 207n29
  network, 45, 92
  supermarkets, 40, 45, 52–3
  suppliers to, 92–3
  weaknesses of, 92–3

Mercosur, 93, 200n14
Ministry for the People's Economy, 9, 41, 56, 92
Ministry of Agriculture, 82, 89, 95
Ministry of Food, 9, 92
Ministry of Labour, 7, 98–9, 99, 189, 204n30
Ministry of Popular Participation, 159, 164
Mission Barrio Adentro, 11, 18–19, 44, 95, 195n2, 196n14
Mission Ribas, 11, 17, 18, 36–7, 54, 168–9, 173, 194n3, 195n2
Mission Robinson I/II, 11, 19, 36, 54, 86, 194, 195n2, 195n3
Mission Sucre, 11, 133, 195n2
Missions, 11, 21, 26, 35–7, 40, 44, 47, 127, 155
  effect of, 18, 180
  funding from oil revenues, 3, 20, 43
  see also Missions by name
Monsanto, 91
Montilla, Avelino, 26, 28, 35, 195n8
Motta, Greydaris, 17, 18, 19, 37, 173
Moyer, Hugo, 44, 47–8
mudslides, 10, 43, 145

National Assembly, 34, 35, 141, 157, 197n20
National Land Institute (INTI), 65, 70, 71, 75, 76, 80, 82, 87, 88, 92, 95, 199n7, 199n8
National Urban Land Office, 29, 31, 32, 34, 70, 196

National Workers' Union (UNT), 6, 99, 190, 200, 201n3, 202n19
natural resources *see* oil
Navas, Raúl, 51
Negro, Toni, 182
neighbourhood associations, 27, 28, 29, 148, 152, 169
neoliberal policies, 42, 186, 192
  anti-neoliberalism, 66
  Bolivarian challenge to, 3, 4, 5, 11, 38, 46, 170, 179–80, 183
  in Venezuela, 2
New Strategic Map, 6, 41, 59, 74, 141, 161, 180
Nieves, Yolanda, 166, 206n21
nucleus for endogenous development (NUDE), 40–1, 58, 59, 62–3, 80, 83, 121
occupation of factories, 102
  see also Maracay, Sanitarios

OCV *see* Organisation for Home Credits (OCV)
oil
  boom of 1970s, 2
  curbing elite control of, 2
  Dutch disease, 24, 46, 70, 88–9, 92
  funding development and Missions, 3, 11, 17, 26, 42
  international prices, 17
  lockout, 10, 20, 42, 92, 99, 101, 123, 158, 183, 196, 201n3
  nationalisation of 1976, 19

production, xiii–xiv, 49,
195n6
reassertion of national
sovereignty, 3, 19–20,
160, 197n4, 205n16
right use of revenues, 38,
58
surge in income of
2004–8, 93
see also PDVSA
Ojeda, Fabricio, 40
Olga, 47
OPEC, 20
Organisation for Home
Credits (OCV), 25
Orsini, Omar, 53
Otaiza, Eliezer, 65, 75, 80,
81, 88, 92

Parra, Martin, 162
participatory budgets, 143,
156, 164, 165, 168,
170, 171, 186, 195n9
limitations of, 159
see also ALCASA,
Brazil, Porto Alegre
participatory democracy,
46, 103, 110, 141, 177,
185–7, 188, 191
see also direct
democracy
Party of Socialism and
Liberty (PSOL), 4
Patria Para Todos (PPT),
169, 206n23
PDVALs, 174
PDVSA, 19, 41–3, 48, 63,
114, 117, 123, 125, 188
bar on privatisation, 20
and Fabricio Ojeda, 40,
41, 43, 45, 47, 53, 56,
58
and Las Salinas, 49–51
lockout see lockout
managers, 19–20

and Missions, 36, 43,
175
see also ALCASA, oil
pensions, 56
Brazil, 4, 8
Perez, Germán, 69, 70, 83,
84
Perez, President Carlos,
24, 25, 30, 144, 204n6
piqueteros, 27
popular power, 123, 129,
156, 158, 160, 177–8,
185
Presidential Commission
on, 158, 170–1
see also co-management,
communal councils,
participatory budgets
Porto Alegre, 15, 26, 114,
156, 198n1
participatory budget,
157–9, 205n9, 205n12,
206n20
Chavez' speech at see
Chavez
private property, 65, 72,
73, 88, 166, 178, 199n6
and Chavez see Chavez
constitutional protection,
33, 164–5, 183
lack of clarity in titles,
23, 33, 37, 75, 76,
77–8, 90, 199n9
problems with, 33–5
Punto Fijo Pact, 2, 204n6

Querales, Mario, 161, 163,
164, 166

Raby, D., 14
Ramirez, Egly, 51
Rangel, Jhonny Yánez, 73,
199n6, 73, 74, 80
Rato, Rodrigo, 17, 22

Recall Referendum 2004,
6, 10, 65, 194n2
reform from below and
above, 12, 32, 38, 43,
62–3
from above? 43, 52, 64
Regional Land
Commission, 76–9
Ribas, 168–9
see also Mission Ribas
Ribas, Claudio, 86, 87
Ribas, José Felix, 168
Ribas, Regina de, 86
Rice, Condoleezza, 2,
207n2
Richards, Tony, 69, 78
right to remain
see latifundios
Rivero, Alcides, 105, 106,
111, 112, 115, 122,
124, 127, 129, 130,
131, 133
Rojas, Felix, 96, 97
Rumsfeld, Donald, 2

San Buenaventura Textile
Co-operative, 118
Sanitarios see Maracay
Sayago, Elio, 107, 116,
122, 130, 133, 208n5
Seattle, 2, 14, 15, 182
self-help/reliance, 25–6,
27, 45
self-management, workers',
12, 43, 56–7, 100–1,
104, 110, 111, 114,
118, 137, 140, 155, 189
see also co-management
self-organisation, 27–30,
37, 42, 95, 140, 142,
155–6, 172
see also NUDEs
self-sufficiency, 58, 63
Sidor, 105, 128, 188–9,
203n23, 204n30

Silva, Trino, 129–30
Singer, Paul, 60–1
SINTRALCASA, 120, 124, 125
social production enterprises (EPS), 59, 121, 137
Soviet bloc, collapse of, 5, 177
squatters, 25
  see also Carapita, El Charcote
state apparatus, old, persistence of in Venezuelan politics, 75, 90, 105, 119, 121, 131, 137, 147–8, 153, 184
  see also Bolivarian revolution, divisions; Bolivarian revolution, tensions; bureaucracy
subsidies
  basic goods, 3, 9, 44, 53, 174
  projects, 58, 59, 94
  see also Mercal
Sucre
  parish, 41
  state, 159
Supreme Court, 2

Tacagua Vieja, 7–9, 10, 11, 42
Thatcher, Margaret, 11, 31
Toro, Hernan, 63, 139, 142, 143, 144, 145, 146, 147, 148, 150, 151, 152, 204n5
Torres, 161, 162, 164, 168, 171, 172, 186
  budget in, 165
trade unions, 28, 102, 103, 131, 132, 196n13, 200n1, 201n3

Brazilian, 26
  subordination to AD, 28
  see also ALCASA, Carapita, Maracay, National Workers' Union
Troconis, Manuel, 49–50
Trotsky, 6, 207
twenty-first-century socialism, 152, 176–93
  chimera?, 16
  and land reform, 65–8
  outline proposal of Carlos Lanz, 135–7
  social or political, 61
  Venezuela as laboratory for, 11, 14, 15–16, 48, 110–11, 181–2

UNESCO, 19
United Socialist Party (PSUV), 13, 32, 160, 179, 191, 194n1
United States, 3, 5, 19, 67, 194n2
  and 2002 coup, 3
  Alliance for Progress, 66
  South American resistance to, 3, 5, 192
  State Department, 2, 10
  Treasury, 2
UNT *see* National Workers' Union
urban land committees (CTUs), 30–3, 36, 155, 196n16, 196n17
  importance of, 37
  scales of, 32–3
  see also Caracas, Carapita
Uzcátegui, Simón, 88–9, 91, 92–3, 96

Vasquez, Rafael, 168

Venalum, 105, 108, 117, 121, 122, 124
Venepal, 101, 104, 113
  co-operative, 101
Verdiospino, Estela, 55, 56
Vestey
  Agroflora, 68, 75, 76, 77, 78, 80, 81, 82, 83, 199n5, 200n10
  Lord 'Spam', 11, 64, 68, 73, 199n5,
  Vestey Group/family, 68, 73, 77, 78, 79, 81, 82, 199n5
  see also El Charcote
Villareal, Giovanny, 51
Villegas, José, 99, 190
voluntary work, 18, 32, 97, 124
Vuelvan Caras, 7, 9, 41, 71, 95, 122, 194n3
  in Cabimas, 50
  in Caracas, 45, 46, 47, 55, 69

wage levels, 54, 55
Wall Street Journal, 2
Walter, General, 145
Washington Consensus, 1, 179
World Bank, 67
World Social Forums, 1, 15, 198n1
  Fifth, 1, 180

Yánez, Jhonny, 73, 199n6, 73, 74, 80

Zamora, Ezequiel, 73–4, 199n6
Zapatista uprising, 15, 182
Zimbabwe, 65